Man-in-Organization

Man-in-Organization

ESSAYS OF F. J. ROETHLISBERGER

THE BELKNAP PRESS OF HARVARD UNIVERSITY PRESS

CAMBRIDGE, MASSACHUSETTS   1968

Contents

The Author: Fritz J. Roethlisberger retired from the Harvard Business School in 1967 after forty years at that institution. His name symbolizes the theory and practice of human relations in industry—the search for more understanding of how individuals interact in organizations.

Foreword

This volume consists of essays I have written over a span of forty years, from 1928 to 1968. They have been addressed mostly to business practitioners, but also in some cases to social scientists. I have arranged them chronologically (with one exception) and now I want to state the central theme which I think ties them together.

I have done this partly by headnotes in which I stated for each piece how it originated and, if published, by whom and hence whose permission to reprint it was granted—and to whom collectively now I would like to express my appreciation. But also in each headnote I tried to say what I thought I was up to when I wrote the paper as well as sometimes something about its latent content, that is, about some of the free-floating bees in my bonnet at the time.

In some pieces I have made a few purely stylistic changes—for example, to improve an awkward sentence without changing the meaning, or to reduce the superfluous platform language in an essay originally given as a talk. Whenever I have done more than this I have indicated it in the headnote. Almost all the original footnotes I kept the same, even though sometimes better references now could be given.

Whenever I felt I would say something different now from what I said then, I have added a postscript to that effect. The curious thing, as I reflect upon it now, is how few postscripts I felt needed to be written. In this strange fact, I believe, lies the central theme of these essays. Perhaps it can be clarified by looking at the external events that were taking place when these essays were written.

During that period of time this country went through the aftermath of World War I; a serious economic depression, the New Deal and a slow economic recovery. It engaged in World War II and emerged in a position of world leadership. And then came the cold war with some of its increasingly hotter engagements. But compared with other nations economically, we were an affluent society, in spite of the minority groups who were still having difficulty in telling the affluent establishment, now called the "white power structure," how things were like for them in this affluent state of affairs.

Meanwhile, outside this country, monarchies fell and colonialism came to an end. All over the world nations began to seek their own kind of self-determination and social justice. But they sought economic development too. Although they wanted to enjoy the economic goods that modern science and technology could produce, they were not so sure about the social goods that seemed to accompany them, and around these issues mighty battles were fought at both verbal and non-verbal levels.

About all these important matters, except for occasional references, I will have little to say in these essays. So the question arises: amidst this strife and dissension, clatter and noise, what was I doing? Was I contemplating my navel on the right bank of the Charles? But this would be difficult to conceive, because, as everyone who knows Harvard knows, on the right bank of the Charles River at the Business School resided the men of practical affairs—the doers and actors—and on its left bank at the College and Graduate School of Arts and Sciences resided the men of theoretical affairs—the thinkers and world policy makers—and although there was a bridge that connected the two sides physically, it did not connect them intellectually because of the mutual fear of contamination. We could not have the right bank start thinking and the left bank begin to implement its own theories, could we now?

Well, if you can believe this now, I thought that we could or at least that we should give it a good try because I thought that the traditional division of labor between theory and practice in most universities was not unrelated to the sound and fury going on outside. It seemed to me that with regard to social and organizational matters, those who theorized were often not practicing what they theorized about and those who practiced were often not theorizing about what they practiced; and, being young, I thought something should be done about it. It was not the fact of differentiation but the lack of traffic between men of thought and men of affairs that had me concerned. So I wanted to build a bridge across the Charles that would increase the two-way traffic between the two sides.

It was to be no modern and technologically efficient superhighway. In fact this would defeat my purposes because this would allow them only to bypass each other more rapidly. Instead there had to be a bump, an encounter or, as we would say today, a confrontation between them. Yet I did not want a boundary line to be drawn now in the middle of the Charles, with each side issuing passports and visas or hurling javelins to the other side. In the rosy hue of my early manhood I wanted this encounter to be more *gemütlich*.

Anyway, the kind of bridge that I wanted to build across the Charles is also the bridge that connects these essays. In most of them I was tempting each side to cross to the other by offering it the goodies that I thought it was short of and the other side was long on. In this manner I hoped to establish the conditions for an equivalence of exchange that would be rewarding to both.

For example, from the right bank, because that is where I was stationed, I would sing to the left bank in my most seductive manner, "Won't you come over to my yard and play like a good little boy?" But then I would follow up this somewhat "dated" and "corny" appeal by pointing out that in the organizations we were trying to train the leaders for, we had the most juicy and luscious *phenomena* and—to boot—all the paradoxes, dilemmas, inconsistencies, contradictions, ambiguities, dissonances, and uncertainties that they could think of and theorize about. But this was not all in which we luxuriated. In addition I would say that we had the damndest mix of cooperation and conflict, rational and nonrational, matters of fact and relations of ideas, prescribed and emergent phenomena, subinstitutional and institutional behavior, and external and internal environments for them to put together in some systemic way. And then I would appeal to the values of the scientific establishment by saying, "You don't want to study the determinants of conflict apart from the determinants of cooperation, do you now? You want to study them together, don't you now?" And so on.

At the same time I also was making safaris from the right bank into the great "productive jungles" of this country, and there I would try to entice their inhabitants to play footsies with the great "verbal jungles" of academia by saying in effect, "Don't let those on the left bank asphyxiate you with their big words; let me provide you with a gas mask when you cross the bridge to the other side." And then, cribbing from Kurt Lewin, I would say, "Really now, there is nothing more practical than a good theory." But then I would add, "Remember that you are dealing with complex facts; so keep your theories simple. And how are those on the other side who are dealing with simple facts by complex theories going to find this out unless you invite them into your establishments? They (the social scientists) want to be helpful but they don't know how. The universities don't teach that." And then I would appeal to the values of the newly emerging group of professional managers by saying, "You want to be competent, don't you now? But how can you be competent if you don't know what you are administering? Without an organization to administer you are a fish out of water and you don't want to be a dead fish, do you now?" And so on.

Thus in this manner in all my early essays, until about 1954, I was preparing the soil for the great confrontation between theory and practice from which I hoped the new society would emerge. But I fear I was naive. Just when I thought I had theory and practice eyeball to eyeball, they bypassed each other (and me) with the greatest of ease and without batting an eyelash. This happened, so it seemed to me, because each side was concerned only with its own practices and could not care less about the practices of the other side. So I could not get one side's theories hitched up to the other side's practices. Scientific theories did not want to be concerned about administrative practices, and scientific practices did not seem to be able to produce administrative theories.

It can be seen that pivotal to my position was the assumption that the producers and utilizers of knowledge could be brought together in the social sciences by the person I called the "administrator." Although by abstraction man could be studied apart from organizations and organizations apart from man, this person I called the administrator could not be studied even abstractly this way. He was *par excellence* man-in-organization, and the relation between what he thought he was doing or should be doing and what he in fact was doing was critical. Only by keeping the focus on man-in-organization could the gap between theory and practice be bridged.

As will be seen, starting around 1954 and especially with Chapter 17 in this book, "Management's Mission in a New Society," this assumption was challenged more and more by the rapid rise in technology which developed at an ever-accelerated pace until, toward the end of the period in which I was writing, it seemed to have taken a quantum jump into a state that bore little resemblance to its earlier stages.

By this time there was no longer any need for me to entice the social scientists to cross the river. They were coming over in droves and with them they brought their models about man and systems of all sorts. But they were not *good little boys;* they were *enfants terribles,* as their training had correctly brought them up to be. So in the shuffle the focus of man-in-organization got lost, knowledge for the administrator became once again an old-fashioned question, and the manager went back to the business of the business and not forward to the business of administration. But perhaps this is not quite accurate. He had learned now to talk to a computer and to level with his fellow men on a cultural island. But in any case specialist knowledge was back in the saddle again and with this trend the question of who the administrator was, besides being a conglomeration of specialties, was thrown into bolder relief.

Thus it seemed to me that by 1968 I was back to where I was in 1928 —except perhaps for being sadder and wiser. But not too sad because it was no peewee puddle but a great big circle I had been around, and although today this might not be the approved method of problem solving, it was one way of learning. But the essays are becoming impatient; so I'll let them tell you about it.

F.J.R.

Cambridge, Massachusetts
March 1968

Man-in-Organization

1 The Nature of Obsessive Thinking

Written in June 1928, this was the first paper I produced after joining Elton Mayo at the Harvard Business School in September 1927, where for the next five years I spent most of my time in counseling students. Although the piece does not pertain directly to matters of organization and administration, I have included it here because its major theme about the "false dichotomy" as a manifestation of "obsessive thought" appeared in many of my later writings when I began to realize that this kind of thinking was not restricted to students but also afflicted academics and business-men.

This paper was never published, although twenty years later in 1947 it was in-cluded in the School's file of mimeographed "cases" copyrighted by the President and Fellows of Harvard College. It was used then as background reading in courses pertaining to matters of human behavior, the School having discovered by then that "people" were one of the elements of administration.

In this paper the reader will see the great influence of Pierre Janet and Elton Mayo on my thinking.

This report summarizes briefly the methods used and the results ob-tained in an investigation extending over a period of a year on the nature and form of "obsessive thinking."[1] The study arose from a more general question, namely, what is the relation between a person's pre-occupations and his capacity for learning and for discriminating atten-tion to his work? With what kind of reflective musings does the skilled thinker interrupt his attentive acts and how does it differ from that employed by the obsessive? Might not the answer to this question be a key to the "neurotic ills"—a difference in technique with which one learns to control and develop this "perpetual internal chatter"? In one case it illuminates life and activity; in the other case it blunts discrim-ination and causes learning to cease. As a result repetition, boredom, and monotony ensue, with the accompanying dissatisfaction and dis-tress.

In the course of the investigation 74 persons were observed and in-terviewed. Of these 61 were students at Harvard University. The rest were for the most part directly or indirectly connected with academic

1. The report is concerned only with certain intellectual findings of the investi-gation: i.e., with describing the form of obsessive thought and its relation to adapta-tion here and now. Questions of therapy, i.e., how to deal with and modify this kind of thinking, are not taken up in this report. Nor is it concerned, except indi-rectly, with the way this kind of thinking is developed from past experiences: i.e., how the obsessive "gets that way."

work in the vicinity. Among the students, 34 were members of the Harvard Graduate School of Business Administration; 19 attended the College; 4, the Law School; and 4 were graduate students in other departments.

The investigation was under the direction of Dr. Elton Mayo; and Miss Emily Osborne, Mr. Osgood Lovekin, and I assisted. Much of the work was conducted in collaboration with the medical department at the Business School and the Department of Hygiene of Harvard University. Students worried and anxious about themselves were referred to us for counseling by the chief medical officer of the Business School. At the Lyman House, where I resided during the year, and where the psychiatrist for the University sent students for rest, quiet, and sympathetic social surroundings, ample opportunity was provided for observation and study. Mrs. Irene Dickson, in charge of the Lyman House, was also of invaluable assistance to us.

METHOD OF INVESTIGATION

The method employed in collecting the data for this study can best be described as the indirect method of "skilled listening." The student was allowed to talk about anything he pleased. No attempt was made to direct the conversation in any particular channels. During this process one's attention was fixed not so much on what the person was saying as on what he was assuming. Adroit questioning offered by such leads never failed to reveal personal reveries and phantasies of a more personal order.

In this connection it might be well to quote from Bjerre's *Psychology of Murder:*

> In our usual association with our fellow creatures, whether at work or at play, we naturally fasten upon the common bonds of social intercourse, work, exchange of thought, amusements, etc., and our attention is usually directed exclusively to what I have called the *formal content of the intercourse of our companion.* But as soon as intercourse with a certain person is no longer governed by common interests, but by a desire to acquire a knowledge of his inmost being, we immediately abandon the formal content of his utterance and begin unconsciously to seek for whatever indication of his inner life appears in his speech independently of, or even in spite of, his conscious will. In this connection it ought to be easy to establish the fact that practically every utterance, if observed and analyzed in this manner, discloses important glimpses into the deepest complex of forces in the life of the speaker.[2]

2. Andreas Bjerre, *The Psychology of Murder* (New York: Longmans, Green, 1927), p. 13.

One of the immediate practical consequences of this principle is, then, that we listen to "what the speaker regards in his own mind as obvious or of universal application" (Bjerre), something which it has never occurred to him to doubt, something which underlies what he says but is itself not expressed. At the Lyman House where subjects of all sorts were frequently discussed among the students residing there, a fertile field was offered for the accumulation of just such kinds of "universal assumptions." There was no "ism" which did not have an ardent exponent or caustic critic—socialism, communism, anarchism, agnosticism, atheism, modernism, fundamentalism, pacifism, neo-Malthusianism, solipsism, idealism, realism, classicism, romanticism, etc. It was surprising to find how many of these "views," far from being products of rational speculation, had their roots in preoccupationally determined emotional attitudes. In short, then, our method was one of "careful and skilled listening" to the internal mutterings, grumblings and musings of persons which appeared unconsciously in conversation and discussion.

One thing had better be said at once so that we be not accused of taking "inferences," "guesses," "hunches," etc., for "facts." It was not a question of merely guessing at what lay behind the formal utterances. Unless what we guessed could actually be found to have been or actually was a present preoccupation on the part of the speaker, the guess was discounted just as is any unverified hypothesis in science. Such guesses were merely taken as "leads" to be verified at that time or later, whenever it was more opportune.

In conclusion it should be said that we never treated the student as a "subject" for psychological investigation. At all times we were concerned with a "living, integral human being in a natural and social environment" and in sympathetic rapport with his hopes and his fears, his loves and his loathings, his interests and his apathies. We always tried to secure such a relationship with the student which would allow him to communicate thoughts to us which he had never quite been able to express explicitly to himself. In every case it was a relation between two human beings enjoying on the whole a similar world, even though they selected different things from it for attention. In no case was the student "talked to," "lectured to," "seriously advised," "worked upon." The question for us was what quirk, if any, was present in the thinking of the person which made it difficult for him to reach a decision, encounter a certain situation, or adjust himself to the world in which he lived.

PSYCHASTHENIA OR OBSESSION DESCRIBED

Before proceeding it is necessary for us to describe quite clearly the area of our investigation, namely, the obsessive or "worrying" type of person. This disability which affects the normal individual has been well described by Pierre Janet under the name of psychasthenia. "Psychasthenia," he says, "is a form of mental depression characterized by the lowering of psychological tension, by the diminution of the functions which permit action on reality and perception of the real, by the substitution of inferior and exaggerated operations under the form of doubts, agitations, anguish, and by obsessing ideas which express the preceding troubles and which present themselves the same characteristics."[3] By a diminution of capacity for perception of or action upon the immediate environment, Janet means a lowered capacity for fixing and sustaining attention on a point in the immediate surroundings. However, by this he does not mean a complete loss or a permanently damaged loss of function, but that this function is exercised *in an incomplete manner.*

This last distinction is extremely important since it is this which differentiates in psychological terms the normal obsessives from those whose mental disabilities can be called abnormal. For the obsessive the primitive awareness of his surroundings is *integrate and whole.* There is no "split," "contraction," or "rift," in his total field of consciousness. He is not suggestible or hypnotizable (there is difference of opinion about this last statement, but we have never found an obsessive capable of being hypnotized unless sleep or the hypnoid state were confused with the hypnotic condition). He does not suffer from amnesias or anesthesias; neither does he exhibit such phenomena as "automatic writing" or "double personality." He does not believe that he is "God" or "Napoleon." He may have and often does have eccentric ideas, but in contrast to the demented he himself realizes their queerness and is acutely distressed about them. He may feel and often does feel he is going insane. But all this only illustrates that this primitive orientation to his surroundings is sufficiently integral to make him painfully aware of his "differences."

To go back to Janet, then, the obsessive has a diminished capacity to fix and sustain his attention on his immediate surroundings. The in-

3. Pierre Janet, *Les Névroses* (Paris: Ernest Flammarion, 1927), p. 367 (my translation). Janet italicized the sentence.

adequate orientation to his environment which follows in his case is due to the diminution of this function. Incapacity to attend is followed by lack of discrimination; lack of proper discrimination ultimately spells erroneous conceptions; misinterpretations thus developed organize themselves into adverse general attitudes, and inadequate orientation of this sort in turn fosters a defective relationship between the individual and his environment. Thus the "vicious circle" of the obsessive is created.

The ill which the obsessive suffers, then, is not due to a disrupted primitive orientation to his surroundings but an adversely conditioned orientation developed from an accumulative misinterpretation of his experience. In his case there is a total object of consciousness to which he can refer his ideas for verification and control. The fault lies in that he assigns erroneous meanings to this total object. The mechanisms which perpetuate these misinterpretations I shall consider later under "revery thinking." Need it be said, however, that his cure lies in his capacity to reassess his defective conceptions, to reassign new and more adequate meanings, and to reinterpret his old experiences?

THE SYMPTOMS OF THE OBSESSIVE

The symptoms which the obsessive presents follow as a natural consequence from his primitive orientation to his surroundings being intact and his secondary orientation (because of diminished capacity to attend as described above) being askew. He complains of a sense of unreality and sense of isolation, an inability to undergo a feeling exactly in accord with his present situation. He suffers from insomnia and finds it difficult to stop his obsessing preoccupations. He has trouble in starting work, and after he has started, with stopping. In order to study he needs absolute quiet and freedom from any distraction. His preoccupations are mainly concerned with the past and the future, and never with the present. He is painfully aware of his differences and shortcomings and yet, on the other hand, in many cases he feels rather superior to other people. Frequently he has a deep sense of guilt and conviction of sin. He wonders what people think of him and whether they like him. In one case, he is apt to be very silent, reticent, and self-conscious; in another case, we find him very forward and rather disagreeably argumentative. He tends either to multiply possible disasters endlessly or to entertain equally absurd and grandiose ideas about success. His life is reduced to a number of "compulsive rituals"—things he must do for no apparent reason, but the nonperformance of which entails in some unspecified and unanalyzed way a certain danger. He washes and rewashes his hands; he is careful regarding the way he forms his letters when writing; he goes back two, three, and sometimes four or more times to see that the door is properly locked; he carefully avoids stepping on the cracks in the sidewalk, etc. Life at this level is for him miserable.

It is needless to say that these "symptoms" are merely "end products" of a total situation and are not to be regarded as "things-in-themselves." The obsessive is only too willing to talk about these symptoms and to feel that something should be done about them as they stand.

Janet also points out that together with the diminution of the attentive function goes an enhancement of exaggerated and inferior forms of thinking. Here he refers to the revery thinking (sometimes called day dreaming, phantasy thinking, autistic thinking, undirected thinking, or dispersed thinking) in which all of us indulge when we are not actively engaged in something in our immediate surroundings. Surely Janet cannot mean that it is indulgence in this sort of thinking which differentiates the normal obsessive from the normal nonobsessive (I use this cumbersome way of expressing the distinction to make it absolutely clear that we consider the obsessive to be essentially a normal person). For, as has frequently been noted, it is this sort of thinking which is the most creative and imaginative. It supplies us with our "hunches," our "leads," our "hypotheses," and our "brilliant ideas." And yet it is in this area that the difference also lies. The obsessive differs from the normal in two respects:

(1) in the lack of relation between his revery thinking and his attentive acts.

(2) in the nature and form of his reveries.

The obsessive's preoccupations are always irrelevant; that is to say, irrelevant to what he is doing or should be attending to. And it is this very irrelevance which hinders his capacity for attention and for discrimination. It is the form of his undirected thinking which allows him to perpetuate the misinterpretations of the world about him.

From this "lead," which Janet offers, then, we take our departure and proceed with our investigation. Just what is the form of the reveries in which the obsessive indulges and how does it differ from that of his normal but more successful contemporary?

CONCERNING THE FALSE DICHOTOMY

Probably one of the first things about the thinking of the obsessive which attracted our attention was its oversimplification and over-exaggeration. In very important departments of living, the obsessive substitutes a false antithesis for an integral attitude. He tries to conduct his life by choosing between two alternatives, both of which are false and unreal. He proposes to respond in either one of two ways to a variety of different situations. It is this oversimplification which constitutes his lack of discrimination and unintelligent adaptation to his social surroundings.

By a "false dichotomy," then, we mean a breaking asunder into two halves of a complex problem of the nature of "either A is true and then B is false or B is true and then A is false" when the halves into which the problem is thus bifurcated are contraries and not contradictories so that "both A and B may be false." Let me illustrate this point, for it is the only logical error we have as yet found which the obsessive commits. Otherwise he is a rigorous and excellent logician and his extensive elaborations of his original false position, from a logical point of view, are flawless and extraordinary. To go back, however, "all A is B" and "some A is not B" are contradictory propositions. If the first is true, then the second is false. Likewise, if the first is false, then the second is true. However, if we take the two propositions, "all A is B" and "no A is B," we cannot argue in the same manner. These are contrary propositions. Here we can *not* argue from the falsity of one to the truth of the other. Only one can be true but—and it is this which the obsessive forgets—*both may be false.* Our criticism is not directed to the splitting of the problem into two contrary positions but in arguing from them, as if they were contradictories.

During the year's work a number of such "false dichotomies" were unearthed. Some of them, and especially those lying in fundamental areas of living, I shall now list and consider in turn.

A. safety–danger
B. success–failure
C. superiority–inferiority
D. good–bad
E. abstinence–promiscuity
F. obedience–rebellion
G. spectator–participant

H. independence–dependence
I. theory–practice
J. work–play

A. Safety–Danger

This was probably one of the most fundamental of all the dichotomies we found. In one student this antithesis was exhibited to a marked degree. The chief symptom he presented at the time he came to us was fear of fainting in the classroom. Actually he had only fainted once in such a situation. This student was the only child of two anxious and watchful parents, who, because they were afraid of their son's contracting contagious diseases, had not sent him to school until the age of thirteen and had kept him away as much as possible from children of his own age. One of his chief preoccupations seemed to be concerned with railroads—i.e., he imagined himself driving a locomotive, attending to a signal tower, etc. Day dreaming in this area had been one of his chief recreations for years. Much of his time—much more than he had ever realized—was taken up with trying to anticipate possible disasters. Before taking any small trip, he would have to plan out each move in detail to be sure nothing dreadful would happen. Nothing could be done spontaneously and free from care and anxiety. The actual danger against which he was desperately striving was vague and unspecified. He must "play safe," "make sure," find a "zone of safety," be free from all dangers. Life at this level was, of course, accompanied by boredom and monotony. And now we see the significance of the preoccupations about locomotives. This was the only outlet he gave himself to "flirt with danger."

Let me cite the case of another student. It was at about the age of 12 or 13 that compulsive ceremonies and tests began to appear. He felt that he must perform certain feats or else something dreadful would happen to his family—especially to his mother—and the family reputation would be in ruins. This vague but terrible foreboding was constantly with him. He would hold his head under the water when he was taking a bath until he was on the point of suffocation. In fact he was averse to bathing because of this compulsion. He would try to drink all the water from the faucet in the bathroom, and felt fearful if he didn't succeed. Often at night in bed he would bury his face in the pillow and try to hold his breath as long as possible. Once he swallowed a pin after a long inner debate about the possible efficacy of this method. Several times he hung over the edge of a roof until he had just strength enough to swing back on the top of the porch rather than crash on the ground below. For a time he felt that he must not permit anyone to pass him on the street, and as a protective measure he would try to pass others. Later he thought that he must outstare other people and keep count. If he succeeded in perhaps seven out of ten cases in staring until the other person dropped his eyes, all was provisionally safe.

In all cases where we found the safety–danger dichotomy foremost, we also found any notion of "adventure" lacking. The idea that mistakes were made, that they were always essentially retrievable, that this is the means by which we learn, was not present. There was no notion of an "experimental attitude" toward life. On the contrary, life for the obsessive perpetually is being on the "thin edge of somewhere," always with the possibility of making an irrevocable mistake. He is forever walking on egg shells. Everything that is not absolutely safe is dangerous.

B. Success–Failure

This dichotomy is a twin sister of the safety–danger dichotomy discussed in the last section. The difference lies in that the former (safety–danger) is wider, more primitive and more fundamental. It is pronounced in the thinking of primitive peoples and in the thinking of the child; whereas the latter (success–failure) is more restricted to the thinking of the intelligent but obsessive adult of modern civilization. It is his new variation of the older theme. It was especially prevalent among the students at the Business School, particularly among those who had gone to the Business School primarily to insure themselves against failure in the business world.

For the obsessive there is nothing which lies between success and failure. He interprets his own activities and the activities of others in terms of these irreducible categories. His preoccupational thinking is thus likely to oscillate between these two levels. Wherever we have found preoccupations about failure, we have also found preoccupations about success. In either case, the important thing was the juvenility of the ideas of success and the overexaggeration of the ideas of failure. One man used to spend considerable time in picturing himself as one who had achieved high eminence and authority in his chosen field of endeavor, and imagining how his associates and the people back home would then regard him. Or maybe he could be President of the United States? Then wouldn't he make things hum. On the other hand, when he was depressed and probably more fatigued, he would be convinced that he could never amount to much. His life had been one failure after another. Then he would picture himself as a butler in a very wealthy family where he could have close contact with luxury and conveniences. Or maybe he could be a criminal, get arrested and sent to jail where the state would take care of him. Between viewing life from the White House or "behind bars," there was no middle point of vantage.

Another man could not believe that a person could be indifferent to or happy without having his name in *Who's Who in America*. It was this which spelled success. In my many discussions with students, and especially those at the Business School, the topic of "success" was frequently brought up. Everything from "going to bed early at night," "taking regular exercise," "putting your pennies in the savings bank," "not drinking coffee or smoking cigarettes," "getting to work every morning before the boss arrived," to "sticking to one thing" was proposed as having a good deal to do with, or constituting the essence of, success. In no case was it proposed that *continuing interest* in your work and in the world in which you lived—so much so in fact that the question as to whether you were or your associates thought you were a success or failure never entered your head—might have some relevance to the subject.

C. Superiority–Inferiority

The very nature of the neurotic disorder is bound to bring as a consequence the feeling of inferiority. It is not of this feeling of inferiority, however, of which I wish to speak. My concern is rather with the alternating preoccupations of superiority and inferiority as well as their logical elaboration by means of which the obsessive tends to isolate himself from his social surroundings, and which in turn make him very sensitive toward them.

Probably more students fall into this group and the following two than any other. These are the adolescent false conflicts *par excellence*. This is natural enough since it is during this period that the student experiences what he describes as his "first disenchantment with the world in which he lives." More accurately stated, however, he is disillusioned with his infantile conception of the world. And it is merely his refusal to give up his childish conception as inadequate and erroneous which makes him interpret his new experiences as bitter disappointments and disillusionments.

Let us cite an example. This student was the only son of a family of two children. During his childhood his father had incurred financial losses which he felt had affected the social position of the family. His sister, although two years his senior, was both physically and mentally retarded, having a mental age of about 12. This had always been a great source of embarrassment to him. Because of his sister and the reduced social position of his family, he never brought any of his schoolmates to his home. At school he never felt that he "belonged to the group." He tried to imitate the popular boy, the boy who was generally liked, who was "smooth" and "polished." But his attempts were never very successful.

So much for his early family situation and upbringing. How did he interpret his social surroundings? On the one hand, toward a certain portion, he was extremely contemptuous and sarcastic, indulging in extreme "hates" and "loathings." This group comprised the "common herd," the socially ineligible people toward whom he need be neither diplomatic nor tactful and on whom he could vent his sarcasm. On the other hand, from the other portion he wished approval and feared disapproval. This group comprised the socially eligible. In the area of men, they were those who belonged to clubs and exclusive social sets; in the area of women, they were the well-bred, the virtuous and the pure. Toward this group he was likely to be reticent and shy, measuring very carefully what he said and wondering what they thought of him.

What about his preoccupations? At one time he would be indulging in the most "heroic" day dreams. He would be "directing other people's minds," "securing other people's admiration," commanding obedience from some and securing admiration from others. He loved to evoke fantastic situations which gave him a sense of "physical and social power." At another time he would reproach himself severely for the poor work he had done and the social mistakes he had made.

Another student illustrated very nicely how an originally false dichotomy may be elaborated in a most rigorously logical fashion to an extreme position. This man felt very inferior when playing ordinary sports and doing things with his hands. In order to compensate for his inadequacies in these departments he built up a complete system of thinking. In the first place, only stupid people of course liked sports and were interested in mechanical things. They were "cookbook engineers" and machinists who worked by formulae and whose interests were narrow. Masculinity, because of its preference for sports and the mechanical, became degraded. Mechanisms, engineering and the applied sciences became objects of contempt—objects for the interest of a "mid-western Babbitt" but not for the intellectually superior person. For the latter there were pure sciences, logic and philosophy. The superior person dealt in ideas and abstract theories. Of course this system did not completely hold water; the more he studied "pure science," the less pure it became. He wondered whether he was a "cynic" and a "skeptic" and this, in turn, raised a conflict for him with religion.

As a child this boy had little companionship of his own age. Because his home bordered on the outskirts of a rather tough section, he was not allowed to play with the "bad boys." Later, in another town his neighbors were Jewish. In both communities he felt superior to the rest of the people. He had always felt set off from the rest of the group. All of his grade work had been taught to him by his mother from lessons obtained from a correspondence school. As a child he read many novels—Thackeray, Scott, Dickens, and Eliot. He considered himself intellectually superior to the rest of the children. He felt it was superior not to pay attention to girls. His mother had an unusual contempt for the silliness of girls. Puppy love, as she called it, was silly and dangerous.

Besides the above two cases and many other similar cases in which the mechanism involved tended to produce the disagreeably argumentative type so well described by Adler, we had another case in which the dichotomy at work was, without question, one of superiority and inferiority, and yet it did not produce the same picture. In this case, it was the inferiority arm of the antithesis which seemed to be elaborated.

This man did not enter college until his early thirties. For years he had felt keenly his lack of education. During all these years he had lived an active life in the oil fields and mining districts of the West. During the (first) World War he had seen active service in France. His experiences both in this country and in France might have aroused the envy of any man his own age as well as many who were older. And yet in the presence of a Harvard freshman he felt his inferiority keenly. As I have said, it was not until at about the age of thirty that he attended college. He had gone to a small teachers' school in the South and at the end of three years had been able to obtain an A.B. From there he came to the Business School at Harvard, and it was while attending his first year there that he came under our attention. With an energy and application that seemed almost superhuman, this man wore himself into a state of complete nervous exhaustion trying to convince himself and his associates that he was intellectually capable of being at Harvard. For him Harvard was a sort of educational heaven to which only the elect could go and manage to stay. At the end of his first term's work, he had made for grades two distinctions, one high pass, and one low pass. When we told him this (at this time he was in the infirmary) he was convinced that either we were not telling him the truth in order that he might get well, or that the professors had not really graded his papers.

D. Good–Bad

In all these dichotomies, there is a tendency to repudiate one side and elaborate the other. Because that one side, however, cannot be completely repudiated and the other side completely elaborated at the expense of empirical facts, the conflict arises. In the good–bad antithesis we have an excellent illustration out of which arise two general attitudes—the very very good and the very very bad.

One man used to spend a good part of his time in trying to fight off low-minded reveries and activities about sex. But the more he fought against their recurrence, the more they came back to annoy and torture him. He was filled with shame and guilt. And in turn they hindered the development of real contacts with boys and girls of his own age. In the presence of girls his conviction of sin was enhanced. He became self-conscious and embarrassed. He chose his language very carefully and saw to it that only proper and respectable topics were discussed. In no respect was he to express any admiration for their physical charms, or make any reference to or gaze too intently at any portion of their bodies. On one occasion, quite accidentally a girl who was planning to be married talked openly about the physical pleasure of marriage. He was duly shocked and felt that she must be a bad woman.

When he first went to college, he roomed with several boys, but they talked freely about sex and he felt it was deplorable and demoralizing. So, before a month had elapsed, he left them and sought a solitary room. All during the year he was religious and sought church services regularly. He meditated upon the possibility of studying for the ministry and listened for guidance from the sermons. He went so far as to adopt quite a favorable attitude toward the League of Nations, although the family tradition was Republican, and one of his obsessions was that he ought to run along with the ideals of the family.

With increasing knowledge, his religious fervor waned. In his junior year he roomed with a young man who was sexually experienced and who talked fairly freely about women. For a while he felt less restrained than previously and began to feel less timid and melancholic. But just a fortnight before the end of the term, as the examinations approached, he felt that a mysterious retribution for this looseness of sex talk would be visited upon him and he packed up his things and prepared to escape the iniquitous scene. Thanks to the intervention of a Dean, he was induced to take his examinations, which he passed quite easily.

Just as one may repudiate an empty bad and chose as the alternative an empty good, so, on the other hand, one may repudiate an abstract good and choose the path of iniquity and vice as the logical alternative. We had a student who illustrated this very beautifully.

This man was a senior at college. For him the normal and good person was stupid and uninteresting. He loathed this type of person for his smugness and complacency, his lack of finer aesthetic sensibilities, his social-mindedness, his seriousness and his conscientiousness. But above all for his stupidity. It was the eccentric and abnormal who were intelligent and interesting. Evil was beautiful. And so he developed an aesthetic theory of evil. He cultivated a taste for the bizarre and the grotesque. He abhorred anything symmetrical, balanced, and harmonious.

During his four years at college, he gathered about him as friends the most weird and outlandish set that could be found outside of a psychopathic hospital. Each afternoon they would gather in one of the rooms, draw down the blinds, burn incense and sip tea, while they indulged in Rabelaisian and ribald conversations and "raised skeptical eyebrows" about the indiscreet practices of their friends and members of the faculty.

If there is one thing more boring than virtue, it is vice. In his attempt to run away from his preposterous and absurd notion of goodness, he had run into an equally absurd notion of wickedness. Both situations were boring and monotonous. And it was that which this student was beginning to realize at the end of his college life. And yet his theory had been so well elaborated that at times he would wonder whether a change in attitude might not be followed by a loss of his literary capacities and a descent into mediocre oblivion.

E. Abstinence–Promiscuity

Only a few words in passing need be said about this dichotomy, since it is but a more particular variation of the one discussed above. It was interesting to find that more of the students with whom we came in contact repudiated promiscuity than approved it. We had several cases of promiscuity, but the majority were not promiscuous.

One man, whose revery thinking about sex oscillated between the extreme poles of "high-minded" and "low-minded," was either imagining himself playing an heroic or chivalrous role before a woman or wondering (when attending a musical show) "how many women in the chorus were diseased." These latter thoughts disturbed him a good deal. He felt he was eternally damned for "he that looketh upon a woman to lust after her hath committed adultery with her already in his heart."

Another man whose heterosexual experiences numbered in the hundreds, according to his story, only thought of a woman as a means of satisfying his own sexual activity. It is a question whether this student ever enjoyed any real sexual experience.

It is needless to say that neither of these two men was satisfied with his sex life. Neither had enjoyed a real and human relation with a girl as a human being. It was either no intimacy with a girl or complete intimacy for them; no other relationship was possible.

F. Obedience–Rebellion

In this case we have the infantile attitudes of complete obedience or complete rebellion perpetuated in adult situations. Here the alternative proposed is either complete acceptance or complete rejection of what any person in authority says. Such wholesale attitudes carry with them as consequences a diminished capacity to discriminate.

In one instance it meant that the student became childishly rebellious to all authority after he had left his home where he had been completely obedient to every wish and fancy of his parents. This infantile obedience to his parents was reflected repeatedly in the things he said. Even though geographically he was separated from them by over 3,000 miles, while attending the Business School, he was as tied to his parents in feelings as though he were living with them. Every move he made had to be made in terms of what he thought his parents would approve or disapprove. He would have quit school instantly but for his parents. On the other hand, he was childishly rebellious toward the academic authorities. When he was disgusted with the way some of his courses were run, he would walk out of a lecture. He liked to enter into serious discussion with his instructor about his work and the methods of the courses. On one occasion, in a certain course in government he was extremely satisfied with himself after he had made the professor agree that he (the professor) and not himself was in the wrong. During his period as a pledge of a fraternity at college, he was reprimanded for having failed to do some work and he was told that he would be paddled in punishment. He felt that he was unjustly accused and threatened to leave the fraternity if he were punished in this manner. When this did not deter the brothers, he actually did renounce the pledge pin and forswear all fraternities. Even an apology from the fraternity president did not induce him to abandon his attitude. Once more he withdrew from social circles in protest against horseplay and was thrown back upon the social resources of his home circle.

In another case the man had elaborated his rebellion into a more complete logical system. He was a complete radical and rejected wholesale the institutions and thought of modern organized society. All modern society was organized for the sole purpose of perpetuating falsehood and preventing people from learning the truth.

G. Spectator–Participant

False dichotomies of a personal order can be found in any variety. So far I have only discussed those I considered to be the most fundamental and those which ran as themes through a large number of cases. The next three antitheses can be grouped together as they all play a similar role, namely as rationalizations whereby man can justify his isolation from his social environment. They are general attitudes, in most cases difficult to express.

First is the idea of being a spectator, of viewing with God-like detachment the world, of observing with amusement and tolerance or perhaps contempt the frailties and weaknesses of mankind. Sometimes it is expressed as the philosophical ideal—to seek the point where all roads lead but none depart and watch from this point of stability the world of flux and change, where things are not what they seem. In many instances I have found that such a philosophical attitude was largely an escape from reality, a fear of being hurt in the "danger" of living and a repudiation of an ordinary level of living before it had been even achieved. Many of them were trying to be extraordinary before they had learned to be ordinary.

In the other case, the man hurled himself into the activities of life and scorned reflection. He was lost in the medley and multiplicity of things. His life became one round of petty trivialities. He bolstered his attitude by telling his friends, "you think too much," "stop introspecting," etc. Although he gave the appearance of close contact to his surroundings, he was equally isolated.

H. Independence–Dependence

Here is another of these general attitudes. In this case the individual tries to achieve something which resembles Descartes' definition of Substance or God—"something which requires nothing but itself to exist." He wants to be completely self-sufficient. Between being a parasite and God, there is no satisfactory human relation possible.

I. Theory–Practice

This antithesis was sung by the students in many keys. I shall give its most extreme expression which underlies as an assumption what they have said.

On one hand was the world of "matters of fact," the brute stubborn existences with which the scientists deal but which ultimately told us nothing except that they exist. On the other hand, there was the "world of ideas," which was logically manipulatable, but which seemingly had no relevance to the things which existed. You played with ideas; you lived in a world of facts. Between the two there was no connection. These students existed in a bi-polar world where the poles could not be hitched together. In the world of ideas, these students were sophisticated young gentlemen, talking a highly sophisticated jargon; in the world of facts they were timid, frightened children, solitary and alone, pathetically demanding reassurances.

On one side were sung the praise of theory and the contempt for practice; on the other side were sung the praise of "experience" and the contempt for "book learning" and academic theoreticians who are teaching merely because "he who can does; he who cannot teaches."

Never was the distinction drawn between good and bad theory, those theories which are elaborated in connection with empirical facts and those theories which are not. In a similar fashion no distinction was made between experience which becomes more and more illuminated by the assignment of more and more adequate meanings and experience which becomes oversimplified and distorted by the perpetuation of false alternatives.

J. Work–Play

In conclusion I wish to mention briefly the obsessive's attitude toward work and play. Like the old Ford cars, he has only two speeds ahead—high and low. Either he works at full steam ahead or does nothing. We had one extreme instance of this in the case of a businessman whose method of living consisted of knocking himself to pieces for a period of six months and then going to a sanitarium to recuperate the other six months. Instead of alternating levels of activity and passivity during the day, he tried to maintain one level for a long period of time. The underlying assumption was that work mysteriously took something out of you, and rest in turn restored it. Any notion of equilibrium between the organism and the environment at different levels of activity was lacking.

CONCLUSION

The chief points which I have tried to bring out and illustrate in this report can be summarized briefly as follows:

1. Any psychology should differentiate between the awareness of an unspecified and undefined whole which persists practically unchanged throughout the lifetime of an individual and the meanings which are assigned to this total object and which do change during the life of the individual.

2. It is in terms of the condition of this "primitive total object" that we differentiate the disintegrated person from the normal but perhaps obsessive person.

3. It is in terms of the adequacy or inadequacy of meanings assigned to the "total object" that we differentiate the normal nonobsessive from the normal obsessive.

4. From experience and reflection is built up this wider awareness of

surroundings or background of meanings, against which the particular events are interpreted or misinterpreted.

5. It is the relation of this total object to the object of attention which constitutes the problem for psychology. In this case there would not be two psychologies—a psychology of the mental hinterland and a psychology of the mental foreground—but one psychology which relates the two.

6. Anything which disturbs this general orientation is bound to affect the kind and quality of discrimination made.

7. The obsessive suffers from an adversely conditioned orientation due to an accumulative misinterpretation of his experience.

8. This in turn is followed by a diminished capacity to fix and sustain attention and enhancement of preoccupational or revery thinking.

9. It is the nature of the obsessive's preoccupation which perpetuates the misinterpretations.

10. The revery thinking of the obsessive suffers from oversimplification and overexaggeration of the "false dichotomy" type.

11. This form of thinking proposes a false alternative for an integral attitude in certain departments of living which in turn prevents the achievement of an effective relation between the individual and his environment.

2 Understanding: A Prerequisite of Leadership

In this volume as first planned, a seventeen-year gap appeared between the first essay (1928) and the next (1945). In order to close the gap I have included this paper written in 1936 and published by Harvard University Press in a previous collection of essays of mine called *Management and Morale* (1941). Most of the essays in that book, including this one, had been speeches to businessmen. The one reprinted below was an address to Professor Philip Cabot's Business Executives' Group, Boston, on February 9, 1936. I chose this particular essay for the present volume because it illustrates well the shift in my thinking from the individual *per se* to the individual-in-organization as the focus for the study of leadership and administration.

Industry is a social as well as an economic phenomenon. An industrial concern is not only an organization for the promotion of economic purposes; it is also a human organization in which the hopes and aspirations of individuals are trying to find expression. In these terms the leader of an industrial enterprise has two functions to fulfill, an economic function and a social function. First, he has to manufacture and distribute a product at a profit. Second, he has to keep individuals and groups of individuals working effectively together. A great deal of attention has been given to the first function. Scientific controls have been introduced to further the economic purposes of a concern and of the individuals within it. Much of this advance has gone on in the name of efficiency or rationalization. Nothing comparable to this advance has gone on in the personal relations between employer and employee. Whatever slight advance there may have been is completely overshadowed by the new and powerful technology of modern industry. One important reason for this difference is not difficult to find. Effective relations between employer and employee largely reside in skills that are personal, empirical, and intuitive—skills which the individual utilizing them cannot make very explicit. Unlike the skills developed in the technological area, they are difficult to communicate. To them science has been little applied.

Numberless examples could be cited to show that these two skills, technical skill and skill in dealing with human relations, do not necessarily go hand in hand in the same individual. There are some men highly intelligent and logical within their areas of specialty who at the

20

same time are bunglers in the art of human relations. Likewise, there are some men, highly skilled in the handling of people, for whose logical capacities one can have little respect. That high logical skill and skill in handling people do not necessarily go together suggests that they are concerned with different factors. It suggests that, in handling human relations, logic alone will not avail.

In matters pertaining to human collaboration, sentiments and the interaction of the sentiments are important phenomena. Any development of communicable skills in the area of human relations, comparable to those in the technical area, therefore presupposes an understanding of the nature of sentiments.

SOME PROPERTIES OF SENTIMENTS

A simple way of explaining what I mean by sentiments is to differentiate them from another class of phenomena with which they are often confused, namely, facts. Facts have two essential properties: they are conclusions about matters of observation, and they involve terms for which there exist certain operations that can be agreed upon as defining them.

Should I say, "The temperature of this room is 72° F.," everyone would agree that that statement is either fact or error. Should anyone wish to challenge my statement, we should all agree as to the method by means of which the statement could be tested, verified, or corroborated, and we should all abide by the decision of this independent judge, the thermometer. But now let me make another judgment. This time I say, "The room is too hot." Some may agree, and others may disagree with this judgment. Let me assume that someone who disagrees with me wishes to convince me that my statement is incorrect. Let me assume that he says, "But, my dear fellow, the temperature in this room is 68°," and he shows me a thermometer to convince me. I look at the thermometer, agree with him that it registers 68° F. But does that convince me? No. I disagree with his assumption that 68° is not "too hot." I may come back at him and say, "Look here, old man, I'm giving a talk in this room and for the speaker a room at 68° is too hot." At this point he is likely to say, "Don't be silly," meaning that he disagrees with my definition of "too hot." Indirectly he is telling me that I can't define a room as "too hot" in this way. Now what do I do? At this point I'm likely to retort, "Says who?" meaning who is he to tell me how I am going to define the term "too hot." In short, all his attempts to convince me end in a verbal argument because any attempts at verification involve an arbitrary definition of what is "too hot,"[1] upon which we cannot agree.

The first judgment I made was capable of verification. It was either fact or error. The second judgment I made was an expression of sentiment. *It was neither fact nor error.* Strictly speaking, expressions of sentiment are neither true nor false. They refer to the personal and social life of the person who expresses them. Apart from such a context they are meaningless. They cannot be assessed apart from the individual who makes them. Or, to put it another way, sentiments are biologically, psychologically, or socially determined. They vary with time, place, sex, age, nationality, personality, social status, and temperament, to mention some of the many factors. To go back to the previous example: a room at 68° may be called "comfortable" by an Englishman, "cold" by an American, "hot" by a man who is doing heavy muscular work, "chilly" by a man sitting at a desk, "suffocating" by Byrd at Little America, and "too hot" by a nervous man unexpectedly called upon to make a speech.

Sentiments refer not only to "hots" and "colds" but also to a vast range of feelings, emotions, and attitudes, some of which are normal, some of which are pathological. They include behavior patterns which may appear ugly—fear, anger, jealousy, and envy, for instance—and behavior patterns regarded as beautiful, such as loyalty, courage, devotion, honesty, truth, and goodness. They include those things within people which are appealed to by such statements as the following: "The Constitution should be preserved"; "There can be only one capital, Washington or Berlin"; and "Woman's place is in the home."

This statement that the human being has sentiments, and that therefore it is very important for the leader to be aware of this fact, does not imply that the human being is "sentimental" according to popular meaning, that the human being is irrational, or that sentiments should be eliminated from human beings. What it does imply is that the human being is a social animal and that a social animal is not merely—in fact, is very seldom—motivated by matters pertaining strictly to fact or logic. However, to conclude from this statement that therefore all human responses not strictly logical are illogical or irra-

1. For a more complete discussion of the difference between fact and sentiment, see L. J. Henderson, "Science, Logic and Human Intercourse," *Harvard Business Review* (April 1934), 317–327.

tional is a false distinction. Most human behavior is neither logical nor irrational; it is nonlogical, that is to say, it is motivated by sentiment. To eliminate such nonlogical conduct would be to destroy all values and significances, everything which for most of us makes life worth living.

The distinctions between logical, nonlogical, and irrational behavior can be explained by the following example: When I put on my hat in order to protect my head from the heat rays of the sun, I am behaving logically. When I take off my hat upon entering a church, I am behaving nonlogically. Likewise, if I put my hat on when entering a synagogue, I am behaving nonlogically. If for no good reason I throw my new hat on the ground and stamp on it, I am behaving irrationally. Let us assume now, however, that I am a college undergraduate and that it is the code of this group not to wear new-looking hats; then stamping on my hat in order to destroy its new appearance becomes nonlogical. It will be noticed that logical behavior presupposes an objective connection among things that are unaffected by my particular beliefs. Nonlogical behavior, such as taking my hat off to a woman, is action in accordance with the sentiments of correct social behavior in the group to which I belong. Such behavior integrates me to that group. Irrational behavior, on the other hand, although motivated by sentiments, is personal and peculiar to me. Such behavior estranges me from, rather than binds me to, human association.

This consideration brings up another interesting property of sentiments: they cannot be modified by logic alone. When my friend brought me a thermometer registering 68° in order to convince me that my statement was false, he, of course, was under a misapprehension. He thought I was making a statement of fact. Actually, I was expressing my state of mind; I was expressing a sentiment. But my friend was not to blame for his confusion. I didn't express my sentiment as sentiment. I did not say, "I feel hot." I said, "This room is hot." I did try to disguise my sentiment as a statement of fact. Now that is another peculiar property of sentiments. They are frequently disguised as fact or logic. Indeed, two of the most important and time-consuming pastimes of the human mind are to rationalize sentiments and to try to modify sentiments by logic.

Now in this last point there may be a clue to the reason why some individuals who are particularly adept in handling matters of fact and logic fall short when it comes to handling human relations. They are constantly confusing fact with sentiment. They are treating expressions of sentiment as if they were statements of fact. When such a man comes home at night and his wife says, "Man's work is from sun to sun; but woman's work is never done," he immediately gets annoyed with her for her disregard of certain elementary facts about the work of men and the broader responsibilities of men.

When an employee, Bill, comes to this same man's office and says, "My piece rates are too low," this kind of employer immediately goes into a long explanation to the effect that the rates have been set in a most scientific manner on the basis of time and motion studies and that, moreover, these rates are in accordance with rates paid by other concerns in the same territory for comparable work. In other words, he defines to Bill what constitutes a "fair rate," just as my friend tried to define to me what was meant by "too hot." Now it may be that Bill will be interested in this logical definition. The chances are, however, that he will not. He may be trying to tell his employer that his wife is in the hospital, his children are sick, doctors' bills are rapidly accumulating, and he cannot pay them. It may be that in Bill's company there is a fund to take care of such cases, a fund which Bill does not know of but his employer does. However, Bill has no chance to tell his story. He leaves the office disgruntled. Instead of getting human understanding, he gets a logical definition which in all probability only succeeds in increasing his conviction that his piece rates are too low and that he is being treated unfairly.

Sentiments have another interesting property. They are such an intimate part of our mental equipment that often we cannot make them explicit. They act in our thinking as a system of absolute truths. For this reason they enter into the determination of our everyday judgments and thoughts. They constitute our ultimate values and significances in terms of which we assess our everyday world.

Probably the most interesting characteristic of certain sentiments is their tendency to build themselves up into systems, patterns, or configurations. These systems of sentiments also have certain properties. They tend to persist and to resist change. For the industrial leader, there is nothing more important than an understanding of the systems of sentiments which bind individuals together into social groups.[2]

2. See T. N. Whitehead, "Leadership Within Industrial Organizations," *Harvard Business Review* (Winter 1936), 161–171. In this article Mr. Whitehead makes four important generalizations about this group of sentiments.

INDUSTRY AS A SYSTEM OF SENTIMENTS

Let us now conceive of an industrial establishment as a system or pattern of sentiments. This way of looking at things will help us to see how every item and event in the industrial environment becomes an object of a system of sentiments. According to this way of looking at things, material goods, physical events, wages, hours of work, and so on, cannot be treated as things in themselves. Instead, they have to be interpreted as carriers of social value.

A cursory examination of any large-scale industrial establishment will reveal that the jobs within it are socially ordered. Some of them carry more prestige and social significance than others. This ordering of significance, it will be found, is reflected in a number of different ways: in methods of payment, in hours of work, and in working conditions. Wages, for example, vary with occupations, and these wage differentials frequently serve to reinforce occupational stratification. Much evidence could be cited to show that the worker is quite as much concerned with these differentials—that is, the relation of his wages to the wages of the other workmen—as with the absolute amount of his wages. In short, the job and all those factors connected with it serve to define the position of the person performing that job in the social organization of the company of which he is a member. That jobs are socially ordered is a fact of the greatest importance. For it will be seen that, in so far as this holds true, any change in the job is likely to alter the existing routine relations between the person whose job it is and other people within the plant. But changes in the social significance of work are not confined to changes in the job alone. The physical task may remain the same, but its social significance may be altered by changes in working conditions. When it is perceived that many such conditions are symbolic of the status of the job, it is easy to understand why this is so. If the only visible difference in two levels of supervision is the size or arrangement of the desk, the color of the carpet, or the kind of calendar pad each supervisor has, that difference, as anyone who has lived in such situations knows, assumes considerable significance, not only to the executives but to the people reporting to them.

The following incident illustrates how important small things may become in a situation permeated with social value: The personnel of a certain department was moved from one building to another. In the new location, because of lack of space, it was found necessary to seat four people across the aisle from the remainder of the group. It happened that there were three women in the department who were to be transferred to other work. These three were given desks across the aisle so that their going would not necessitate a rearrangement of desks. The fourth person, a man, was also given a desk there, simply because there was no other place for him to sit. In choosing the fourth person, the supervisor was undoubtedly influenced by the fact that he was older than the rest of the group and was well acquainted with the three women. But, beyond that, nothing was implied by the fact that he was chosen. Now see how he interpreted this change. He felt that his supervisor regarded him as one of the women. The women were being transferred to other types of work; consequently he too would be transferred before long. Two of the women were being transferred to jobs in the shop. He, himself, might be transferred to the shop; and there was nothing he dreaded more. Having dwelt on speculations like this for a while, the employee recalled with alarm that his name had been omitted from the current issue of the house telephone directory. This omission had been quite accidental. The house telephone directory, however, constituted in this concern a sort of social register. Names of shop people below the rank of assistant foreman were not printed unless they were employed in some special capacity requiring contacts with other organizations. With the exception of typists and certain clerical groups, the names of all office people were listed. The fact that his name had been omitted now took on new significance. It tended to reinforce his growing conviction that he was about to be transferred to an unimportant shop position. He became so preoccupied with the problem that he could not work. He was completely demoralized.

Now from a rational point of view it may seem silly for this employee to have drawn so many erroneous conclusions; but, like most social beings, he was responding to certain social signals. In this case, however, the signals got twisted.

FIVE SOCIAL GROUPS IN INDUSTRY

Looking at an industrial plant from the point of view of sentiments reveals another important fact. It shows that no simple twofold classification of the personnel can be made—into employers and employees, for instance, or management and workers, or supervisors and employees. In any plant of moderate size such an inspection will reveal at least five groups whose interrelations need to be considered:

(1) A group of people in whom responsibility for the concern as a whole is vested, which is generally called management.

(2) A group of supervisors through whom in part management exercises control. This group is not so much concerned with general administrative problems as with getting a job done and carrying out the orders of the managerial group.

(3) A group of technical specialists through whom in part management also exercises control, which includes the highly trained engineer, the efficiency expert, the cost accountant, and the rate setter.

(4) A group of office workers and clerical assistants.

(5) A group of shop, bench, and machine workers.

A study of the interrelations among these five groups reveals some interesting results. It shows how, unwittingly, the attempt to rationalize industry at the expense of social sentiments may produce a constraint type of morality. Consider first the relation between the technologist and the worker.

The Relation between the Technologist and the Worker

Perhaps the chief characteristic of the technologist group of persons is that they are experimentally minded. They think in terms of the logic of efficiency, and they scrutinize everything that comes within their scope in these terms. This group is constantly striving to make improvements in machines, mechanical processes, and products. Sometimes they devise ingenious ways of bringing the worker's actions in line with the logic of efficiency. If the assumptions on which such plans are based be granted, they are perfectly sound. Certainly the technologist has no intention of foisting an arbitrary set of rules upon the worker. In fact, most of his plans are designed to help the worker. Carefully thought out wage plans are intended to reimburse the worker with a wage proportional to his efforts. The simplification of his job, whether through a change in process, division of labor, or elimination of random movements, is supposed to make his work easier and less fatiguing. If fatigue is eliminated, the worker, theoretically, can produce more and can thereby earn more money.

Now it happens frequently that these logical plans to promote efficiency and collaboration do not work out as intended. From the point of view of sentiments, they involve consequences which sometimes defeat the logical purposes of the plan as conceived. Let me point out some of these possible nonlogical consequences. When skill is divorced from the job at the work level and put in the hands of a group of technologists, a situation is created whereby the worker is put in a position of having to accommodate himself continually to changes which he does not initiate. And not only is he asked to accommodate himself to changes which he does not initiate, but also many of these changes deprive him of those very things which give meaning and significance to his work. In the language of the sentiments, it is as if the worker were told that his own individual skills, his acquired routines of work, his cultural traditions of craftmanship, his personal interrelations, had absolutely no value. Now, such nonlogical consequences have devastating effects on the individual. They make him feel insecure, frustrated, or exasperated.

The Relation between the Supervisor and the Worker

Unlike the technologist, the supervisor is related to the worker in a direct, personal, face-to-face way. Moreover, the supervisor has disciplinary authority over the worker. To say that one person has disciplinary authority over another is to say that the superior is under the obligation of seeing that his subordinate's conduct is in accord with certain prescribed norms. The father-son relationship, for example, contains this element of disciplinary authority. But let us see how it differs from the supervisor-employee relationship in terms of the norms of conduct with reference to which discipline is exercised. In the case of the father-son relationship these norms are set by society at large. The father disciplines the son into socially controlled and socially approved modes of behavior, and he is aided in the process by numerous social institutions, such as the church and school. In the case of the supervisor-employee relationship, no similar social codes exist. The criterion in terms of which the supervisor must exercise discipline is not the convention of ordinary social living, but the logic of efficiency. He has to be constantly insisting that the worker's behavior correspond to what the logic of efficiency represents it to be. But what does the logic of efficiency represent the worker's behavior to be? It assumes that the worker is a logical being, primarily motivated by economic interest, who will see the various technical systems set up for his economic interests as the creators of these systems see them; namely, as logical, coherent schemes which the worker can use, and should use, to his own advantage. However, some matters do not work out as the strict logic of the situation dictates. In human situations things do not mean to individuals what they are logically intended to mean. They are or they mean what human sentiments interpret them to be or to mean. And so here we have the paradox: The very schemes management devises to promote collaboration may become the very factors which prevent effective collaboration. What in the language of efficiency is intended as a source of help may become, when translated into the language of sentiments, a source of constraint.

The supervisor is in a difficult situation. More than any other person, he knows that it is impossible to uphold strictly the logic of efficiency without sometimes demoralizing his group. Many rules which he is supposed to enforce and which, in terms of technical efficiency, should promote efficiency and thereby redound to the worker's advantage, become in terms of the worker's sentiments petty annoyances which deprive his work of social significance. So the supervisor is put in a position of having to give lip service to a point of view which it would be suicidal to practice. He has to talk in one way and behave in another.

In one department, for example, where three occupational groups were working together (wiremen, soldermen, and inspectors) there was an unwritten rule to the effect that not more than two wiremen should help each other in wiring the same equipment. This rule received its sanction from the logic of efficiency, which said that the wiremen could turn out more work by working only on the equipments to which they were assigned. There would be less opportunity for talking, less likelihood of their getting in one another's way, and less likelihood of their delaying the soldermen. To the wiremen, however, this was just another arbitrary rule. Many of them preferred to work together occasionally. It was one of the ways in which they expressed their social solidarity. The supervisor recognized this situation. Moreover, he knew that working together did not necessitate slowing down. In fact, the evidence showed that when the wiremen were refused the privilege of helping one another, they became more inefficient. So occasionally he allowed this type of behavior to continue. By so doing, however, he was running counter to the logic of efficiency, the logic he was under obligation to uphold.

It can be seen that one of the chief sources of constraint in a working group can be a logic of efficiency which does not take into account the worker's sentiments. Any activity not strictly in accordance with the logic of efficiency (and sometimes this means most forms of social be-havior) becomes wrong and can only be indulged in surreptitiously. Social activity is driven into the ground, where it forms at a lower level in opposition to the technical organization.

CONCERNING APPLICABILITY

The time has come to restate the question. We started with two assertions: first, that one of the chief functions of an industrial leader is to secure collaboration, and, second, that in matters pertaining to collaboration the sentiments and their interactions are very important. On the ground, therefore, that it is wise to know something about the nature of the phenomenon to be controlled, we looked at the proper-ties of sentiments. We noticed their stubborn, persistent character in their resistance to rapid change and to modification by logic. We observed their ubiquitous nature. With these characteristics in mind, we examined the industrial environment. We noticed how sentiments are being reflected in the worker's job and in his surrounding condi-tions. We noticed that even in simple matters, such as the moving of desks and chairs, sentiments are also likely to be manipulated. We saw how the logic of efficiency may appear to the worker as something quite different from what it is intended to be. In short, we elaborated a way of looking at things from the point of view of the sentiments. We erected a more explicit framework for ideas already intuitively derived. But now the question can be raised: Granted that this is a useful way of looking at things, how can it be applied? What are the methods of application?

The application of this point of view to practice is something which some people are doing intuitively all the time. Its skillful application has gone under a number of different names: good breeding, manners, tact, diplomacy, courtesy, personality, charm, wisdom, and understand-ing. However, there is a method which applies this point of view to practice more explicitly and systematically.

THE INTERVIEWING METHOD

This method is called interviewing. It is a method of assessing a per-son's attitudes and the factors determining them. Whenever one under-goes this experience of sitting down and patiently listening to an individual, not with the purpose of making any moral judgments, but with the purpose of trying to understand why he feels and acts as he does, a new outlook is likely to develop. One discerns the beginnings of a new method of human control.

During the period from 1928 to 1930 members of the industrial relations staff of the Hawthorne plant of the Western Electric Company interviewed some 20,000 employees. In the beginning they hoped to get "facts" in the strict sense. From these data they hoped to improve working conditions and company policy. But what they did get from the interviews was an inextricable mixture of fact and sentiment. This outpouring of human sentiments could not be used in the simple fashion originally conceived. However, it is to the credit of management that they did not throw this material into the rubbish heap. They began to see that sentiments, when properly understood and interpreted, constituted social data of the greatest importance.

Probably one of the most interesting developments of this interviewing program was the experience which the interviewers themselves received and in turn communicated to supervisors. When some of the more enterprising of the interviewers realized the nature of the material they were eliciting from employees, they began to devise rules and techniques for ferreting out and trying to understand the employees' sentiments. Curiously enough, the very rules they devised to improve their interviewing technique, they found were easily translatable into simple rules for the supervisor in handling his personal relations. These rules apply to the first-line supervisor, as well as to the higher executive, in his relation to individuals with whom he has face-to-face contacts.[3]

The first rule is that the supervisor should listen patiently to what his subordinate has to say before making any comment himself. Probably the quickest way to stop a person from sufficiently expressing himself is to interrupt. Of course, it follows that, besides actively listening and not interrupting, the supervisor should try to understand what his subordinate is saying. Moreover, he should show his interest in what is being said.

The second rule is that the supervisor should refrain from hasty disapprobation of his subordinate's conduct. It is not his business, in

3. Some of these rules have already been reported in a preliminary statement of some of the Western Electric Company researches. See Elton Mayo, *The Human Problems of an Industrial Civilization* (New York: Macmillan, 1933), pp. 77–121.

the first instance at least, to give advice or moral admonition. If the employee says, "This is a hell of a company to work for," the attitude of the supervisor should not be, "Tut, tut, my good man, you are not displaying the proper spirit." Instead, he should try to get the employee to express himself more fully by asking why he feels as he does. In many instances employees by themselves are not able to state precisely the particular source of their dissatisfaction, but if they are encouraged to talk freely the effect is not merely emotional relief but also the revelation to the critical listener (and sometimes even to the speaker himself) of the locus of the complaint.

The third rule is that the supervisor should not argue with his subordinate. It is futile to try to change sentiments by logic. The best way for the supervisor to avoid arguments is to see that the employee's sentiments do not act on his own. It will be remembered that when Bill told his employer that his piece rates were too low he acted upon his employer's sentiments. The employer felt that he had to defend his wage rates.

The fourth rule is that the supervisor should not pay exclusive attention to the manifest content of the conversation. The interviewers had discovered that there is a tendency to rationalize sentiments and that in ordinary social intercourse the participants are likely to become more interested in the truth of the rationalizations than in the sentiments that are being expressed. Bill's employer, it will be remembered, paid attention only to the manifest content of Bill's complaint, with the result that he failed to learn anything about Bill's personal situation.

The fifth rule is that the supervisor should listen not only to what a person wants to say but also to what he does not want to say or cannot say without assistance. A person has difficulty in talking about matters which are associated with unpleasant and painful experiences, and many sentiments tend to remain so much in the background of a person's thinking that he is unaware of them. It is important to listen for what a person regards as so obvious and so common that it never occurs to him to doubt or question it. These implicit assumptions are of the greatest importance in assessing a person's values and significances. How often one discerns when listening to people the following assumptions: that everything that is not perfectly safe is dangerous (the common assumption of the hypochondriac); that everything that is not perfectly clean is dirty (the fussy housekeeper); that everything that is not perfectly good is bad (the Puritan); that everything that is not perfectly efficient is inefficient (some efficiency engineers). These are all false distinctions and oversimplifications.[4]

A NEW CONCEPTION OF COLLABORATION AND LEADERSHIP

In short, then, as a result of interviewing experience at Hawthorne, a new conception of leadership was developed. This conception began to percolate to the higher ranks of supervision and to the higher executives of the company. They found that one of their functions as supervisors and managers was to listen to, and become better acquainted with, the sentiments of their employees and with the nature of that social structure, or system of sentiments, called "the company." They began to see that each industrial concern had a social structure, that this social structure was related to the wider social structure of the community. They began to see that it was very important for them to understand their own social structure, for this structure defined the limits and degree of collaboration. When they listened to the complaints of their employees, they realized they were listening to the creakings and groanings of their own social structure. When they saw the newly arrived young college man making an ass of himself, annoyed at the red tape which seemed to block his movements at every turn, they began to realize they were watching the painful adaptations of a logically tutored individual to a complicated social structure with which he was unacquainted. They began to understand better the battered and mutilated state in which their own neat plans and policies finally reached the worker, after have been transmitted through an elaborate supervisory hierarchy. Also they began to understand better why the reports they received from their immediate subordinates as to what was happening at the front line, after having been transmitted through an elaborate supervisory hierarchy, did not quite coincide with what they learned from the interviewing program.

In short, they began to see that right before their eyes was occurring a very complicated phenomenon, a phenomenon which was very different from what it was represented to be in their blueprint plans. This complicated phenomenon was an intricate web of human rela-

4. For an interesting discussion of these rules of interviewing as applied to fields other than industry, see L. J. Henderson, "Physician and Patient as a Social System," *New England Journal of Medicine* (May 1935), 819–823.

tions bound together by a system of sentiments. Such a social structure is riddled with social routines which define our attitudes and feelings, our duties and obligations to one another. It tells us what kind of behavior is expected of us, as well as the kind of behavior we can expect from others.

Many industrial problems need to be redefined in terms of social structure. In the first place, we have to understand better the particular social structures of industry. Industrial organizations make for socially ordered, if not logical, living. In terms of social routines they control and regulate the behavior and the attitudes of the individuals within them. Not only do such organizations make for efficient social living; they also make for stability. Any serious disruption of them arouses feelings of insecurity among their members.

However, this respect for social structure in general should not blind us to the limitations of certain social structures in particular. Social structures not only make for stability; in some instances they make for red tape. They also make for difficulties in communication, difficulties in transmitting orders down the line as well as in obtaining accurate information up the line. There are certain types of structures which prevent the right kind of men from reaching the top rather than facilitating their progress. In other words, *the social structure of any particular company determines the kind of collaboration, the kind of people who will stay in the company, and the kind of people who will reach the top.*

Postscript, 1968

I had one other reason for including this essay in this present collection, and it was personal. This was my first attempt as a young man to talk to an audience of prominent business executives, whom at this period in my career I viewed with mixed feelings of a "false dichotomy" character, such as could be illustrated by the question, for example, were they to remain the robber barons or to become the saviors of our industrial civilization?

But the warm and enthusiastic reception this talk received from this distinguished audience I found so rewarding that like one of B. F. Skinner's obsessive pigeons I have continued pecking away for now nearly thirty years at what I thought was the same target. But upon reflection now I fear that in the interim, the target changed. The robber barons or saviors-to-become turned into "organization men." Nevertheless, my behavior did not change because the new organization men kept rewarding my speeches in the same way that the old robber barons or saviors-to-become had done.

3 The Foreman: Master and Victim of Double Talk

This article was first published in the *Harvard Business Review*, Spring 1945 (copyright 1945 by the President and Fellows of Harvard College), and that version is reproduced here. It is one of the most popular articles I ever wrote. The *Review* has sold thousands of reprints and the piece has been included in several books of readings. The essay was republished by the *Harvard Business Review* twenty years later in 1965 in their series of *HBR Classics*, at which time they asked me for my further reflections about it. I will add them at the end of the essay.

The increasing dissastisfaction of foremen in mass production industries, as evidenced by the rise of foremen's unions, calls for more human understanding of the foreman's situation. This dissatisfaction of foremen is no new, nor static, problem. It arises from the dynamic interaction of many social forces and is part and parcel of the structure of modern industrial organization. In its present manifestation it is merely a new form and outbreak of an old disease, which management has repeatedly failed to recognize, let alone diagnose or treat correctly. Master and victim of double talk, the foreman is management's contribution to the social pathology of American culture.

Some of the reasons cited in the current situation for the increasing receptiveness of foremen to unionization in mass production industries are:

(1) The weekly take-home of many foremen is less than that of the men working under them; this condition has been aggravated under war conditions in those factories where foremen do not receive extra compensation for working overtime.

(2) The influx of inexperienced workers, under war demands, has made the foremen's jobs more difficult.

(3) The rise of industrial unions has stripped the foremen of most of their authority.

(4) Many union-minded workers have been upgraded to supervisory positions.

(5) Many production workers promoted to the rank of foremen during the war expansion face the possibility of demotion after the war and the sacrifice of seniority credits in the unions from which they came for the period spent as foremen.[1]

1. See Herbert R. Northrup, "The Foreman's Association of America," *Harvard Business Review* (Winter, 1945), 187.

It would be absurd to argue that these factors, particularly as they are aggravated by war conditions, have not contributed to the grievances which foremen hope to correct by unionization. In a number of companies it is only fair to say that management has recognized some of these grievances and, when possible, has taken corrective steps. But is the correction of these grievances alone enough? Unfortunately, the possibility still exists that too little attention will be given to the underlying situation. The symptom-by-symptom attack that management is prone to take in solving its human affairs will fail to go below the surface. Failing to recognize the hydraheaded character of the social situation with which it is faced, management will cut off one head, only to have two new heads appear.

The major thesis of this article therefore will be that once again "management's chickens have come home to roost."[2] And this question is raised: Can management afford not to take responsibility for its own social creations—one of which is the situation in which foremen find themselves?

THE POSITION OF THE FOREMAN

Nowhere in the industrial structure more than at the foreman level is there so great a discrepancy between what a position ought to be and what a position is. This may account in part for the wide range of names which foremen have been called—shall we say "informally"? —and the equally great variety of definitions which have been applied to them in a more strictly formal and legal sense. Some managements have been eloquent in citing the foremen's importance with such phrases as: "arms of management," "grass-roots level of management," "key men in production," "front-line personnel men," and the like. Not so definite is the status of foremen under the National Labor Relations Act, since they can be included under the definitions given both for "employers" and "employees." To many foremen themselves they are merely the "go-betweeners," the "forgotten men," the "stepchildren" of industry. And what some employees call some foremen we shall leave to the reader's imagination.

But even without this diversity of names, it is clear that from the point of view of the individual foreman the discrepancy between what

2. See Clinton S. Golden and Harold J. Ruttenberg, *The Dynamics of Industrial Democracy* (New York: Harper & Brothers, 1942).

he should be and what he is cannot fail to be disconcerting. At times it is likely to influence adversely what he actually does or does not do, communicates or does not communicate to his superiors, his associates, and his subordinates. For this reason let us try to understand better the foreman's position in the modern industrial scene.

It is in his new streamlined social setting, far different from the "good old days," that we must learn to understand the modern foreman's anomalous position. The modern foreman has to get results— turn out production, maintain quality, hold costs down, keep his employees satisfied—under a set of technical conditions, social relations, and logical abstractions far different from those which existed 25 years ago.

For one thing, he has to "know" more than his old-time counterpart. Any cursory examination of modern foreman training programs will reveal that the modern foreman has to know (and understand) not only (1) the company's policies, rules, and regulations and (2) the company's cost system, payment system, manufacturing methods, and inspection regulations, in particular, but also frequently (3) something about the theories of production control, cost control, quality control, and time and motion study, in general. He also has to know (4) the labor laws of the United States, (5) the labor laws of the state in which the company operates, and (6) the specific labor contract which exists between his company and the local union. He has to know (7) how to induct, instruct, and train new workers; (8) how to handle and, where possible, prevent grievances; (9) how to improve conditions of safety; (10) how to correct workers and maintain discipline; (11) how never to lose his temper and always to be "fair"; (12) how to get and obtain cooperation from the wide assortment of people with whom he has to deal; and, especially, (13) how to get along with the shop steward. And in some companies he is supposed to know (14) how to do the jobs he supervises better than the employees themselves. Indeed, as some foreman training programs seem to conceive the foreman's job, he has to be a manager, a cost accountant, an engineer, a lawyer, a teacher, a leader, an inspector, a disciplinarian, a counselor, a friend, and, above all, an "example."

One might expect that this superior knowledge would tend to make the modern foreman feel more secure as well as to be more effective. Unfortunately some things do not work out the way they are intended. Quite naturally the foreman is bewildered by the many different roles and functions he is supposed to fulfill. He is worried in particular by what the boss will think if he takes the time to do the many things his many training courses tell him to do. And in 99 cases out of 100 what the boss thinks, or what the foreman thinks the boss thinks, will determine what the foreman does. As a result, the foreman gives lip service in his courses to things which in the concrete shop situation he feels it would be suicidal to practice. In the shop, for the most part, he does his best to perform by hook or by crook the one function clearly left him, the one function for which there is no definite staff counterpart, the one function for which the boss is sure to hold him responsible; namely, getting the workers to turn the work out on time. And about this function he feels his courses do not say enough—given the particular conditions, technical, human, and organizational, under which he has to operate.

Curiously enough, knowledge is not power for the modern foreman. Although he has to know a great deal about many things, he is no longer "the cock of the walk" he once was. Under modern conditions of operation, for example, there seems to be always somebody in the organization in a staff capacity who is supposed to know more than he does, and generally has more to say, about almost every matter that comes up; somebody, in addition to his boss, with whom he is supposed to consult and sometimes to share responsibility; somebody by whom he is constantly advised and often even ordered.

To the foreman it seems as if he is being held responsible for functions over which he no longer has any real authority. For some time he has not been able to hire and fire and set production standards. And now he cannot even transfer employees, adjust the wage inequalities of his men, promote deserving men, develop better machines, methods, and processes, or plan the work of his department, with anything approaching complete freedom of action. All these matters for which he is completely or partially responsible have now become involved with other persons and groups, or they have become matters of company policy and union agreement. He is hedged in on all sides with cost standards, production standards, quality standards, standard methods and procedures, specifications, rules, regulations, policies, laws, contracts, and agreements; and most of them are formulated without his participation.

Far better than the old-timer of 25 years ago the modern foreman knows how much work should be done in what length of time; how much it is worth; what the best methods to be used are; what his material, labor, and burden costs should be; and what the tolerances are that his product should meet. But in the acquisition of all this untold wealth of knowledge, somehow something is missing. In some sense, not too clearly defined, he feels he has become less rather than more effective, less rather than more secure, less rather than more important, and has received less rather than more recognition.

INTERACTIONS WITH MANY PEOPLE

Let us explore further this feeling of the modern foreman. Not only does he have to know more than his old-time counterpart about the "logics" of management, but also he has to relate himself to a wider range of people. In any mass production industry the foreman each day is likely to be interacting (1) with his boss, the man to whom he formally reports in the line organization; (2) with certain staff specialists, varying from one to a dozen people depending on the size and kind of organization—production control men, inspectors, standards men, efficiency engineers, safety engineers, maintenance and repair men, methods men, personnel men, counselors; (3) with the heads of other departments to which his department relates; (4) with his subordinates —sub-foremen, straw bosses, leadmen, group leaders, section chiefs; (5) with the workers directly, numbering anywhere from 10 to 300 people; and (6) in a union-organized plant, with the shop steward. Exploring the interdependence of each of these relationships as they impinge in toto upon the foreman makes it easier to understand how the modern foreman may feel in his everyday life. A diagram may help to make this clear (see EXHIBIT 3.1).

Foreman-Superior

In the modern business structure there is probably no relation more important than that of the subordinate to his immediate superior.[3] This statement applies straight up the line from worker to president. It is in the relation between a subordinate and his immediate superior that most breakdowns of coordination and communication between various parts of the industrial structure finally show up. It is here that distortions of personal attitude and emotional disturbances become

3. See B. B. Gardner, *Human Relations in Industry* (Chicago: Richard D. Irwin, 1945).

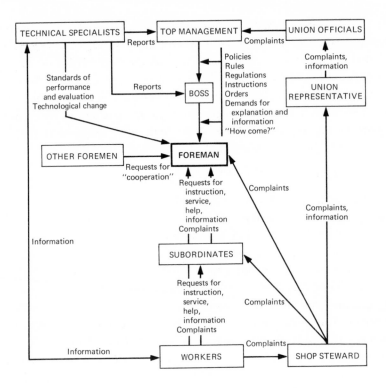

EXHIBIT 3.1. Forces Impinging upon the Foreman

This diagram shows only those forces impinging upon the foreman through the actions of other people. It is not designed to show the reaction of the foreman to these actions, either in terms of feelings or overt behavior, or to show the reactions of the workers to management's actions, which in turn become one of the chief forces acting upon the foreman. These reactions will be considered in the text.

more pronounced. Why this relation is so important could be indicated in any number of ways. But it is clear that any adequate analysis would go far beyond the confines of this article, since it would involve a critique of modern business organization and the individual's relation to authority and, in part, an examination of the ideologies held by the leaders and executives of business.[4] It is enough that the importance of this relation and its consequences in terms of behavior,

4. See Chester I. Barnard, *The Functions of the Executive* (Cambridge: Harvard University Press, 1938), pp. 161–184.

particularly at the foreman level, are matters of common observation; and it will be at this level of behavior and its associated *feelings* that we shall remain.

Personal dependence upon the judgments and decisions of his superiors, so characteristic of the subordinate–superior relation in modern industry, makes the foreman's situation basically insecure.[5] He feels constant need to adjust himself to the demands of his superior and to seek the approval of his superior. Everything that he does he tries to evaluate in terms of his superior's reaction. Everything that his superior does he tries to evaluate in terms of what it means or implies about his superior's relation to him. Everything that his subordinates and workers do he immediately tries to evaluate in terms of the criticism it may call forth from his superior. In some cases this preoccupation with what the boss thinks becomes so acute that it accounts for virtually everything the foreman says or does and all his thinking about what goes on around him. He will refrain from doing anything, even to the point of dodging responsibility, for fear of bringing disapproval from the boss. Hours at work and at home are spent in figuring and anticipating what explanations or reasons he will need to give the boss. And the boss's most innocent and unintentional acts—failure to say "good morning," for instance—are taken perhaps to imply disapproval.

It is hard to realize how much those who are interested in improving the efficiency of industry have neglected this area. If the man-hours spent by subordinates both on and off the job in preoccupation about what the boss thinks were added up, the total hours would be staggering—not to mention the results this phenomenon has produced in nervous breakdowns and other forms of mental anguish. Stranger still, it almost appears as if modern industrial organization, which prides itself so much on its efficiency, has aggravated rather than reduced the amount of this preoccupation, with disastrous consequences for health and thus for efficiency. All this applies to the foreman in particular.

The crux of the foreman's problem is that he is constantly faced with the dilemma of (1) having to keep his superior informed with what is happening at the work level (in many cases so that his superior may prepare in turn for the unfavorable reaction of his superior and so on up the line) and (2) needing to communicate this information in such

5. For an excellent statement on this point, see Douglas McGregor, "Conditions of effective Leadership in the Industrial Organization," originally published in the *Journal of Consulting Psychiatry* (1944) and reprinted in the *Massachusetts Institute of Technology Publications in Social Science*, Series 2, No. 16.

a way that it does not bring unfavorable criticism on himself for not doing his job correctly or adequately. Discrepancies between the way things are at the work level and the way they are represented to be by management cannot be overlooked, and yet the foreman feels obliged to overlook them when talking to his boss. This makes the foreman's job particularly "tough" and encourages him to talk out of both sides of his mouth at the same time—to become a master of double talk.

Each foreman, of course, resolves the conflict in terms of his own personal history, personality, and temperament. Some foremen become voluble in the face of this situation; others are reduced to stony silence, feeling that anything they say will be held against them. Some keep out of the boss's way, while others devise all sorts of ways for approaching him and trying to direct attention to certain things they have accomplished. And extraordinary are the skills which some more verbally articulate foremen develop in translating *what is* into a semblance of *the way it ought to be* in order to appease their superiors and keep them happy.

But, for the most part, the foreman, being loyal and above all wanting to be secure, resolves the conflict and maintains good relations with his superiors by acting strictly in accordance with his functional relations and the logics of management. In spite of what this may lead to in his relations to workers and other groups, his relations with his superiors at least are not jeopardized.

Thus the foreman, like each individual in the modern industrial structure, is in effect painfully tutored to focus his attention upward to his immediate superiors and the logics of evaluation they represent, rather than downward to his subordinates and the feelings they have. So rigid does the conditioning of supervisors and executives in the industrial structure become in this respect that it is almost impossible for them to pay attention to the concrete human situations below them, rich in sentiments and feelings. For them, this world of feeling does not exist; the territory is merely populated with the abstractions which they have been taught to see and the terms in which they communicate —"base rates," "man-hours," "budgets," "cost curves," "production schedules," and so on.

Foreman–Specialist

Also of extreme importance are the foreman's relations to the technical specialists who *originate* the standards of performance which he must *uphold* and to which his subordinates and workers must *conform*. This experimentally minded group of engineers, accountants, and technologists can become one of the chief sources of change, and rapid change, at the work level; through them changes can be introduced at the work level at a more rapid rate than they can be assimilated by customary shop codes and practices. Through them, also, "controls" can be exercised far more precisely than heretofore. It is one thing for a foreman to know what his cost performance has been; it is another matter to know what his actual costs should be in relation to a standard. What was heretofore a matter of experiential judgment after the fact becomes now a matter of projective evaluation and of constantly shooting at a target—a target whose outlines become increasingly more clear-cut and demanding, at least in one area of his job.

It is little wonder that this group can become (although it does not need to become, as we shall discuss later) a constant source of threat to the foreman's feelings of security. These men of course affect and often make more difficult his relations to workers. They also provide reports to management which can make his relations to his boss exceedingly uncomfortable. The result: more double talk.

It is well to note that these control groups can (as can the union) short-circuit foremen and levels of supervision lower in the line by providing information direct to higher levels of supervision.[6] Whatever the value of this information in evaluating the foreman's performance, it results in certain pressures upon him. Each superior can request explanations from, or give orders to, his foreman based on such information; yet the foreman cannot control it and indeed may be unaware of it until his superior initiates action. Information flowing through the line the foreman can censor before it reaches the boss; but this way the boss can get information at the same time he does, or even before, and the foreman is no longer able to foresee or to gauge the boss's reaction. The results of this in mental anguish, in preoccupations, in worries about what the boss may think or do, in preparation of explanations, "good reasons," and alibis, are tremendous. Because of the subjective nature of the data, the technologists of industry have not as yet decided to study this area or even to give it much attention. But the modern foreman, from the point of view of both his effectiveness and his satisfaction at work, finds the actual phenomena only too real.

6. Discussed more fully by Gardner, *Human Relations.*

Foreman–Foreman

By the very nature of the closely knit technological processes of a manufacturing organization, the foreman of one department often has to work very closely with a foreman of another department. These lateral relations are not formally defined, and their functioning depends largely upon the informal understandings which exist between foremen. Thus, the kind and amount of cooperation which one foreman is likely to obtain from another foreman is in good part determined by their interpersonal relations. Here again, the boss comes in, because the preoccupation with what the boss thinks may also affect the foreman's relation to his colleagues at the same level.

Although all foremen have equal formal status, they do not, as everyone in a shop situation knows, enjoy equal informal status. The individual foreman's relative status is determined by such factors as age, sex, service, earnings, and social symbols of one sort or another. But the chief determining factor is his direct relation to the boss, i.e., how close he is to the boss. Not only the foreman's need for security but also the closely allied strivings for status and recognition are therefore directed to his superior. He needs to feel "close" to him. Thus he may constantly be comparing his relation to the boss with that of his colleagues. If this comparison indicates his position to be weak, he may enter into competition with his colleagues for recognition from the boss. As can be imagined, such emotional disturbances in the work situation may impede rather than facilitate cooperation among foremen, and they constitute a peculiar kind of "headache" for the superior.

Foreman–Worker

It is in his relation to the workers, however, with the rise of "scientific" management and with the growth of industrial unions, that the modern foreman's position becomes especially difficult. Here "the straw that breaks the camel's back" is finally reached. Here the problem of getting smooth operation becomes acute because, as we have seen, the foreman according to the logic of industrial organization must (1) *uphold* at the work level the standards, policies, rules, and regulations which have been *originated* by other groups and see to it that the workers *conform* to them and, at the same time, (2) obtain if possible the workers' spontaneous *cooperation* to this way of doing business. As anyone who has been in such a position knows, this is not a very easy task. As a rule, people do not like to conform to matters when they have no say in them, when they do not participate or feel that their point of view is taken into account. This is not a popular way of evoking spontaneity of cooperation; it is not consistent with our basic social values. Yet over and over again both foremen and workers are told, merely told, to conform to conditions over which they have very little or no say—conditions, moreover, which shockingly fail at times to take into account what is of vital importance to them in their work situations.

This state of affairs affects the foreman's personal situation: his strivings to satisfy his needs for security, personal integrity, and recognition in the work situation. Further, it makes his job in relation to his workers very difficult. Again and again, he is put in a position either of getting the workers' cooperation and being "disloyal" to management or of being "loyal" to management and incurring the resentment and overt opposition of his subordinates.

For those who do not fully appreciate the conflicting position in which the foreman is placed, it may be desirable to show the nature of the two contrasting worlds in the middle of which the foreman stands and spends his workaday life. In business, as in any organized human activity, there are two sets of social processes going on:

(1) There are those social processes which are directly related to the achievement of purpose and which result in "formal organization." In business, for example, formal organization leads to such things as practices established by legal enactment or policy, specifications, standard methods, standard procedures, standards of time, output, quality, cost, and so on. They are concerned with those means most appropriate to achieve certain ends. And as such they can be changed rapidly.

It should be noted that these manifestations of formal organization are essentially logical in character. Through formal organization man expresses his logical capacities; in fact, it is one of the chief outlets for the expression of man's logical capacities. It should also be noted that in the past 25 years there has been a tremendous amount of attention given to this aspect of business organization. It is in part because of this that, as we tried to show, the modern foreman's environment is so radically different from the good old days. And yet the foreman, unlike some higher executives, cannot stay only in this logically sheltered atmosphere.

(2) There are those spontaneous social processes going on in any organized human activity which have no specific, conscious common

purpose and which result in "informal organization." Informal organization leads to such things as custom, mores, folkway, tradition, social norms, and ideals. In business, for example, it expresses itself at the work level in such things as what constitutes fair wages, decent conditions of work, fair treatment, a fair day's work, and traditions of the craft. It takes the form of different status systems: e.g., old-timers should get preferential treatment; supervisors should get more money than their subordinates; and office workers are superior to shop workers. These are attitudes and understandings based on feeling and sentiment. They are manifestations of "belonging," and they do not change rapidly.

It should be especially noted that these manifestations of informal organization are not logical in character. They are concerned with values, ways of life, and ends in themselves—those aspects of social life which people strive to protect and preserve and for which at times they are willing to fight and even die. It should also be noted that a cursory examination of the periodicals, books, formal statements, and speeches of business executives and business experts shows that little systematic attention has been given to this aspect of business organization. This is indeed a curious state of affairs since, as every foreman intuitively knows, it is only through informal organization and its manifestations that he can secure spontaneity of cooperation at the work level.

Informal organization in any organized human activity serves a very healthy function. It binds people together in routine activity. It gives people a social place and feeling of belonging. It provides the framework for the fulfillment of human satisfaction. It gives people a feeling of self-respect, of independent choice, of not being just cogs in a machine. Far from being a hindrance to greater effectiveness, informal organization provides the setting which makes men willing to contribute their services.

Yet what is management's attitude toward these informal groups which form at the work level? Curiously enough, their appearance makes management uneasy. And sometimes management willfully tries to break them up. Such ill-conceived attempts inevitably produce open hostility to the aims of management. For informal organization cannot be prevented; it is a spontaneous phenomenon necessary wherever coordinated human activities exist.

More important still—for it is more often the case—these informal groups are ignored and not even recognized. Having no representation in the formal organization, which to many an executive is by definition the "reality," they just do not exist. As a result—not from malicious design but from sheer oversight born of overlogicized training—these informal groups at the work level become inadvertently the victims of change, disruption, and dislocation. Technical changes are introduced without any attention to what is happening to the members of these groups in terms of their group associations. New methods of work and new standards are initiated, newcomers are added, someone is transferred, upgraded, or promoted, and all as if this group life did not exist. What happens? There develops a feeling of being "pushed around"—a very uncomfortable feeling which most people dislike and which often provokes the reaction of trying to push the pusher with equal intensity in the opposite direction.

Because their way of life is constantly in jeopardy from technological changes, new methods, raised standards, and constant manipulation of one kind or another by logically minded individuals, these groups in industry take on a highly defensive and protective character. Their major function becomes, unfortunately, the resistance to change and innovation, and their codes and practices develop at variance with the economic purpose of the enterprise. Much pegging of output at a certain level by employees is an expression of this need to protect their ways of life, as well as their livelihood, from too rapid change.

As might be expected, these defensive and protective characteristics of many informal groups at the work level—and they exist full blown in many factories even before any formal union appears—have serious consequences for foremen (not to mention new workers and other individuals). Any supervisor or foreman in charge of such groups has two, if not three, strikes against him to begin with. Anything he does in relation to them is likely to be "wrong." To ignore them completely would be to invite overt hostility; to accept them completely would be to fail in fulfilling his responsibilities to management. Yet the foreman is the key man of management in administering technical changes. He often has the impossible task of taking plans made by the specialists without thought of the realities of human situations and relating them to just such situations.

Foreman–Union

Once these patterns of behavior become formalized in a union, the foreman's debacle becomes complete. Into this situation, now, is introduced a new set of logics, verbal definitions, rules, and regulations, by means of which he is supposed to set his conduct toward the workers. The last vestiges of initiative, of judgment, and, what is perhaps more important, of personal relations with his subordinates are taken away from him. Literally the foreman is left "holding the bag"—a bag containing (1) the maximum of exquisitely logical rules, definitions, procedures, policies, standards that the human mind can devise, by means of which he is now supposed to do his job, and (2) the minimum of those relationships and their associated feelings through which he can obtain the wholehearted cooperation of people. Standing in the middle of a now formally bifurcated situation, where one-half is trying to introduce changes and improvements into the factory situation and the other half by habit and conditioning is trying to prevent or resist them, the modern foreman is expected to "cooperate."

SUMMARY OF THE FOREMAN'S SITUATION

The salient features of the foreman's situation should now be clear. In very broad outline—tentatively and approximately formulated—the failure on the part of top management, in mass production industries in particular, to understand the social implications of its way of doing "business" has resulted in the development of certain rigidities which do not make for cooperation in the industrial structure.

(1) At the bottom of the organization there are people called *employees* who are in general merely supposed to *conform* to changes which they do not originate. Too often the attitude is that employees are merely supposed to do what they are told and get paid for it. Directing them there is—

(2) A group of *supervisors* who again are merely supposed to *uphold* —"administer" is the popular word—the standards of performance and policies determined by other groups, one of which is—

(3) A group of *technical specialists* who are supposed to *originate* better ways and better standards through which the economic purpose of the organization can be better secured and more effectively controlled by—

(4) A group of *top management* men who in their *evaluation* of the workers' behavior assume that the major inducement they can offer to people to cooperate is financial (i.e., that they are merely providing a livelihood, rather than a way of life); that informal organization is either "bad" or not "present"; and that authority comes from the top,

somewhat removed from but not unrelated to the concrete and the particular. And although concerned with "a moving equilibrium" and the social forces working both for and against it, nevertheless up to now he has paid almost exclusive attention to those social forces operating to upset stability—simply in order to bring out inescapably the fact that the forces making for unbalance do exist, in latent if not in active form, in *every* mass production industry. The picture presented thus far has been therefore a picture of the inexorable grinding out of the social forces and logics that modern technology has unleashed—in the raw, so to speak, and uncontrolled by the "administrative process." But we must not forget that there is, often equally present and equally strong, the compensatory function of the "administrator."

In the last analysis the forces acting upon the foreman, as upon any other individual in the industrial structure, are the actions of other people. It was for this reason that the actions of the principal people with whom the foreman has relations in his working environment were examined. It should be clear, however, that the actions of these different characters are not always the same. Bosses, technical specialists, foremen, workers, and shop stewards differ in their behavior, sometimes very radically. This fact cannot be ignored; indeed, its implications are tremendous. And if *management's* actions are different, foremen's reactions are likely to be different.

In business (and in unions too) there are not only "men of goodwill" but also men with extraordinary skill in the direction of securing cooperative effort. These men, at all levels, perform an "administrative" function the importance of which is too little recognized. Much of their time is spent in facilitating the process of communication and in gaining the wholehearted cooperation of men. Many of them are not too logically articulate, but they have appreciation for a point of view different from their own. Not only can they appreciate the fact that a person can be different from themselves, but more important still they can accept his right to be different. They always seem to have the time to listen to the problems and difficulties of others. They do not pose as "experts"; they know when to secure the appropriate aid from others.

Such "administrators," selfless and sometimes acting in a way which appears to be lacking in ambition, understand the importance of achieving group solidarity—the importance of "getting along," rather than of "getting ahead." They take personal responsibility for the mixed situations, both technical and human, that they administer. They see to it that the newcomer has an effective and happy relationship with his fellow workers, as well as gets the work out. Accomplishing their results through leisurely social interaction rather than vigorous formal action, more interested in getting their human relationships straight than in getting their words and logics straight, more interested in being "friendly" to their fellow men than in being abstractly "fair," and never allowing their "paper work" to interfere with this process of friendliness, they offer a healthy antidote to the formal logics of the modern factory organization previously described.

The importance of the "administrative" functions these men perform for the smooth running of any organization is incalculable, and fortunately industry has its fair share of such men. It is the author's impression that a greater proportion of them are found at the lower levels of management, because the logics of promotion in business organization seldom recognize their skills. Were it not for them, it is the author's opinion that the unleashed forces of modern technology would spin themselves out to doom and destruction. Aware of the two-fold function of industrial leadership, i.e., the social organization of teamwork and the logical organization of operations, they maintain that healthy balance which makes for individual growth and development and, ultimately, for survival of the organization.

Yet, curiously enough, the theories of administration, as frequently expressed by business leaders, experts, and teachers, bear little resemblance to the functions these men actually perform and give little justification to their actions. As a result, they sometimes suffer from feelings of inferiority and lose confidence in themselves, an unfortunate consequence for them as individuals and also for the organization they serve. It is not comfortable to think that industry may depend for its stability on the personal and intuitive skills of a few such gifted people. Can the "administrative" skills they practice, the skills of getting action through social interaction, be made explicit and communicated?

WHAT IS THE SOLUTION?

In the author's opinion, the foreman's dissatisfaction in large part results from actions of management. These actions of management are not the expression of maliciousness, bad faith, or lack of goodwill on the part of business executives. Far from it; they are merely the inexorable working out of the social forces which modern technology has produced and which we have not learned to recognize or control. They are the result of our ignorance and of our failure to pay as much explicit attention to the social organization of teamwork as to the logical organization of operations in our modern industrial enterprises.

The solution of the problem, therefore, seems to depend on a better realization of the "administrative process" as it operates to secure the cooperation of people in the furtherance of the economic objectives of business organizations. More than anything else, the modern world needs men who understand better the nature of, and give more explicit attention to, the social systems they administer. This is the challenge the modern world presents to business leadership; this is the great adventure for the coming generation. The business leaders of today and tomorrow, like the foremen, are facing a new "society," a stream-lined "adaptive" society, a world which modern technology has produced and which is far different from the "established" society of their forefathers.[8] For their effectiveness, as well as for their survival, the coming "administrators" must be given new skills and new insights.

Can this job be done? The signs of the times are promising. In all quarters of business there are resolute young men who "when hope is dead will hope by faith," who will build the new world. In this connection it is well to remember that man's enormous capacity for adaptation, readjustment, and growth is his most striking characteristic, and it is upon this strength that we can hopefully rely.[9] In business and educational institutions, a fresh breath of life is beginning to stir. The possibilities of new courses and new methods of teaching and training are being explored.

A NEW CONCEPT OF ADMINISTRATION

Can the outlines of this new "administration" be even dimly envisaged? What will these new "administrators" be like, and in what skills will they be trained? Here we can only guess and express some personal opinions and hopes:

(1) The new "administrator" will need to know and understand better the nature of "organization"—its structure and dynamic inter-

8. For an elaboration of this distinction between an "established" and an "adaptive" society, see Mayo, *Social Problems*.

9. On this point, see Carl R. Rogers, *Counseling and Psychotherapy* (Boston: Houghton Mifflin Co., 1942).

relations. It is indeed a strange remark to make, in the year 1945, that an executive will have to know something about "organization," the very phenomenon with which he daily deals. But strange as the remark may seem, the average executive knows little or nothing, except for what is implicitly registered in his nervous system, about the "social organization" of his business. Most of his explicit concern, most of his logical thinking is only about "formal organization." About the other aspects of organization, he only stews, frets, and gets stomach ulcers.

(2) "Administrators" of the future, to do their new jobs effectively, will have to develop a common language structure which represents accurately the interdependent realities of the phenomena with which they deal—technical, economic, organizational, social, and human. Too many different and often times conflicting "languages" riddle present business. No longer can the human beings who contribute their services to a business organization be regarded as "so many beads on a string." For the new world a new language has to be created which will keep together in words, rather than keep separate by words, those things that are together in the territory. This will be a language of mutually interdependent relations, of togetherness, of equilibrium, of adaptation, and of growth.[10]

(3) The new "administrator" will have to understand better the problem of communication—and not only the aspect of communication which by persuasion attempts to sell one's own point of view, but that which tries to understand and has respect for another's point of view. In the systematic practice of taking into account another person's point of view as the first step in obtaining that person's cooperation— a most difficult skill—he should have daily and continuous drill. He should be taught to listen, in addition to being logically lucid and clear. He should learn to practice the "democratic method" *at the level of daily interaction* in the work situation.

(4) New methods and new skills will have to be developed whereby change can be introduced into the work situation without provoking resistance. About no urgent and pressing problem of modern industry is there so little systematic knowledge—so little understanding and so much misunderstanding. In no area has it been so convincingly demonstrated, again and again and again, that people refuse to cooperate in meeting a standard of performance when they have not been allowed

10. For a good example of this, see the articles by Benjamin M. Selekman in this number [Spring 1945] and the preceding number of the *Harvard Business Review*.

to participate in setting it up or, many times, even to "understand" it. In no area are the ordinary methods of "salesmanship" so woefully lacking.

For this particular aspect of "administration," the introduction of changes into the shop, we shall need to exercise and practice new insights regarding human motivation. These insights will have to envisage how technological progress and improvement can go hand in hand with individual and social development. Technological change will have to be introduced at the work level so that the group affected will see it, in T. North Whitehead's phrase, as "an enlargement of its own way of life rather than as an interruption to it." And for the working out of these new methods and skills, more time and more effort will have to be given; more ingenuity and more understanding will have to be exercised.

(5) The new "administrator" will have to understand better the dependent relation of the subordinate to the superior in business organizations and the feelings of insecurity this dependence arouses. He will have to learn new methods and techniques of assuring his subordinate of those minimum conditions of security, not merely financial, without which the subordinate's position becomes intolerable. For this he will have to learn something about the principles of individual growth and development through active participation and assumption of responsibility, and these principles he will have to learn to practice in relation to his subordinates in an atmosphere of approval. He will have to learn to be responsible for people, not merely responsible for abstract and logical categories.

We will not obtain this type of "administrator" merely through verbal definition, i.e., by defining what his formal responsibilities and duties are. He has to be fostered and made to feel secure, allowed to grow and, occasionally, to make mistakes and thereby learn. He has to be nurtured like a plant; and the environment in which he grows, the care and human understanding he gets, will determine whether he flourishes or withers, gets bugs, and so on. Unlike our present foremen, who have suffered from too many logical definitions and too little human understanding, he must not be allowed to "wither" and be forced to join a union in order to recapture the zest of growth and life again.

(6) The new "administrator" will have to learn to distinguish the world of feelings from the world of facts and logic. And for dealing effectively with this world of feelings, he will have to learn new tech-

niques—which at first may seem strange, after having been ignored and misunderstood for so long. Particularly, of course, he will have to learn about "informal organization," that aspect of organization which is the manifestation of feeling and sentiment. Only by paying as much attention to informal organization as to formal organization will he become aware of what can and cannot be accomplished by policy formulation at the concrete level of behavior. He will have to learn new techniques of "control." He will see clearly that "feelings" cannot be verbally legislated out of existence; that, as a first step in their "control," they need to be expressed and recognized.

These and many other new methods and skills the new "administrator" will have to learn. He will have to learn to "control" the future by first learning to "control" the present. He will have to learn to formulate goals and ideals which make the present in which we live more, rather than less, meaningful. And to achieve these new levels of insight and practice, he will have to throw overboard completely, finally, and irrevocably—this will be difficult—the ideologies of the "established society" of the eighteenth and nineteenth centuries. This new. representative of a new "adaptive society" at all cost must not be the representative of an "ism." For he does not represent any particular way of life: he is only the guarantor of the "ways of life"—plural—that are important to many different people. In this task he can only represent what Elton Mayo calls "polyphasic methods" of dealing with the complex human, social, economic, and organizational problems of our industrial civilization.

Can we develop a group of such "administrators"? This of course is a matter of opinion. To the author it seems that, if only $\frac{1}{2}$ of 1% of the time, effort, and money that have been spent in the direction of technological improvement were to be devoted to seeking better and improved methods of securing cooperation, the accomplishment would be considerable—and that is an intentional understatement. It just does not seem sensible to suppose that man's ingenuity, if given free scope, would fail in this undertaking. The task is tremendous; the challenge is great; the stakes are high; but only by traveling some such arduous road, in the author's opinion, can business leadership face up to its real social responsibilities.

Retrospective Commentary, 1965

Today's readers of the *Harvard Business Review* are probably most interested in two questions. *First,* from an over-all point of view, what in this article is most relevant today? *Second,* more specifically, what is the foreman's situation today compared with what it was 20 years ago?

Relevance

In my opinion, the most significant element of the article resides in the method of analysis. Twenty years ago I made what today would be called a "role analysis" of the foreman's job. I looked at his relationships to the other members of his "role set," that is, to the other groups with whom he had to interact and who had something to say about what his role should be. Within these groups, I not only found no consensus but also discovered *conflicting expectations* about what the foreman was supposed to be doing. He suffered seriously from what today would be called "role conflict and ambiguity." He was "the man in the middle"—what I called then, "Master and Victim of Double Talk."

During the past two decades, continued researches from this point of view have shown that the foreman's dilemma is merely a "special case" of a more general problem. In modern industry the foreman is not the only man or position suffering from this "disease." Some of his colleagues on the staff and superiors in the line seem to have caught it too. As a result of the advance of science and technology, the acceleration of change, and the introduction of many new roles, modern industry seems to be riddled with role conflict and ambiguity. A recent study would seem to indicate that about 80% of the work force, from worker to president, may be suffering from some such strains, and that role conflict increases with supervisory rank in a curvilinear relationship "in which the maximum of conflict occurs at what might be called the upper middle levels of management." *

Role analysis, like any other method, is a useful but limited tool. Applied to the diagnosis of a particular situation, it can reveal some of the factors that may be making for trouble. Applied as a general model for the analysis of organizational behavior, it may find only what it is looking for. As the authors of the above-mentioned study cautioned, if one focuses too much on disease rather than on health, one can find only too easily that the whole world is ridden with disease.

So I too should like to warn my new readers to treat "role conflict" not as a disease to be eliminated but, rather, as something that needs to be better understood and managed. This is the difficult lesson to learn from the many disease-sounding syndromes, typologies, concepts, and words that the behavioral sciences have generated. The trick is how to use them—as Adlai Stevenson would have said—"without inhaling."

Foreman's Situation Today

Having made these preliminary remarks, I am now prepared to entertain the question, "Is there more or less role conflict at the foreman level in 1965 than 1945?"

---

* Robert L. Kahn et al., *Organizational Stress: Studies in Role Conflict and Ambiguity* (New York: John Wiley, 1964), p. 382.

The Foreman: Master and Victim of Double Talk

My first, honest answer is "I don't know," but I realize this may be unsatisfactory, so let me give you my second-best answer, which is closer to a guess.

In my judgment, the chances are better than even (say, 60%) that there is more conflict at the foreman level now than there was 20 years ago, but the conflict is probably being better managed, both by the foreman himself and by his boss and his boss's bosses. In 1945, the foreman seldom talked freely with other members of his "role set" in 1965, he can be found more often meeting with them in "natural groups." The manager of 1945 spent more of his time bossing the individual foremen; the manager of 1965 is spending more time managing "role sets." If the human relations movement in industry has made any difference, it is along these dimensions that I would be looking for it to show up. Otherwise, I fear that once again the experts in communication have failed to communicate. If so, I fear that we may have been spending too much time inhaling a new vocabulary and not enough time with the phenomena.

F.J.R.

4 Human Relations: Rare, Medium, or Well-Done

This article was published in the *Harvard Business Review*, January 1948 (copyright 1948 by the President and Fellows of Harvard College). It was my first attempt to separate out "human relations" from "scientific management," "personnel relations," "labor relations," and "administration"—areas with which I thought it was being confused and confounded. I thought that "human relations," at least as I conceived it, was slicing the cake quite differently from these other areas and that this difference of conceptualization should be recognized.

Man's proclivity for putting things together, for combining elements previously dissociated, for making new combinations, and his ever-continuing faith in the efficacy of his own combinations—a manifestation of behavior referred to by the Italian sociologist, Pareto, as "the instinct for combination"—has been vividly brought to this reviewer's attention by five recent books which, despite their varied approaches, all belong roughly in the same area. The books in question, which will be referred to in detail later, are Filipetti's *Industrial Management in Transition,* Milward's *An Approach to Management,* Maier's *Psychology in Industry,* Moore's *Industrial Relations and the Social Order,* and Pigors and Myers' *Personnel Administration.* What makes these books especially interesting to me is the way in which more or less the same topics are broken down, reshuffled, and put together in five different ways.

Each author seeks for first principles. Each author tries to put together a wide range of scattered materials. Each author looks in his scattered materials for the common thread that ties them all together and makes every part a subdivision of a larger whole, and does his best to show that they all branch out from a common source. Yet, depending upon whether the author is an economist, psychologist, sociologist, or administrator, the combinations that result are quite different. All this makes for good, exciting, and stimulating reading, particularly for those who themselves share to a high degree the bent for making bigger and better combinations.

On the other hand, those readers whose impulses to try something new are weak and whose particular combinations have tended to become congealed into fixed aggregates may find reading these five books together an overstimulating dose. For, peculiarly enough, what appears as a whole in one book becomes a subdivision in another book, and in each case "the common thread" bears a different label. Thus some readers may not like, for example, to see their pet combination, industrial psychology," which they consider a whole, made a subdivision of somebody else's whole called "scientific management"; and other readers will be equally shocked to find their whole, "scientific management," treated as a very small and, to boot, unscientific subdivision of a while called "industrial sociology." For it is an equally strong sentiment among men that they dislike to have their pet combinations reduced to the status of a subdivision.

I was particularly conscious of this feeling when reading the five books, because the research which my associates and I have done at the Harvard Business School, although most graciously acknowledged by all five authors, becomes finally in each case a subdivision of a larger whole. In one book we are "buddies" of Mr. Frederick Taylor—a small but important link in the "unfolding pattern of the scientific management movement." In another book our work becomes part of the field of "industrial psychology." In the other three books we are significant contributors to the fields of "industrial sociology," "personnel administration," and "management." To find our work such a vitalizing subdivision of so many different combinations was, of course, most flattering; nevertheless I had a very strong "they-can't-do-that-to-us" feeling, if you know what I mean. Man's liking for his own particular intellectual combination is very strong. He dislikes to be indiscriminately adopted by, or adapted to, "wholes" which he has not chosen for himself.

That this reaction on my part was highly subjective, nonlogical, and inappropriate to the situation I soon realized. In the present state of affairs in the social sciences, particularly on their applied side, this babel of nomenclature is bound to exist. In fact, if not too confusing, it may be a most healthy sign, since it may indicate that "something is cooking." Moreover the particular combination my associates and I represent in a very real sense *is* closely related to the areas of administration, labor and personnel relations, scientific management, industrial psychology, and industrial sociology. For some time I have been shouting this from the house tops. Why should I get disturbed now?

What is needed, of course, is the answer to these two questions: (1) Is the combination that my associates and I represent a combination which can stand on its own feet? (2) If so, how is it related to the other important combinations which seemingly it has vitalized? Is it a chronological relation—one merely following the others in time or vice versa? Is it a relation of part to whole or whole to part? Is it a relation of one combination being a substitute for the others? Or is it a relation of one supplementing the others?

Although it is not a matter of first importance, I feel that the time has come to christen this combination which my associates and I, and of course many others too, are interested in developing—not in a vacuum of course. For want of a better name I shall hereafter refer to it as *human relations*. It is my belief that human relations is a legitimate field of study which can be developed in its own right from the point of view of (1) theory and research, as well as (2) professional formulation and practice—indeed, of both simultaneously. In fact this hand-in-hand development of both theory and practice is essential to the continuing growth and development of the combination. Its relation to existing experimental and applied sciences, on the one hand, and to professional formulation and practice, on the other, is one of supplementation.

This point can be developed better, however, after the five books have been considered separately. And surely the reader has been alerted sufficiently to the point of view which will animate those reviews: The baby that my associates and I have nursed for some years is not up for adoption. He is not looking for a foster home. He has grown up now and is searching for active independence—a most healthy and normal desire, as the authors of the books reviewed, who are also parents, will surely recognize.

But let it be emphasized—if the reader has not realized it fully already—this reviewer is no slouch himself when it comes to combining things. It is both my strength and my weakness, and in this respect I am like the authors I am reviewing. Anyway it is this bent which has got me into the predicament of combining together for purposes of review five very different books which might customarily remain dissociated for many readers. In getting out of this predicament—fortunately not an egocentric one—I hope to clarify for myself as well as for the reader the field of human relations today. In each case, therefore, I shall first consider the book in general and then try to point out the bearing of its approach on human relations.

"INDUSTRIAL MANAGEMENT IN TRANSITION"[1]

The purpose of the author, George Filipetti, who is Professor of Economics and Business Administration, University of Minnesota, is to survey and evaluate the growth and development of the industrial management movement. In Part I he starts with the birth of the movement by Frederick W. Taylor and his associates. He examines its early growth prior to World War I and its acceleration following the war. Roughly this covers the years from 1900 to 1921. In Part II he observes the unfolding pattern in Europe and America, in both its labor and managerial aspects, up to World War II. He also offers some previews of its future course of development. Mr. Filipetti achieves his purposes by reviewing the writings of Taylor, Gantt, Gilbreth, Cooke, Emerson, Hoxie, Thompson, Fayol, Devinat, Roethlisberger and Dickson, Cooke and Murray, Golden and Ruttenberg, McCormick, Holden, Fish and Smith, Follett, Tugwell, Burnham, Urwick, and Johnston.

Mr. Filipetti's approach rests on three propositions: (1) Modern industrial management is "essentially the expansion and development of what has been designated as 'scientific management,'" (2) Scientific management, in turn, is "the application of the scientific method to the problems of business management" or "the displacement of tradition by science in the managerial field." And (3) the scientific method, in turn, is "the collection and classification of data, analysis of data, and the formulation of laws and principles based upon such analysis." Mr. Filipetti makes no attempt to discuss these propositions but treats them as perfectly self-evident and clear. Starting with them, he has of course little difficulty in wrapping up the above-mentioned people and showing "how they all branch from a common source." It is this almost primitive and totemistic concept of relationship (i.e., all people of a certain clan, living and dead, can be traced back to a common source) that vitiates what would otherwise be interesting reading.

Mr. Filipetti is at his best when he is giving a résumé of the work of some particular person. This is especially true in the two chapters where he considers the work of Frederick W. Taylor and in the one chapter devoted to the contributions of H. L. Gantt, Frank Gilbreth, and Harrington Emerson. But even in these chapters, where he seems to be most at home, he spoils things a little by going out of his way to show the importance which Taylor and his associates placed upon

1. Chicago: Richard D. Irwin, 1946.

the human factor — an importance which unfortunately too many of his followers, Mr. Filipetti feels, did not appreciate.

Scientific Management—Human Relations

This need of "humanizing" Taylor and his associates, which seems to be so popular these days in certain circles,[2] puzzles me. What is it all about anyway? Perhaps I am naive in supposing that no one ever seriously questioned the good intentions and integrity of the founders of scientific management. I for one have never doubted that they were men of goodwill, motivated by the best of intentions. It never occurred to me that they might be the kind of men who would willfully introduce a "sweat system" or who had any less milk of human kindness than their fellow men. It would be as absurd to think this as to think that the alchemists of old disseminated falsehoods on purpose and pulled the wool over people's eyes just for the hell of it. But if there are people who do think such things, it is of course in the interests of common decency to see that this erroneous picture is corrected.

On the other hand, it would equally distort history if Taylor and his associates were made so wise and omniscient that any future discoveries or developments in the field with regard to matters of fact had to be referred back to Taylor for final approval. Such an attempt would be most unscientific and according to Mr. Filipetti's own definition should expel the offender immediately from the elect circle.

That Taylor's early hypotheses, theories, and generalizations may become inadequate in the light of future research is nothing for his disciples to be frightened about. In fact it should fill them with pride. When Taylor's theories finally do repose in that "graveyard of abandoned hypotheses" where ultimately all "good" scientific theories rest, he will have taken his place in the true scientific tradition. Only if his generalizations are regarded as immutable and universal principles should his followers worry, for then someone becomes suspect of making Taylor into a cult.

One would think that Taylor's works could stand on their own feet, without so much apology. In the long list of notable books that Mr. Filipetti covers, Taylor's works have at least the merit of talking about one thing at a time. Whether or not Taylor was actually aware of the

2. See L. Urwick and E. F. L. Brech, *The Making of Scientific Management*, Vol. I (London: Management Publications Trust, 1945), and also the review of this book by Harry A. Hopf in *The Management Review* of the American Management Association, January 1947 and February 1947.

social implications of what he was up to may be open to question. But that he tried to think systematically about a few variables at a time (no matter how inadequate in number these variables may have been for understanding of the total situation) is all to his credit—a virtue unfortunately which too many other names on Mr. Filipetti's list do not have.

To return, however, to the original point: Mr. Filipetti is at his best when giving résumés of particular persons. It is only when he tries to tie them all together that the reader should become wary. A good example of the hand's being quicker than the reader's eye occurs on page 215 in connection with *Management and the Worker*,[3] a book of which this reviewer is particularly fond. Mr. Filipetti says:

> Under such circumstances there is little point to one of the criticisms of this study that it has sent the "time and motion study boys" into a back seat, if not into oblivion. The time and motion study technique and its application by properly qualified people is very much in the *front* seat. Such a study has brought industrial psychology into a front seat where any student of scientific industrial management has always maintained that it belonged.

In these three most extraordinary sentences Mr. Filipetti gives one of his best verbal demonstrations of a trapeze artist. With the skill of an acrobat who leaves one secure holding, makes three complete somersaults in mid-air, and finally lands safely on another ring, Mr. Filipetti leaves his reader gasping, exhausted but satiated. All is well again with "scientific industrial management"! But when the reader feels his heart has stopped thumping, the reviewer urges him to try reading these three sentences again—slowly this time.

In the same way with regard to the notable list of contributors to the industrial management movement (all the milestones unfortunately could not be included), it would seem that for the "unscientific" lay reader, i.e., the reader with no preconceptions, a most cursory examination of this list could hardly fail to reveal what a diversified kettle of fish it is. It would be difficult to find greater differences in background, in emphasis and level of treatment, and in understanding of scientific method, industry, and people. Far from illustrating Mr. Filipetti's thesis of a common source, this list would seem to show that modern industrial management is made up of many things, that it is not just the development of one thing. Many different people—mostly non-scientific—have contributed to it.

3. F. J. Roethlisberger and William J. Dickson, *Management and the Worker* (Cambridge: Harvard University Press, 1939).

"AN APPROACH TO MANAGEMENT"[4]

G. E. Milward compresses a great deal of material into a very short space. He claims nothing more for his book than that it constitutes his working notes developed from wide experience, reading, and study in the field. Yet he hopes the material will encourage the publication of more material with "intellectual content of a sound mental discipline." As an introduction to the many varied aspects of management and administration, this book will serve a useful function.

It appears that Mr. Milward is interested in reconciling what may seem to some to be two warring approaches to management, the human approach and the efficiency approach. Accordingly, his book is divided into two parts, (I) The Management of People and (II) The Management of Work. In Part I Mr. Milward pays his respects to the human element—the importance of human desires, motives, and idiosyncrasies. In Part II he outlines the more formal, scientific, and analytical approach to management problems. This second part is heavily condensed into "principles."

By a principle the author means "a hypothesis which has been or can be sufficiently proved by experiment or observation to be a safe guide for action or understanding." Unfortunately these principles when enunciated become so general that they say very little about anything in particular. Mr. Milward does not go into the problem of how these principles are to be applied. For example, he enunciates a management principle, "to bring to all processes of measurement or judgment a complete impartiality," but makes no attempt at all to show how this is to be done. Nor does he show how such a principle may be compounded with other principles (e.g., "to simplify all work by the elimination of any superfluous operation, product, or record") and thus be used without conflict in handling a concrete situation.

The Human Approach—The Human Relations Approach

It is unfortunate that such an iron curtain exists between Part I and Part II of this book, dealing with people and work respectively. It would seem to me that the keeping and thinking together of these two parts constitute the real challenge for those who are interested in providing intellectual content to theories of management. I should like to suggest that the manager is neither managing men nor managing work, but that he is managing a coordinated set of activities; he is administer-

4. Cambridge: Harvard University Press, 1947.

ing a social system. This is the human relations approach as contrasted with an approach which implies that people at work can be considered separately from their work. I do not mean that the human relations approach is incompatible with a "human approach," but it is more than (and not to be identified with) just the expression of humane sentiments, of which in the world today there seems to be no dearth.

For the responsible manager, people apart from work and work apart from people are both abstractions from the total situation. If this be so, it is difficult to see how principles drawn from either area to the exclusion of the other can be the safe guides for action which Mr. Milward seeks. It is the impression of the reviewer that the second part of the book suffers more from this fallacy of misplaced concreteness than does the first part, as is perhaps to be expected because of its greater use of "principles."

One thing for which the reader should be grateful to Mr. Milward is that he advances no claim that management is a science. And although the book falls short in providing *intellectual concepts* for the systematic and orderly thinking together of both aspects of management (the human relations approach), it does succeed in stimulating an *appreciation* of the importance of combining the human factor with a more logical approach to management.

"PSYCHOLOGY IN INDUSTRY"[5]

For being clear, concise, simple, and well-written, this book, written by Mr. Norman R. F. Maier, who is Professor of Psychology, University of Michigan, should reach a wide audience. Almost always one knows what the author is talking about. He takes up one thing at a time. He tries to be systematic in bringing together "the principal facts and theories of pure and applied psychology which are important in industry and business." Accordingly his nineteen chapters break down roughly into twelve subdivisions: (1) attitudes and morale; (2) types of leadership; (3) frustration; (4) individual differences in mental abilities, aptitudes, and personality traits, and the use of psychological tests in industry; (5) measuring proficiency; (6) motion and time analysis; (7) training; (8) motivation; (9) fatigue; (10) accidents; (11) job environment; and (12) labor turnover.

5. Boston: Houghton Mifflin, 1946.

Mr. Maier's way of conceiving the relationships among some of the above concepts is interesting and illuminating. Schematically they can be represented thus:

1. Aptitude = unpracticed or natural ability or talent for a particular kind of work.

2. Aptitude × training = achievement, or ability to do a given job.

3. Achievement × motivation = production, or the actual work accomplished.

4. Production × attitude = merit, or a man's total value on the job.

It is very clear from reading Mr. Maier's book that he is primarily oriented toward the individual. He shows little interest in matters of group relations or organization. He is particularly concerned with "psychological techniques" as they can be applied to specific industrial or business problems relating to the individual. Although it is true that he spends much less time on techniques of employee selection and testing than do the majority of writers on applied psychology, nevertheless he is most at home when he is considering questions of measurement, whether they be matters of measuring attitudes, proficiency, mental abilities, aptitudes, skills, motions, choices, fatigue, monotony, accidents, illumination, noise, or labor turnover.

In a very interesting last chapter Mr. Maier spells out, (1) for first-line supervision, (2) for counselors, and (3) for higher levels of management, the importance of his techniques and intellectual understandings about individuals. Were it not for the fact that I have chosen a rather different framework within which to review the five books in this article, my review would stop here. I would merely reiterate that the author has succeeded very well in achieving without pretension and fanfare the job he set out for himself. But inasmuch as Mr. Maier's type of combination is so important and represents so well a common school of thought with regard to applied science, it should be identified and its bearing on human relations clarified.

Applied Science—Human Relations

According to Mr. Maier, "psychology as a science is related to applied psychology in much the same way as physics and chemistry are related to the techniques of engineering." Mr. Maier goes on to say: "In the last analysis the science and its application must be consistent. To attempt to develop an applied field into an independent body of knowledge is to lose sight of the importance of systematization in arriving at principles."

Inasmuch as the author does not tell us just how he conceives the way in which engineering is related to physics and chemistry, the above statements remain somewhat unclear. If all he means is that theory and practice should go hand-in-hand in the acquisition of knowledge, one can hardly disagree. But there is some indirect evidence that he means a little more. He seems to suggest also that professional practice is merely the application of principles and techniques derived from science. As this point of view has serious implications for balanced development, it needs careful consideration. The notion which associates applied science with certain techniques is very common; although most important and useful for some purposes, it would be unfortunate if this were the only way the term "applied science" could be legitimately used. It seems to me there are *three* different orientations involved which need to be differentiated before their interrelations can be fully understood:

1. *Experimental or laboratory orientation*—This is the orientation where one seeks for certain relationships under controlled conditions among a few carefully chosen variables in a certain class of phenomena. It leads not only to the establishment of "laws," but also to a great deal of other conceptual formulation (theories, generalizations, definitions, "big words," and the like). This orientation generally does *not* come first in the development of a "science."

2. *Application of techniques and principles*—This is the orientation where one seeks to apply to concrete situations certain principles and techniques derived from science or some other unspecified source. For many people this orientation is called "applied science." I would place Mr. Maier's orientation in this category. I should also include much of what is called "scientific management" here, with one important qualification: unlike "applied psychology," scientific management has a much smaller body of theoretical formulation behind it.

3. *Situational orientation*—This is the clinical orientation of the practitioner—the person who has to act and decide under the burden of responsibility. It is the orientation of dealing with complex facts as they arise in experience. It leads to skills of diagnosis and judgment derived from long experience and intuitive familiarity with the facts. It is a clinical approach, and in the development of "science" generally precedes the experimental or laboratory orientation.

The fields of medicine and engineering are marked by a very close relationship among these three orientations. They have developed hand-in-hand. Here it is well understood that the orientation of the practitioner is not merely the orientation of the "applied" scientist (as defined by Orientation 2, above). The practitioner of medicine is not merely applying to the patient the principles and techniques of physiology and anatomy. The engineer when building a bridge is not merely applying the principles and techniques of physics and chemistry. Of course, the physician and engineer make use of those principles and techniques. But they depend also to a great extent on the well-recognized and well-appreciated skills they have derived from long experience in diagnosing and dealing with complex situations.

In these areas the skills the physician and engineer exercise and the observations they make are not ignored by those who are interested in more theoretical formulations. Questions and facts which arise in the clinic or during construction are taken to the laboratory for further investigation and speculation. In turn, the facts observed and the theories and techniques developed in the laboratory illuminate and make more effective the actual day-to-day practice. It is this hand-in-hand development of theory and practice that characterizes the fields of medicine and engineering, and in my opinion is responsible for much of the progress they have made.

In the social sciences on their applied side this situation does not obtain. In their endeavor to become "legitimate," these sciences have aped too quickly the present form of the more exact sciences and have tried to draw too soon a dividing line between theory and practice. As a result a most lopsided development has occurred. Let us consider, for example, the case of industrial psychology. Very few laboratory experiments in psychology have been performed which have arisen from the problems and questions perplexing the practitioner of human relations in industry. Very little use has been made of the data or skills these practitioners have acquired in making decisions and taking action under the burden of responsibility. Little cross-fertilization exists. Instead we find two separate groups:

(1) On the one hand, there are people who can only take into account the limited data which certain specialized techniques can produce. These people in industry are generally called "industrial" or "applied psychologists." They are subservient to the "science" which they apply. They cannot study a complex situation for what it is worth without

running the risk of being called "unscientific." They merely apply certain "techniques," many of which, curiously enough, did not originate in industry itself (e.g., psychometric techniques and public opinion polling techniques). As a result they have merely become just one of the many "technical specialist" groups with which modern industry is riddled.

(2) On the other hand, sitting in a quite separate corner, are the business executives, supervisors, and other people whom I think of as "practitioners of human relations." Are they "applied psychologists"? If by this is meant, "Are they applying to practice the principles and techniques of psychology?" the answer is, "No." Most executives and supervisors have not heard of these techniques, and those who have generally hire experts to perform them. Yet it remains true that the executive is daily dealing with matters of attitude, aptitude, morale, leadership, frustration, motivation, individual differences, fatigues, and so on—all the topics in fact with which Mr. Maier's book deals. The conclusion one reaches, therefore, seems to be that although the executive is dealing with psychological matters, he is not doing so with the specific techniques associated with "science"; so he is not an "applied psychologist" in the sense Mr. Maier means it. If the executive were to go around with a questionnaire and ask his employees certain questions upon which he performed certain elementary statistical operations, he would then become an "applied psychologist." But when he sits around the bargaining table with his union representatives and asks them certain questions, he is not one.

The problem I am raising is not just a verbal one; I am not trying to split hairs. It is of little importance whether or not the executive is called an "applied psychologist." What is important is that the problem does reveal a serious hiatus between theory and practice in the field. The people who are practicing, on the one hand, and the people who are experimenting and applying techniques, on the other hand, bear very little relation to each other. They have developed independently of each other. No amount of integration later on can bring them together except in the manner previously noted, whereby practice is subordinated to theory and professional practice is conceived as merely the application of principles and techniques derived from the sciences. As a result psychology is not related to applied psychology in the same way that physics and chemistry are related to engineering or that anatomy and physiology are related to the practice of medicine.

In engineering and medicine the people who do and the people who theorize are the same people or at least know one another; in applied psychology, they are not even acquainted.

Mr. Maier's book never quite comes to grips with the problem which I am calling to the reader's attention. He does a good job of relating experimental psychology to "applied psychology" (again, in the sense of applying certain techniques and intellectual understandings). But he never relates "applied psychology" to what I call "the practice of human relations." Granted he shows how supervisors and higher levels of management would profit from better psychological understandings and techniques; this demonstration is nonetheless primarily intellectual. What he fails to understand is (1) that the setting of the supervisor or executive is not the setting of the "applied psychologist"; (2) that the situations of an executive or supervisor are more comparable to those of a clinician; (3) that they are faced with difficult problems of diagnosis, of persuasion, of communication, of getting things done through people, of providing adequate incentives, and so on; (4) that these functions are part of their job and cannot be delegated to "applied psychologists"; (5) that more often than not they are dealing with mixed situations where attitudes, morale, skill, motivation, and the like are all involved in varying degrees; (6) that in the performance of these duties and functions, they are exercising skills; (7) that these skills have not been considered of sufficient importance to be investigated, studied, and developed in relation to the theoretical speculations of of the psychologist.

In a way I have been unfair to use Mr. Maier's book as a vehicle for the point I am trying to make. Mr. Maier's book is a good one, and the combination he represents is an important and useful one. Moreover, the lack of relation which exists between this combination and professional practice runs throughout all the social sciences. I have felt it important to point out this problem now primarily in order to state my case for the field of human relations.

Human relations can do much to bridge this gap between theory and practice. Starting with the data and the skills derived from responsible practice in a particular area involving a certain class of phenomena, it seeks for simple uniformities in these data. Thus theory and practice are kept together from the beginning. The practice of responsible people who have an intuitive familiarity with the facts provides the data for theoretical formulation; in turn these theoretical formulations illuminate professional practice. Under this conception executives, labor leaders, personnel administrators, supervisors, and others are at least in part "practitioners of human relations." Some may practice poorly, and some may practice well. It would be the concern of human relations to make them as competent practitioners as possible by articulating the skills they practice as well as the human situations to which they are applied. For professional practice such a development would go a long way in supplementing—not supplanting—the knowledge derived merely from the techniques of applied science.

"INDUSTRIAL RELATIONS AND THE SOCIAL ORDER"[6]

Wilbert E. Moore, of the Department of Economics and Social Institutions and Office of Population Research, Princeton University, paints his picture on a much broader canvas than do the other authors reviewed. His book divides into six parts. After an introduction stating his point of view (Part I), he considers the development of modern industry (Part II). Unlike Mr. Filipetti, he sees many ingredients which go to make it up: he sees technological and economic changes, i.e., changes in methods and relationships of production; and he sees various ideas, values, and sentiments forming a system under which these changes have taken place—discussed under the headings of (1) capitalism, (2) science, (3) technology, (4) individualism, and (5) rational division of labor. Together these ideas "form a general climate of opinion, which had major importance in the formative stages of factory production, and continues to influence the organization of modern industry." Once understood, they "should provide warning against any crude economic or technological determinism in the analysis of modern industry."

In Part III Mr. Moore considers modern industrial organization from the point of view of management. He discusses (1) the rise and growth of professional management, (2) the managerial function of executives, technical specialists, and supervisors; and (3) managerial beliefs, policies, and practices in the supervision of employees. Under this last heading he scrutinizes "scientific management"—"the possible application of science to the practical aims of industrial organization and administration."

In Part IV Mr. Moore looks at modern industrial organization from

6. New York: Macmillan, 1946.

the point of view of labor. Some of the topics in this section will give an idea of the scope of Mr. Moore's treatment: (1) the sources of labor supply, (2) wastes of labor resources, (3) the worker and the machine, (4) informal organization of workers, and (5) the question of motives and of worker's aspirations.

With this analysis Mr. Moore is now ready to look at the modern industrial relations scene. Here in Part V he discusses (1) the purposes and functions of unions, (2) the nature of collective bargaining, and (3) the sources and points of industrial conflict.

In Part VI Mr. Moore concludes with an investigation of the relation of industry to society—the functional relationship between industrial production and other aspects of societal organization. As Mr. Moore states so well:

> For many purposes . . . it is possible and proper to consider the industrial plant, the association of manufacturers or the labor union as an isolated unit. It is equally true that such a treatment is abstract, that is, overlooks other important aspects of industrial life and organization. The single organizational unit is related not only to the whole structure of economic production and distribution, but to the society and culture as a whole. A treatise on industrial relations which overlooked this range of social phenomena would do violence not only to logic but to utility as well.

Accordingly, in this section Mr. Moore looks at (1) the interdependence of industry and the community, (2) social classes and the industrial order, (3) the social controls of industry. He concludes with a chapter on "The Prospects and Problems of Economic Planning."

Applied Sociology—Human Relations

As the reader can see, Mr. Moore has attempted to combine many fields rarely brought together. Most of the facts, as he says, are well known to industrial managers, to labor leaders, and to various specialists. "But facts gain their significance in relation to other facts. If the social scientist in industry has any virtue, it is chiefly that of 'seeing industry whole': as a functioning organization made up of persons in various official and unofficial relationships, and as an organization which is in some way or other related to other organizations, to the community, and to society as a whole." To this approach Mr. Moore gives the name "applied sociology"—"the application of sociological (or social scientific) principles to the analysis of a concrete set of social relationships." From it the reader obtains a panoramic view of industry as a complex social organization that is most suggestive and provocative.

Although Mr. Moore claims that the social aspects of modern industrial organization are of the most practical sort, he never quite shows how this is so. His analysis of social relationships in industry remains at a very high level. He seems too interested in painting "the big picture" to get down to concrete cases. Or maybe he feels that getting down to this level would be premature in the present stage of development of "applied sociology." Anyway the reader who is eager to see how this new applied science can work will be disappointed that no case material is provided. In this respect Mr. Moore's position is quite far from my understanding of the field of human relations—as a much more mundane and pedestrian sort of affair. Furthermore, although Mr. Moore's conception of applied sociology is not the application of techniques, it does involve the application of "sociological principles." (The way each author uses this word, "principles," in a different sense is more than slightly confusing; we may return to this point later.)

"PERSONNEL ADMINISTRATION"[7]

Paul Pigors and Charles A. Myers, who are Associate Professors of Industrial Relations, Industrial Relations Section, Department of Economics and Social Sciences, Massachusetts Institute of Technology, have prepared a most significant and satisfying book. It is unusually well written, well organized, and should be required reading for any personnel administrator. According to their subtitle, the authors are most interested in providing "a point of view and a method" for personnel administration. Unlike the previous authors who have tried to integrate their varied materials through the application of principles, these men have taken the point of view and method as their unifying theme. Through this attempt they go a long way in presenting a formulation for professional practice. The results are most rewarding indeed.

The book divides into two parts. Part I presents the text material divided into six sections: (A) The Nature of Personnel Administration, (B) Handling Personnel Problems, (C) Diagnosing Organizational Stability, (D) Building and Maintaining Work Teams, (E) Wages and Hours, (F) Employee Services and Programs.

Part II gives case material to illustrate the subject matter of the chapters in Part I. In thus providing concrete case material this book

7. New York: McGraw-Hill, 1947.

also is unique among the books reviewed. One feels very strongly that these authors have an intuitive familiarity with the phenomena which they are dealing with and trying to organize. Theirs is no ivory tower or merely intellectual approach; they give the impression that they are ready to accept the brute, stubborn, and recalcitrant data of human relations which they find.

In Section A of Part I, on the Nature of Personnel Administration, the authors discuss their articles of faith: (1) "Good management means getting effective results with people." (2) "Management and personnel administration are one and the same." (3) "Management is personnel administration"; (4) "This does not mean, however, that an organization can dispense with an officially designated personnel administrator." (5) A personnel administrator is not to be regarded as "something superficial, like the frosting on a cake." (6) Personnel administrators are staff men, and they should *not* take over the duties and responsibilities of the line. (7) Although the personnel administrator is not responsible for making policies, he can influence top management policies, particularly toward unions.

In Section B the authors start developing a useful point of view for personnel administrators. In a very interesting chapter on "Situational Thinking," they break down into four interrelated basic elements the "total situation" confronting the personnel administrator: (1) technical features, (2) the human element, (3) principles and policies, and (4) the time factor. Here they differentiate between the approach which may be called *person-centered thinking* from the approach which may be called *policy-centered thinking*. The former is particularly useful when one is studying the human element. It is the approach which realizes that each person's situation is unique and which stresses the need of understanding the person first in terms of his own situation. But exclusive emphasis on the person-centered approach would be misleading. It needs to be combined with the approach "in which generally valid principles of behavior are formulated as guides to action in specific types of situations," i.e., policy-centered thinking.

To these two useful modes of thought must also be added "thinking about time as process." It is this third mode of thought that sees that both persons and policies are in a stage of development. They appear in time contexts and hence cannot be regarded as things that are final, fixed, and static. By thinking about time as a process, one obtains a different perspective on evolving situations. These useful modes of thinking taken together with the *technical features* help the personnel administrator in getting a picture of the essential relationships which constitute his "reality." In a chapter on "Getting Down to Cases," the authors show how this method of understanding can be used in actual cases. They conclude this section with a chapter on "Interviewing" as a method of understanding personal situations.

In Section C the authors develop their point of view as a method of diagnosing and evaluating individual and organizational stability. As indexes of employee morale, they consider (1) data on production efficiency, (2) tardiness and absence, (3) accident records, (4) health records, (5) labor turnover, (6) transfer data, and (7) complaints and grievances. Throughout this section the authors stress the importance of considering these data not as things in themselves but as symptoms of total situations that need to be diagnosed. What is behind the figures? What attitudes and needs of people do they reveal? What attitudes and circumstances determine them? What do they tell us about management and supervision? What preventive action might be taken? And so on.

I have a very strong feeling, although there is no formal indication to this effect, that a differentiation of approach exists between Sections A, B, and C, on the one hand, and Sections D, E, and F, on the other. In the latter sections the authors become concerned with the procedures and policies that build and maintain work teams and that promote stability in the organization: (1) recruitment, selection, and placement; (2) selection and training of supervisors; (3) employee induction and training; (4) employee rating and promotion; (5) transfer, downgrading, and layoff; (6) discipline and discharge; (7) wages and hours; and (8) employee services and programs. These last three sections contain the topics one is most likely to find in a book on personnel administration, except that the authors present them with new emphases. They emphasize how all these procedures should be integrated into a single policy system. They also show how all these procedures are aimed at organizational stability whereby policy requirements and individual needs are balanced.

Personnel Administration—Human Relations

Sections B and C present a point of view and method which are not too dissimilar from what the reviewer conceives of as "human relations." It seems unfortunate that the authors do not continue with this approach in Section D on "Building and Maintaining Work Teams" before they take up the more formal functioning of a personnel department in relation to this process. It would seem to the reviewer that something more in the direction of stating the nature of organic and evolving social systems in relation to the maintaining of teamwork and the administrator's function in relation to this process would have provided a broader framework for the discussion of this problem before going to the level of personnel procedures and policies.

However, this is of small matter. It is obvious that at some point—actually it is somewhere near the beginning of Section D—their human relations orientation has to shift because human relations and personnel administration, although very closely related, are not one and the same thing. Human relations is a very important ingredient but not the sole ingredient in the personnel administrator's job. In Sections D to F there is an acceptance of a particular structure and certain procedures to do the job that stops further exploration and growth. The authors become committed to a particular organizational point of view, and they talk about specific matters highly important for the understanding of the best accepted practices of personnel administration. But the result is not "human relations" as I conceive it.

CONCLUSION

In the process of reviewing these five books, I have also been interested in separating out *human relations* from other closely associated combinations in order that I could state more clearly what I conceive *human relations* to be and its bearing on these other important and useful combinations. For purposes of convenience I have prepared a schematic diagram to show the existing state of development in the integration of various related fields and how *human relations* as a field fits, or might fit, into this picture (see EXHIBIT 4.1). Let it be clear that I am not trying to legislate how things should be among these various related fields; I realize the futility of this process. I am merely making certain discriminations so that those who will may choose more discriminately.

In the diagram the reader can find ten boxes designating ten fields of knowledge with which this review has been concerned. To this list two more boxes have been added—*anthropology* and *applied anthropology*—even though no books in this general area have been reviewed. These fields need to be included because they have also made

	A	B	C	D
	Science	**Techniques**	**A clinical point of view and method**	**Professional formulation and practice**
1.	Psychology	Applied Psychology		Administration
2.	Sociology	Applied Sociology	Human Relations	Personnel Relations
3.	Anthropology	Applied Anthropology		Labor Relations
4.		Scientific Management		
5.		Technical specialist groups in business and industry		

EXHIBIT 4.1. Diagram Showing the Integration of Various Related Fields

significant contributions to the emerging integration.[8] Omitted from column D are certain boxes which easily could be included; e.g., political administration, general education, the administration of many different kinds of formal organizations besides business, such as labor unions, Army, Navy, and so on. For the purpose of this article their inclusion does not seem necessary.

Concerning Four Useful Combinations, and One Not So Useful

If the reader will draw a line around the boxes B_1, B_2, B_3, and B_4, in column B, he will obtain a grouping of subjects which we will refer to as *Combination 1*. This combination has contributed to the fields represented by all the boxes in column D primarily by supplying them with facts derived from the application of techniques. It should be noted that these techniques have been practiced primarily by specialists and technicians (see B_5) and not so much by the people in positions of administrative responsibility represented by boxes D_1, D_2, and D_3. To put it another way, this combination has contributed to the development of technical specialists in business and industry far more than to the development of concepts and skills directly relating to the responsible practice of administrators. Of the utility of this combination to business and industry there can be little question. It has provided business management with techniques and, through the application of these techniques, with standards by means of which the purposes of the organization can be better evaluated. It is this development which Mr. Filipetti identifies with modern industrial organization. It is this combination with which Mr. Maier's book is primarily concerned.

I have included *scientific management* in this combination because in orientation it has also been primarily concerned with the application of techniques and the setting of standards—time standards, performance standards, standard methods, cost standards, and so on. The bearing of this combination on human relations will be mentioned in connection with Combination 3.

By drawing a line around boxes C_2, D_1, D_2, and D_3, the reader will obtain a grouping of subjects which we will refer to as *Combination 2*. This combination has grown in importance during the past ten years. It is the combination which has been primarily concerned with making more explicit the skills of handling organized human activity

8. See *Applied Anthropology, Problems of Human Organization*, the journal published by the Society for Applied Anthropology.

which are practiced by people in positions of responsibility—executives, supervisors, personnel men, and labor relations men. Its utility to business and industry is also great. Unlike Combination 1, however, its significance is often overlooked; it is also much less highly developed or articulated. It is still in its infancy, but to the reviewer it promises to be one of the most significant developments for the immediate future.

Recent books have attested to the growing interests in this area. Mr. Milward sees the importance of this combination, but he does not go much further. The book by Paul Pigors and Charles A. Myers is an excellent example of the attempt to relate *personnel relations* and *human relations*. B. M. Selekman's *Labor Relations and Human Relations*,[9] as its title indicates, integrates the fields represented by boxes C_2 and D_3. Chester Barnard's *The Functions of the Executive*[10] is the outstanding attempt to relate *human relations* to *administration*. Burleigh Gardner's *Human Relations in Industry*[11] is also a good example of a book representing the articulation of this combination.[12]

Drawing a line around boxes B_4, B_5, and C_2—*Combination 3*—indicates a development that is sorely needed if the fields represented in boxes B_4 and B_5 are to make their contribution more directly to the professional formulation and practice of *administration*. A great deal of empirical knowledge in this area already exists. All the groups in industry who have been concerned with the problem of introducing and administering standards know that there is not only the technical problem of setting standards correctly, but also the problem of getting them logically, understandingly, and emotionally accepted. How to obtain the cooperation of people with regard to these standards—this is a *human relations* problem with which all technical specialists who devise and install "control systems" as well as supervisors who have to administer them, are in one way or another concerned. And yet—a matter of astonishment to me—I can find no book which attempts to put this kind of material together. This is an important combination —not merely to write a book about, but for further research. Its development would have great immediate significance for industry.

9. New York: McGraw-Hill, 1947.
10. Cambridge: Harvard University Press, 1938.
11. Chicago: Richard D. Irwin, 1945.
12. For an excellent book which articulates this combination for an organization other than business, see Alexander H. Leighton, *The Governing of Men* (Princeton: Princeton University Press, 1945). Also see the works of Mary Parker Follett.

A line drawn around boxes A_1, A_2, A_3, B_1, B_2, B_3, and C_2 forms *Combination 4,* a grouping which could be of the greatest long-range significance. Many social scientists believe that there are certain aspects of the fields of *psychology, sociology,* and *anthropology* (e.g., clinical psychology, social psychology, matters of group, social, institutional, and cultural behavior) which could be more closely integrated with the theory and practice of *human relations.* Each of these fields has already contributed a great deal to the field of *human relations* in terms of methods, conceptual formulations, and some concrete data.[13] Recent techniques have also appeared which may have more direct application to the development of *human relations*—e.g., psychodrama techniques, sociometric techniques, nondirective counseling techniques, group dynamics, and the measurement of interaction rates.[14]

This new integration, however, envisages a much closer relation between those who theorize and those who practice. Such a combination would be an intellectual achievement of the highest order, and also would require an apprenticeship—not only in the library but also in the hard, persistent, and unremitting labor of responsible practice in the handling of concrete human data. Although this integration would be ultimately of the greatest importance and utility, its development cannot be accelerated. If this integration is to be achieved at not merely a verbal level, it requires many years of patient labor at a clinical level before any significant experimental work can be done. Difficult problems of terminology, method, and theoretical formulation beset it from all sides. For its successful achievement a new theory of action is required. It presents unquestionably the greatest intellectual challenge of the modern world. The Newton or the Copernicus of this combination has not yet appeared.

To some readers it may seem as if Mr. Moore's book comes closest among all the books reviewed to this kind of combination. In intent this may be true, but in achievement it falls far short of accomplishing what I have in mind. At the present date the field of general semantics seems to offer a fruitful lead to the development of this combination.[15]

Although it has no representation in the above diagram, there is a *fifth combination* which deserves to be mentioned primarily because

13. See the works of Karen Horney, Eric Fromm, Conrad Arensberg, Ruth Benedict, Margaret Mead, B. Malinowski, W. Lloyd Warner.

14. See the works of J. L. Moreno, Carl Rogers, R. Likert, K. Lewin, R. Lippitt, D. P. Cartwright, Eliot D. Chapple.

15. See the works of Alfred Korzybski, S. I. Hayakawa, Wendell Johnson.

for many people it is the one most frequently associated with the term *human relations*. It is that combination which attempts to give people rules for "success," on how to get other people to do what you want them to, on how to make friends, and on how to be "happy" and "human" at the same time. No book was reviewed in this area. It is the combination which can be most readily packaged and unquestionably has the greatest sales appeal. Although for some people this particular combination may have proved useful, to the reviewer it seems the least fruitful combination to be developed. It misses entirely the tremendous complexity of the problem with which the field of *human relations* is concerned.

What Is Human Relations?

I am now in a position to crystallize my understanding of *human relations*. I should like to do this by answering three questions:

First, what does it include? To the growing body of data that is resulting from the study of concrete situations of human beings at work in an organized human activity, to the point of view and methods characteristic of such study, and to the results obtained therefrom both in terms of more explicit skills and of better theoretical formulation for adjusting to and administering change, I give the name of *human relations*. Some of the problems with which it is concerned are: (1) general problems of communication and understanding between individuals, between individuals and groups, and between groups under different conditions and varying relationships, (2) general problems of securing action and cooperation under different conditions and in varying formal organizations, and (3) general problems of maintaining individual and organizational equilibrium through change. Its methods both from the point of view of research and of taking action are clinical and diagnostic. Its methods of instruction are the problem case and clinical experience. It looks at its data from the point of view of growing and evolving social systems.

To the reviewer these data, methods, and points of view are of a piece and allow *human relations* to develop as a legitimate field of study, both in relation to the social sciences, on the one hand, and practitioners of *human relations,* on the other. As can be seen, the problems with which it deals are not the exclusive concern of any one social science, although singly or collectively they can significantly contribute to it. Moreover, the skills with which it is concerned are applicable to any person in a position of responsibility who has to relate himself to individuals and groups, whether he be a supervisor, executive, personnel administrator, labor union leader, or captain of a ship.

Second, is it a science? Depending upon our understanding of the things to which the word "science" refers, our answer can vary. *Human relations* is certainly not a science as we think of the more exact sciences in the sense of (1) a body of techniques or (2) a body of definitive knowledge about man at work contained in well-articulated theories, laws, and principles. Certainly it is too young for that. Perhaps—and this is my personal opinion at the present—it will never attain that stature. However, it is a "science" in the following senses: (1) It has a method and a useful point of reference for looking at a particular class of phenomena in order to seek for simple uniformities among the facts in that class of phenomena. (2) It can ask simple and clear questions in order to direct its observations. (3) It can seek for those clusters of things which recurrently tend to appear together in experience—like a "syndrome" in medicine, a clinical entity (e.g., the measles) which people who have an intuitive familiarity with the facts in a given area learn to recognize. (4) It can develop simple "theories" and "hypotheses" which it has derived from its observations in order to seek for new observations and to illuminate practice.

Third, has it principles? Words being what they are, perhaps many readers will be shocked to learn that *human relations* has no "principles"; but that is my opinion of the matter, particularly reinforced by my reading of the five books reviewed. Just what are these holy and sacred entities for which each author seeks and which at times are made to appear as the only valid justification for practice? In modern science, as the reviewer understands it, principles like all the other holies—theories, generalizations, and so on—are subordinate to facts. Principles are merely useful ways of synthesizing facts, of picturing facts, of summarizing facts and theories. They are not lords either by divine right or by popular election. They are merely convenient tools of synthesis—useful for certain purposes and under certain limits.

In this latter sense, then, it is not strange but obvious that *human relations,* being such a new field and having yet too few facts and well-established theories, should have few, if any, "principles." What is needed is more practice of *human relations* skills and less talk about verbal principles. The former might help to integrate the world; the latter, as history seems to show, has only succeeded in dividing it.

In conclusion I would like to say that I hope all readers will get as much profit and enjoyment from reading the five books as I did. The fact that the reviewer happens to disagree about certain matters should not deter anyone from looking at them. For those who are seriously and sincerely interested in the area, they are all very much worth while.

Postscript, 1968

At the time, I thought it was important for the development of human relations that the distinctions I made in this article be recognized. But it is a difficult communication to make without inviting invidious comparisons. Although I still think these distinctions are important, I am not recommending the way I went about making them. Differences in conceptualization or ways of thinking can be justified only in terms of their utility for dealing with specified problems, and I do not think now that I stressed this point enough.

5 The Secret of Success

This was a talk given on April 29, 1948, over the Harvard Business School radio station, WHBS, and it was not published. Although chronologically it belongs here, logically it is an extension of my ideas in Chapter 1 about the nature of obsessive thinking. Because I was talking to B-School students I chose as the subject of my remarks the false dichotomy of success–failure, from which it seemed to me they suffered most.

This piece includes some local B-School jargon. *Administrative Practices* was the name of a required first-year course introduced in 1947 at the School. The students referred to it often as *Ad Prac*, and they also used it in the form of a verb, such as *to ad-prac* someone. This often meant listening to someone. Because for them taking action meant *telling* instead of *listening*, and because taking action was what an executive did, it followed that to *ad-prac* someone was not to do anything and thus to assume a non-stereotypical executive posture. In this piece I played with the telling–listening dichotomy too.

I have chosen to talk to you tonight on the question "What is the secret of success?" From my point of view this question is silly, meaningless, and unanswerable, and frankly I have no intention of answering it. However, as some people have a tendency to ask themselves silly, meaningless, and unanswerable questions—for which I don't hold myself responsible in the slightest—it seems to me that it is not the answers, but the tendency to ask such questions, that needs attention.

Most of us in academic circles would profit from a consideration of this problem, because after all we spend a good bit of our time in an environment where questions are being asked that are never quite satisfactorily answered. Instructors ask you questions which you don't answer, at least to the instructor's satisfaction. You ask questions of instructors who in turn do not give answers that satisfy you. This, as you know, can be a most frustrating experience.

Now this frustrating experience can be easily remedied, theoretically at least. Everyone is so concerned with the answers to questions that no one bothers to look carefully at the questions they are asking. Everyone seems to assume that there must be an answer to any question which any damn fool can ask. Our whole educational process—except of course at the Business School—is committed to trying to give answers to silly questions. Very few students are taught to scrutinize with as much care the questions they ask or are asked as the answers they give or that are given to them. As a result they become steadily more and more disillusioned with themselves and their instructors.

Let me therefore start by examining carefully the question, "What is the secret of success?" I suppose most of you feel you know what. success means. *"Success is success. Period."* But just stop and reflect a moment. Remember your first few weeks at the Business School when you naively assumed, "Business is business," and the emotional blockage some of you suffered in Administrative Practices as a result. Remember those of you who kept pounding the desk and insisting that "business is business," in the face of such cases as Willy Maguire and Mary at Ripton Company. Do you remember those wails of anguish, those cries of defiance—"This is not a typical foreman," "Mary is a crackpot," "Things like this don't happen in business." Maybe you have forgotten this now but at least you will remember the "low passes" and "unsats" which accompanied this period.

And then do you remember that period of quiet and contentment (at least for most of you, I hope) which followed this turbulent period when you were emotionally incapable of accepting or even entertaining any idea other than that "Business is business"? Perhaps some of you can even recall the exact moment when this transformation occurred —when something snapped within you, and you surrendered yourself completely and wholeheartedly to the brute and stubborn facts of life and business. Perhaps with a last convulsive wail of rage you had said, "I'm through," "I give up," "I'm licked," "To hell with those 'ad practitioners.' " And then in this—your darkest moment—ready to pack your bag and leave the institution in disgust—an abysmal failure —lo and behold a miracle occurred. With this last convulsive gasp, some compulsive inner core liquidated. You gave up completely a silly but highly cherished idea. And with this inner act of renunciation, a peace and calm descended upon you. For the first time you were emotionally capable of accepting and entertaining the idea that maybe "business also includes monkey business." How simple, but how difficult a transformation! In defeat you found victory; in failure you found success. Do you remember that warm glow (nonalcoholic I mean) in which you now felt bathed, the steady stream of "high passes" and distinctions which now became your daily monotonous lot? How kindly you now felt about poor Willy Maguire and Mary.

Poor Willy who wanted his bosses to listen to him in the same way that his bosses expected Willy to listen to his workers. And poor Mary who couldn't emotionaly hear what she had been logically told, and poor Mary's bosses who insisted in telling poor Mary again and again what she couldn't emotionally accept. I even like to think that in this moment of dispassionate understanding you even began to entertain some kindly feelings toward your Administrative Practices instructors. Poor benighted folk too, suffering the common lot of humanity—being misunderstood and wanting to be understood by their students.

I fear I am being carried away by my enthusiasm and imagination. I realize that for many of you this transformation did not reach the high emotional pitch and fervor which I have described. For most of you the change was more gradual and prosaic. No great crisis preceded the calm. With a shrug of the shoulder, probably assisted by some sympathetic girl and some alcoholic beverage, you walked into emotional maturity, and for a few I understand no transformation, precipitous or gradual, has yet occurred. But let me get back to my point from which I may have seriously digressed—or have I?

"Success," like many words, has many meanings, not just one meaning. It is absurd to think that because there is one word, there is one thing to which it refers. There are probably as many meanings as there are people who use the word and situations to which the word is referred. Probably ninety out of a hundred times when the word is used it has little or no meaning, apart from the personal situation and feelings of the person who used it. In the experience I described above I gave an extreme example of a situation where failure and success are so inextricably intertwined that some people have difficulty in knowing that when they have failed, they have succeeded. I can also think of situations where the more successful you are in one respect, the more you have failed in another respect.

PREOCCUPATION AND ADAPTATION

There is one aspect of this problem in which I have been interested for some time and that is the preoccupation about success with which so many students are concerned. For many years I have been interested in this preoccupation with the future which prevented so many able young men from relating themselves effectively to the present. About fifteen years ago it was part of my job to interview a good many students—very good and able students—in the University. In my many discussions with them and especially at the Business School, the topic of "success" was frequently brought up. Everything including "going to bed early at night," "taking regular exercise," "not drinking coffee or smoking cigarettes," "getting good grades," and "sticking to one thing" was proposed as having a good deal to do with, or constituting the essence of, success. One student I remember kept a collection of maxims about success. Perhaps you would like to hear some of these maxims. Let me read some from his notebook.

1. The expert should be on tap, not on top.

2. Qualities necessary to success: ambition with a will to work.

3. Requisites of success: strong arm, clean mind, brave heart.

4. The essence of success: health, ability, and character.

5. The secret of success (now we have it) is for a man to be ready for opportunity when it comes.

6. The best substitute for brains is silence.

7. The man who wakes up and finds himself famous hasn't been asleep.

8. If you are a self starter, the boss won't have to be a crank.

As you can imagine, this student had a difficult time in living up to all these rules. This rat race for success left him in a perpetual state of agitation and with little opportunity to attend to his immediate surroundings. It has always interested me to observe that the more preoccupied people are with this "success," the more unsuccessful they are likely to be in relating themselves to people here and now. This was particularly true of the student I just mentioned. He had few friends. All his life he felt he had lacked personal and intimate relationships with his fellow men. This was particularly true in his relations to women. This inability to relate himself to women was well reflected in his notebook which also contained maxims on the topic of "women." When I read you some of these maxims I think that most of you, without being psychiatrists, will be able to see that he was better acquainted with the word "woman" than with the many particular and different creatures to whom this word refers. Here are some.

1. There are two places where to be a coward is the worst of all things: one is in war, the other in love.

2. Let your words be as clean as those from the lips of a good woman and as few as those from an Indian.

3. You gaze at a star for two motives, because it is luminous, because it is impenetrable. You have by your side a sweeter radiance, a greater mystery, woman.

4. The hardest thing for a man to forgive in a woman is that of falling in love with him when he doesn't want her to and the hardest thing for a woman to forgive in a man is not falling in love with her when she wants him to.

5. Sexual intercourse is something "no gentleman would propose nor no gentleman would refuse."

It is needless to go on with this list of maxims. They well illustrate two uniformities in experience I have frequently observed: (1) excessive preoccupations about success prevent rather than facilitate the process of giving and sustaining one's attention to the present, and (2) people with such preoccupations do not seem to have the capacity for easy, intimate, and friendly association with other people. Like the student I mentioned above they become enamored about words rather than the things to which words refer. As a result they have a greater facility in relating themselves to words and abstractions than to concrete events, things, and people.

There is a third uniformity which is also worthy of comment. An excessive preoccupation about success always seems to be accompanied by an equally excessive preoccupation about failure. I have frequently encountered these alternating preoccupations of success and failure by means of which some people tend to isolate themselves from their social surroundings. For some people there is nothing which lies between success and failure. They interpret their own activities as well as the activities of others in terms of these irreducible categories. Anything which is not completely successful is failure. One man I knew, for example, used to spend considerable time in picturing himself as one who had achieved high eminence and authority in his chosen field of endeavor and imagining how his associates and the people back home would then regard him. Maybe he could be President of the United States? Then wouldn't he make things hum. On the other hand when he was depressed and probably more fatigued, he would be convinced that he would never amount to much. His life had been one failure after another. Then he would picture himself as a butler in a very wealthy family where he could have close contact with luxury and conveniences. Or maybe he could get arrested and sent to jail where the state would take care of him. Between viewing life from the White

House or "behind bars" there was no middle point of vantage. In the thinking of such people the notion of adventure is lacking. There is little or no place for exploration and experiment. They work so hard in preventing themselves from making mistakes that they never learn anything at all.

WHAT PREVENTS GROWTH AND ADJUSTMENT?

Instead of asking the question "What is the secret of success?" it might be more sensible to ask "What prevents me from adjusting to and growing in my situation here and now?" or "What prevents me from learning here and now?" To these questions experience can give a partial answer.

It should be obvious that growth, adjustment, and learning take place in the present. One cannot adjust easily to the past or future. The past is gone and the future is uncertain. If a person therefore is excessively preoccupied with the past or future, he ceases to pay attention to the present where growth, learning, and adjustment is most likely to take place. To be overly preoccupied with the mistakes, failure, and sins of the past or to be overly preoccupied with vague, absolutistic, and unrealistic goals is the best way I know of preventing growth, learning, and adjustment here and now. This statement is an induction from experience which can be checked in your own experience as well as in the experience of others. It points to the two chief sources of interference with the adequacy of relationship to your present situation.

(1) One source of interference comes from the past. We may bring to our present situation erroneous meanings derived from past experiences. We may have misunderstood and misinterpreted our past experience. This is something which the advocates of "learning from experience" often ignore. It is just as likely that we learn the wrong as the right lessons from experience. The experience of most of us is limited and insufficient. Moreover, experience doesn't speak or reveal its significance or meaning in the raw, so to speak. It has to be constantly and continuously cross-examined if misunderstanding and misinterpretation are not to result. One never learns from experience by asking silly and unanswerable questions of it. What I am trying to say has been well expressed in a truism with which most of you are familiar. "It's not what people don't know that causes trouble; it's

what they do know that ain't so that prevents learning and growth." Too many of us know too many things that ain't so. It is this factor as much as any that makes the teaching of Administrative Practices difficult. It takes many years for most of us to see the significance of our experience and to draw from it correctly the lessons it teaches. Elton Mayo, with whom I was associated for many years, used to put this idea tersely by saying, "People are not born sane or insane. Sanity, particularly in our modern complex world, is a difficult achievement."

(2) The second source of interference to adequacy of relationship to one's present situation comes, peculiarly enough, from the future. It comes from the vague, unrealistic, and absolutistic goals we set for ourselves, in terms of which we constantly frustrate our daily sense of accomplishment. "Success," as envisaged by some, is one of such goals. It is a word with such a vague, unrealistic, and absolutist referent that it prevents growth and adjustment here and now. I know of no word which has gotten more people into more trouble. To go around asking of life "Am I a success or a failure?" is one of those silly questions which people ask which has no answer. It's like asking "Am I a man or a mouse?"—another one of those questions which make many students miserable. The closest we can come to an answer is one which is unsatisfactory for most people. Everyone is both a success and a failure. Everyone is both a man and a mouse. This is the lesson which experience, when sufficiently cross-examined, teaches—for many of us the hard way. This applies to you as well as your professors. I hope I'm not disillusioning some of you too quickly. Curiously enough, however, these statements, once they have been emotionally accepted, release you from a silly and fretful worry. You can go to bed at night and chuckle instead of stewing about the "riddle of the universe."

PRESENT AND FUTURE

This brings me to the last point I want to make. It will be the most difficult one for most of you to accept. It makes more sense at the age of forty than at the age of twenty. But then you know when life begins, particularly for Harvard professors, who take a longer time than most people to grow up. In spite of their erudition from books they too have to learn some things the hard way.

Some of you, I fear, tend to think of the present as a means and the future as an end. Many of you treat the Business School, for example, as a means, to some glorious end—"success." You go through the dreary round of case discussion merely as a routine preparation for that great day when you will be finally in touch with that brute and stubborn reality called "business" where you will find "success." As a result some of you don't learn very much while you are here. I suspect that for some of you this state of affairs may continue. Each job you have will be viewed merely as a stepping stone to the next higher job in the ladder to "success."

What if I suggested to you that the future is the means, and the present is the end? Would that sound too silly? Before throwing it out as absurd, however, let's consider it for a moment. You can't live in the past or in the future, can you? And when the future comes, it is a "present," isn't it? When a businessman retires at the age of sixty-five he doesn't have the same organism he had when he was twenty. Isn't it likely—or am I just daydreaming?—that he won't be able to enjoy at the age of sixty-five some of the things he thought he would enjoy at the age of twenty? Why is it then that so many of us feel that we can't settle down and enjoy the present until we have achieved success? Why do we constantly take all meaning and significance out of the present and put it in the future? Isn't it because we treat the present as a means and the future as an end? Aren't we assuming that when we arrive at this point, everything will be "hunky-dory"? But isn't it likely that if this is our basic attitude, we will continue to act in our old way? When the future comes, it will be a present, and as we have taught ourselves to treat the present as insignificant, won't we have to posit more and new goals, bigger and better goals to strive for—ad infinitum?

The question I am raising is this: are there not two different kinds of goals?—(1) one kind of goal which takes all significance and meaning out of the present and (2) another kind of goal which makes the present more meaningful and significant.

(1) A good example of the first kind of goal is the excessive preoccupation about success of which I have been speaking. By means of it we make ourselves miserable in the present. We prevent ourselves from learning and growing here and now. In this frame of reference we create a target just in order to shoot at it and we make ourselves miserable every time we fail to hit the bull's-eye.

(2) In the case of the second kind of goal we create a target in order to perfect our shooting here and now. This kind of goal works for us.

It makes meaningful and significant the present. It facilitates growth, learning, the sense of adventure and exploration. In this frame of reference hitting the bull's eye isn't an end in itself. The bull's eye merely becomes a means for correcting the source of error here and now. Are not such goals treating the future as a means and the present as an end? If so, what are these goals which allow us to retain our zest for growth and learning and adaptation until the day we die. This question, I suggest, rather than the goal of "success" might be an appropriate subject for your mature reflection.

CONCLUSION

Curiously enough, in the process of debunking the word "success" I have made certain statements about how to deal successfully with the present. These statements can be summarized as follows:

(1) Stop right here and now asking yourself unanswerable questions. Avoid this practice as you would the plague. Give up the notion that every question has an answer. Trying to answer unanswerable questions has much more serious consequences than many so-called "vices." People who indulge in this pastime fill our mental hospitals and educational institutions. Some of them may even become "successes" and get to be political and business leaders. But so what?

(2) Stop right here and now trying to answer the silly and unanswerable questions that are asked of you. Do this to the point of rudeness if you have to, but in most cases all you will need to do is to listen politely. You will find, as you get more experience in this technique, that the last thing a person wants is your answer to his silly question, anyway.

(3) Only ask questions to which experience can give you an answer here and now—not a final answer but a tentative answer which will facilitate new and better discriminations here and now. Keep cross-examining experience with better questions. As you put less effort into answering unanswerable questions, begin to put more effort into finding one good question worth asking of experience here and now. There are not too many lying about; so don't rush. Take it easy.

(4) Stop reflecting morbidly about the mistakes of the past and the goals of the future. As Professor Meriam has told you, the Business School provides a wonderful opportunity, if you will avail yourself of it, for making mistakes and learning. If I understand him correctly,

what he is saying to you is: Don't let your eagerness for future high passes and distinctions prevent you from learning here and now. Don't make of "grades" a goal which deprives the work you do here and now of being interesting, stimulating, and fun. If you have to hitch your wagon to a star, don't choose a star for its inscrutability, impenetrability, and sweet mystery—like the grades you get, for example. That, as you well know, is the road to despair. Choose a star—preferably a few —that will partially illuminate and reinforce the significance of your present experience. Excessive preoccupation about grades and "success" won't do this for you.

(5) What will? Most fortunately for me my time is running short, so that I won't have the time to answer this question I am probably raising in your minds. How can we choose goals which will allow us to retain a zest for living in the present until the day we die? Is this an unanswerable question? In part I think it is. The question contains quite a few vague words. In it the word "choose" is crucial. Most of us don't choose our goals. We live with goals that have been borrowed or handed down to us by our parents and society. Nevertheless I think this is a better question than the one with which we started, "What is the secret of success?" It is less absolutistic. It at least implies that the satisfactions we get from the present are relative to the expectations we have and the demands we make of the present situation. It also implies that goals are not static things—like most other matters they are subject to change. It suggests that occasionally they need renovation and that they can be renovated in the direction of making the present more significant if we so choose. Unfortunately many people do not choose to tinker with their goals in this way. They use their borrowed goals to make themselves miserable. Lastly I think that this is a better question in that it is one to which at least each person can obtain a partial answer for himself in his own experience.

I hope I have amply demonstrated to you the difficulty of asking a sensible question.

6 Efficiency and Cooperative Behavior

This was a talk given April 9, 1949, at Ohio University before the American Society for Engineering Education and published in their *Journal of Engineering Education* for December 1949. It is reproduced here with the permission of that periodical. I had said some of the same things to the American Management Association on June 9, 1948, in a talk entitled "A 'New Look' for Management." In both pieces I was trying to put together in one formulation certain matters about the nature of motivation, organization, and communication that for me constituted the new area of "human relations," and to show their implications for management.

Modern industry presents an interesting contrast. On the one hand tremendous advances have been made in the application of science and technical skill to the economic purposes of business. Scientific controls have been introduced to further the practical purposes of industrial organization. Operations have been logically organized to achieve more efficient ends. Much of this advance has gone on in the name of efficiency, and to this development engineering has contributed a great deal.

On the other hand, nothing comparable to this advance has gone on in the area of human relations. Our capacity to work together has not improved with our advance in material efficiency. Matters of morale and cooperation in our modern factories show no great improvement from what they were 50 or 100 years ago. Whatever slight advance there may have been is completely overshadowed by the new and powerful technology of modern industry. Our social skills have not advanced step by step with our technical skills.

This striking contrast between technical efficiency on one hand and matters of human cooperation on the other presents the number one problem of our present industrial civilization. It is obvious that we know a great deal more about machines than people. The technical skills of modern technology can be made explicit and communicated. To them science has been applied. Our social skills, on the other hand, are largely personal, empirical, and intuitive. They are so rooted in tradition that they cannot be made explicit. To them science has been little applied.

It is my opinion that there is no way of dealing with this problem other than the way that all the sciences have taken. We need to know more about what happens to people at work, and particularly we need to have more first-hand knowledge. In the field of human relations, as in other areas, there is no substitute for first-hand knowledge. We need a knowledge of acquaintance with the facts of cooperative behavior and simple skills of dealing with them.

Once this road is taken—and we have not traveled on it very far—I have become more convinced of the following observations. I find little justification for the prevailing assumption that so long as we turn out goods efficiently of good quality and of low cost, matters of cooperation can be left to chance. I find little evidence for the popular beliefs that cooperation is a matter of logical and technical contrivance or a matter of verbal exhortation—something that can be willed into being by verbal persuasion or efforts of personality. I find that there are just as brute and stubborn facts that determine matters of cooperation as there are brute and stubborn facts that determine matters of technical efficiency, and I find that there are just as specific methods, skills, and a point of view which can be employed to ensure cooperation as there are equivalent tools for ensuring technical efficiency. To the relevant methods, skills, and point of view of dealing with the simple facts of cooperative behavior, I give the name of "human relations."

I want to consider two questions: (1) What do we know about the determinants of cooperative behavior and (2) how can we apply what we know? Let me begin by looking at the determinants of cooperative behavior first from the point of view of the individual.

COOPERATIVE BEHAVIOR FROM THE POINT OF VIEW OF THE INDIVIDUAL

There is a widely held notion that people at work are primarily motivated by economic interest and that in their pursuit of economic gain they are essentially logical. According to this version the major inducement to cooperate is the factor of monetary return. Wherever and whenever this assumption has been seriously investigated in the light of facts, its universal validity has been seriously questioned. Investigator after investigator has agreed on this point. Far from being the prime and sole mover of human activity in business, economic interest has run far behind in the list of incentives that make men willing to work.

Although it would be incorrect to say that this oversimplified version of the economic motivation of people at work has been completely discarded, nevertheless in the past twenty-five years another picture has grown up with which it at least has to compete. According to this view, people at work are not too different from people in many other walks of life. Whether they work at the top or middle or bottom of an organization, they are not entirely creatures of logic; they too have feelings. For example, they like to be praised rather than blamed. They do not like to have to admit their mistakes—at least not publicly. They like to feel important and to have their work recognized as important. They like to feel secure and independent in their relations with their superiors. Moreover, also, they like to express their feelings. They like to be listened to and have their feelings and points of view taken into account. They like to be consulted about and participate in the changes which will personally affect them. In short, they too like to belong and be an integral part of some group.

According to this version man at work is a social creature as well as an "economic man." He has personal and social as well as economic needs. Work provides him with a way of life as well as a means of livelihood. To understand his satisfactions and dissatisfactions at work, one has to understand the social as well as the physical and economic setting in which his work takes place. One has to understand the kinds of relationships he has developed or can develop with his bosses, his subordinates, his co-workers, as well as with other people and groups in the organization. One has to understand the opportunity for social development and for the satisfaction of needs these relationships afford. Within these relationships can his basic social and emotional needs be satisfied?

From this point of view, therefore, cooperation depends upon two factors: (1) the social needs of people and (2) the opportunity which the environments offer for the fulfillment of these needs. This point of view, it should be noted, forces us to look as carefully at the social as at the material environment of the worker. It forces us to look at his social as well as his economic needs.

Any attempt to clarify the needs of people is admittedly an arbitrary one for the sake of convenience. I merely want to point out two very basic needs which often are in conflict.[1] On the one hand we want to be liked and approved of. We want to be able to do those things which give us a sense of belonging. This need to belong and to be an accepted member of a group is very important and necessary for all of us. On the other hand, we also all want to be independent and express our

1. See Nathaniel Cantor, *The Dynamics of Learning* (Buffalo: Foster & Stewart Publishing Corp., 1946).

own differences. We want to do things in our own way, to express our own unique feelings, to be ourselves in order to maintain our own feelings of self-esteem.

These two needs—for dependence on one hand and for independence on the other—are often in conflict. Too often we want to have our cake and eat it too. We want the approval of others and the sense of security which such approval gives us. At the same time we want to tell people off—we want to tell them "to go to hell" and yet fear the loss of support which such behavior might engender. It is obvious that if these needs are out of balance, the feelings they manifest do not make for cooperation. In modern industry, I find this conflict fairly acute. Too many people are in the position of wanting to tell their bosses to go to hell and yet are afraid to do so. (In this connection it should be noted that the union often offers a socially accepted form of expressing some of these feelings.)

Now, although many psychologists would have us believe that the resolution of this conflict can only be achieved by a better understanding of ourselves, I should like to turn to another aspect of cooperation before we reach this conclusion. Let us look at cooperation not only from the point of view of the individual, but also from the point of view of the group.

COOPERATIVE BEHAVIOR FROM THE POINT OF VIEW OF THE GROUP

People at work are related to each other in many different ways, many of which are not represented in the organization chart or manual. Not only are they organized in terms of the technical requirements of the job, but also they are organized in terms of sentiments, social customs, codes of behavior, status, friendships, and cliques. In their daily associations together, people at work tend to develop routine patterns of relationships and social codes of behavior. They come to accept these patterns of behavior as obvious and to react as they dictate. Within this system of relationships each task performed has a rank in an established prestige scale. Each work group becomes a carrier of social value. Each job has its own social values and its rank in the social scale. Each worker has a social as well as a physical place in the organization.

In any coordinated human activity, people belong to small work groups. It is in these small work groups that their meaningful associations and activities take place. It is only through their activities and associations in these small work groups that they become related to the larger total enterprise. In business each small work group has its technical and economic purpose in terms of which its members are formally related. But also, each of these groups has its own informal codes of behavior, its own norms of conduct, and its common ways of thinking. These common codes and beliefs not only provide important functions for the individual; they also provide an effective basis for cooperation. They have the effect of making each individual feel an integral part of the group. They bind people into routine collaborative activity. They give people a social place and feeling of belonging. They provide the framework for the fulfillment of human satisfaction. They give people a feeling of self-respect, of independent choice, of not just being cogs in a machine. Far from being a hindrance to greater effectiveness, informal organization provides the setting which makes men willing to cooperate. It is in this setting that man's needs for dependence and independence can be brought into working balance.

It should be noted that these manifestations of informal organization are spontaneous phenomena which arise wherever coordinated human activities exist. They cannot be prevented because they are the product of man's inherent desire to be a part of and belong to a group. They are not logical in character because they are concerned with values, ways of life, and ends in themselves. They are those aspects of social life which people try to protect and preserve and hence they cannot be changed quickly.

The importance to people at work of these informal groups can best be seen in relation to the introduction of change, when new methods or standards are initiated, newcomers are added, someone is transferred. upgraded, or promoted. Any supervisor knows the time it takes for such groups to accommodate to such changes. Any change which can be regarded as an interference to their customary routines and personal interrelations is viewed with alarm and suspicion. Although these informal groups appear at all levels in the organization, the character of these groups in modern industry at the bottom of the organization is peculiarly significant, because, at this level more than at any other, the ways of life of these groups are constantly in jeopardy from technological changes, new methods, raised standards, and manipulation of one kind or another. As a result, these groups in industry take on a highly defensive and protective character. Their major function becomes unfortunately the resistance to change and innovation, and the codes and practices develop at variance with the economic purpose of the enterprise. These defensive and protective characteristics of many informal groups at the work level exist full blown in many factories, even before any formal union appears.

From the point of view of group behavior, then, cooperation, far from being a matter of logical and technical contrivance, is much more a product of relationships involving feeling and sentiment. Far from being something which can be willed into being by legislation, verbal persuasion, and efforts of personality, cooperation can only take place within the framework of established and accepted social structures. It is not something which springs up overnight, something which is here today and gone tomorrow, something which can be put into a group from the outside. Cooperation is dependent upon routine relationships developed and practiced over a long period of time. It is dependent upon codes of behavior by means of which people work together in a group without any conscious choice as to whether they will or will not cooperate. It is dependent upon a certain stability in the ways of life of groups. Only under these stable social structures can people's needs for achievement, security, independence, participation, status, and growth be realized.

COOPERATIVE BEHAVIOR FROM THE POINT OF VIEW OF MODERN TECHNOLOGY

So far I have looked at cooperation from the point of view of the individual and his feelings and needs. I have also looked at cooperation from the point of view of the group and its social codes, routines, and sentiments. In each case I have wanted to show that cooperative behavior is a product of feeling and relationship. In essence, it is not something logical in character.

Let us now look at cooperation from the point of view of modern technology. From this point of view industry is not primarily organized to ensure cooperation. It is primarily directed to the production of goods of good quality at low cost. But more than this, modern industry is no longer turning out customary products in customary ways for customary customers. It is committed to turning out new and different products in more efficient ways and at lower costs for more quality-and-price-conscious consumers. To this end science and technology have committed themselves, with the result that the environment of the modern factory is quite different from the old know-how shop. In the modern standard shop there are a large number of people whose sole purpose is to originate better ways, more efficient and less costly ways of doing things, as well as to devise standards and controls to see to it that these goals are secured. The far-reaching repercussions of their activities for the social organization of industrial concerns is serious. Introduced without awareness of their effects upon the informal social organization, these activities can easily (1) dislocate people, (2) interfere with their established ways, (3) break up work groups, (4) prevent the development and practice of routine relationships, and (5) produce feelings of anxiety, insecurity, and frustration—what is often referred to as the feeling of being "pushed around." In short, the logical organization of efficient operation can operate against the social organization of teamwork. Many of the changes modern technology originates can collide head on with the social organization of the company and its attempts to maintain internal stability—a necessary precondition, as we have seen, for cooperative behavior. With the very best of intentions, modern technology can unwittingly foster the segmentation of the social structure of industry into groups with radically different points of view. It can unwittingly assist in the development of rigidities of relationship between segments of the structure that make cooperation difficult, if not in some cases impossible. The patterns of behavior produced by modern technology do not in and by themselves make for cooperation.

COOPERATIVE BEHAVIOR FROM THE POINT OF VIEW OF THE EXECUTIVE

So far we have been looking at cooperation from the point of view of the people whose cooperation is being sought. Let us look briefly at cooperation from the point of view of those who are trying to secure it. It is one of the functions of the executive to secure the understanding of people to the purposes of the organization. How does he do this? According to one version the executive gets things done through the authority of his position and the clarity of his communication. How these assumptions came about I do not know because so far I have found little evidence to support them.

Most of us know people who, with all the formal authority in the world and with an unusual capacity to express themselves logically, have great difficulty in getting cooperation. Likewise, many of my more inarticulate friends in positions of little formal authority seem to have no difficulty in securing the understanding of people. It has frequently been noted how some people lose what little authority they have by issuing orders they know cannot or will not be obeyed. Authority does not reside in the superior individual; it resides in the kind of relationship the superior has developed with his subordinates. Without the cooperative attitudes of subordinates, the voice of authority can speak, but the big booming voices it makes do not register upon people.

An extraordinary blindness to this point about securing the understanding of people is well manifested by what I shall refer to as the "tell-'em, sell-'em, explain-it-to-'em" school of thought. Whenever situations arise where people are reluctant to follow or accept cheerfully certain management orders, policies, changes, goals, aims, or what not, this school of thought immediately assumes that this state of affairs exists only because the people involved do not logically understand the need for the order, change, new objective, or what not. This school of thought assumes that a clear order is automatically always obeyed; that the logical and lucid exposition of an aim is sufficient for people to accept it; that any change is cheerfully accepted when the need for it is logically understood. As a result, all problems relating to the securing of people's understanding are resolved by the "tell-'em, sell-'em, explain-it-to-'em" technique. People are told most solemnly how their rates of pay have been determined, how and why this is the best method to do their work, why this is the best company to work for, etc. Whenever this method fails and people still don't understand all that is told them, this school of thought, being unable to question its assumption about matters of human understanding, is forced into either one of two conclusions: (1) "These clucks are just too damn dumb to understand," or (2) they still have not been clear enough. In this latter case they continue feverishly to draw more charts and diagrams, prepare more manuals and bulletins, and hire more experts in communication to explain policy in words of one syllable, so that this time even a moron will really understand management's good intentions and purposes.

The Case of Mary

In this connection I can think of a young married woman, whom I shall call Mary, who was hired for a temporary job because it was against the policy of the company to hire married women for permanent employment. When Mary was hired she was told about this policy, and six months later when she was told that her services were no longer required, she was again reminded about the policy of the company against the permanent employment of married women. Because her work had been of good quality, the office manager even gave her two weeks' advance notice and two weeks' advance pay. At this point, Mary, instead of being appreciative, began to accuse the office manager and the company of giving her a "raw deal." She told her story to many people: how she had been allowed to stay on for six months, how during this period another person had been hired, and why therefore she shouldn't be the one to go, etc. The assistant manager, the office manager, the credit manager all reasoned with Mary unsuccessfully. They told her over and over again about the company policy regarding married women. But she would have none of it. Before she left she succeeded in raising such a rumpus that she finally got the attention of the president of the company. The poor office manager was bewildered and hurt at Mary's unreasonable response.

Although we can all sympathize with the well-intentioned office manager, the interesting point in this situation is that what Mary was told and what Mary heard were two quite different things. People are more likely to hear things in terms of their feelings and personal situation. Mary was the sole support of an unemployed husband and a child—a fact which the office manager, when hiring Mary, did not find out. Temporary work, therefore, was no solution to Mary's personal problem. If the office manager had talked to her about that before hiring her, or at least during the six months' period of her employment, she might have heard what he said. But he was trying to get her to understand the policy of the company. In this process he was crystal clear, but in terms of Mary's situation and her feelings of permanent status after six months' employment, it was certainly the last thing Mary was capable of hearing.

This instance may be trivial, but it illustrates simply the futility of trying to explain things to people merely in terms of the speaker's point of view and without taking into account the point of view of the person to whom the explanation is being given. This approach assumes that people emotionally accept what they logically understand. It refuses to accept the fact that people are motivated more by matters of feeling and sentiment than matters of fact and logic. No amount of logical explanation from management's point of view will be emotionally accepted by people if it fails to take into account their personal situations and feelings. It only provokes argument and irritation—a feeling of being misunderstood.

Effective communication between superior and subordinate generally starts with listening on the part of the superior and trying to understand what the subordinate means within his own frame of reference before the superior starts talking. And when the superior does talk, he is more likely to be understood if he addresses himself to the needs and feelings of the subordinate as well as the purposes of the organization.

What Skills Does the Executive Need?

If my analysis is correct, modern industry needs more executives trained in more explicit skills of securing understanding and cooperation. The complex social system the executive has to administer requires more explicit human relations skills. If the intuitive and traditional ways of handling our human relations no longer work, what are these new skills the executive needs? Can we specify them more clearly?

Inasmuch as these skills are closely related to the phenomena I have been describing, I have already indicated my answer in part. From what I have already said about the nature of cooperative behavior, it should be clear that the practitioner of these skills has to be oriented in the following manner:

1. He has to address himself to what is important to people from their point of view as well as from his own and to make sure he does not confuse the two.

2. He has to address himself to people's feelings, attitudes, and personal background as well as to their more logical motives and purposes.

3. He has to look at the relationships people have with one another from the needs of individuals these relationships satisfy, as well as from the more logical purposes that are secured through them.

4. He has to think in terms of organic rather than mechanical analogies.

5. He has to be clinically, rather than merely logically, oriented.

6. He has to have a capacity to size up total situations and responses to them.

7. But more than practicing these skills of diagnosis, he also has to practice skills of communication and action. He has to develop a skill

of helping people to feel secure, to learn from their own experience, to reach their own decisions, and to become more mature and independent.

I hope that these very brief statements will help to convey in a very general way the nature of these human relations skills. But I would be very remiss indeed if I did not point out to you that to specify these skills, though difficult, is not nearly so difficult as to practice them.

Can These Skills Be Learned and Practiced?

The learning and practice of these skills are extremely difficult. About this there can be little question. The difficulty does not seem to arise because these skills are difficult to understand intellectually. Nor is it due solely to the fact that these skills, like any skill, have to be practiced in order to be learned, and that they cannot be learned merely from a textbook. These difficulties are present, of course, but the blockage goes deeper than this. During the many years I have tried to practice and teach these skills, I have come to believe that the major difficulty arises from the uncomfortable feelings which the practice of these skills sets up in the practitioner.

As I have said, for most of us these skills are rooted in the personal, the intuitive, the customary, and the traditional. To make them explicit makes many of us uncomfortable and uneasy. It forces us to become more conscious of ourselves—our own attitudes and feelings—and how they affect what we do and say. It makes us conscious of our own unconscious manipulations. But more than this, the practice of this skill requires an emotional acceptance on the part of the practitioner of two propositions which often go against our traditional attitudes.

1. It requires a willingness to accept the importance and inevitability of nonlogical behavior.

2. It requires a willingness to see and appreciate points of view different from our own.

For most of us these propositions are difficult to accept emotionally. It is not difficult for us to understand that people are motivated more by matters of feeling and sentiment than by matters of fact and logic. It is not difficult to see that people are members of groups and act in accordance with the sentiments of these groups (which is all that I mean by nonlogical behavior). But to practice this understanding is another matter.

It is obvious, for example, that we all do not perceive the world the same way. What is important to one person or group is not important to another. Matters that are of importance to management are not of the same importance to employees. Older service employees do not share the same values as younger service employees. What is important to professors may not have the same weight with students. And so on an so on. I shall not belabor this commonplace observation. All of us have had sufficient experience to realize that we do not perceive the reality quite in the same way as our parents, our teachers, our bosses, our wives, or our children.

It is also obvious that people respond to the reality as they perceive it to be and not as it actually is. Two workers may perceive their common boss in quite different ways. If worker A perceives his boss as a domineering individual, he will respond in terms of that reality; if worker B perceives this boss as a rather pathetic, insecure person, he will respond to that perception. It is very likely that neither perception resembles the perception that the boss has of himself nor the perception the boss's boss has of him.

But what makes the situation still worse is that although many people can understand these matters intellectually, they cannot accept them emotionally so that they can apply their understanding with any skill. The emotional acceptance of individual differences—our own as well as that of others—is a painful process of maturation.

How Can the Skills Be Learned and Taught?

Because of the emotional difficulties in learning these skills, I have come to have a few simple ideas about a method of learning and teaching them. Some of the elements of this method, which I shall call the case method, I should like to call to your attention.

In this method of instruction we start with a "case," i.e., a simple description of what actual people said, did, and felt in a concrete situation. The student is asked what he would do in such a situation were he in a position of responsibility in it. Moreover, he is asked not only what he would do, but how he would do it—what needs to be done and how to do it. By stressing this latter half, the student is made to realize the difference, for example, between "being tactful" in general and what the particular tactful remark in this particular situation would be.

In the human relations area I cannot stress enough the importance of this distinction. Too often our solutions are merely verbal because we do not address ourselves sufficiently to how we are to accomplish what needs to be done in a concrete situation with particular people who have particular feelings, needs, and relationships. It is always easier to deal with the "average person" than a particular person in a particular situation.

In the discussion of this case, therefore, the student is forced to face up to the attitudes and feelings of different people in the case. He comes to see how the same situation may look different to different people and groups. He comes to realize that he has to take into account these feelings and attitudes as one of the important determinants of the situation with which he has to deal. Emotionally he comes to accept the fact that these elements are just as brute and stubborn data as other aspects of the situation.

In the discussion of the case the student is also encouraged to express freely his own feelings and attitudes about the people and problems being discussed. Gradually in this way we hope that he comes to recognize his own feelings and attitudes and the important part they play in what he says and does when he tries to deal with a concrete situation. It should be noted that in this process the instructor does not try to change or evaluate the feelings the student expresses. He tries to get the student to recognize his attitudes; it is up to the student to change them if he wants to.

As you can see, this method also requires skills of the instructor. But the skills he practices—it should be noted—are of a piece with the skills he is trying to communicate. The student therefore learns by example. It is no use for the instructor to tell his students about the importance of feelings and sentiments in the behavior of people if in the classroom he ignores the feelings and sentiments of his own students. Somehow the communication does not quite register.

It should be noted that this method is quite different from the "tell-'em, sell-'em, explain-it-to-'em" approach. It is based upon quite a different set of assumptions. It does not assume that knowledge is something handed down on authority and that the acquisition of such knowledge is educative in itself. Learning is not based upon the student's ability to hand back abstractions. Learning is not based upon the student's ability to answer questions which the instructor asks. To the contrary, the case method assumes that the learning process is different for different people. It assumes that learning cannot take place apart from the experiences, attitudes, and feelings of the learner. In the case method, therefore, the student is allowed to raise and answer his own questions—not the instructor's.[2]

The case method stresses the importance and subjectivity of personal experiences. Granted that people learn from their experience, it is a fact that people may learn the "wrong" as well as the "right" lessons from experience. People often generalize from too limited experience. Because of certain attitudes they may misinterpret their experience. They may not see the significance of their experience. Before they can learn some things, therefore, they have to unlearn "many things that ain't so." The case method, therefore, assumes that people have to be helped to learn from their own experience. This assistance is the instructor's chief role.

The case method further assumes that learning must start with "concretions" (not "abstractions"), with what we may call action-oriented situations at the "how-to-do" level. Not until the student obtains some intuitive familiarity with these "concretions" and confidence in dealing with them can he begin the process of formulating adequate generalizations from experience.

It is by this approach that I feel we can in a small way begin to face up to some of the very difficult problems underlying the learning of these human relations skills.

2. See Earl C. Kelley, *Education for What Is Real* (New York: Harper & Brothers, 1947).

7 Problems in Applying What We Know

This is an unpublished talk given to the Society for Applied Anthropology in Cambridge, Massachusetts, on May 28, 1949. Here for the first time I was addressing social scientists instead of practitioners. This kind of social scientist consisted of those "behavioral scientists," as they were soon to be called, who were "impure" enough from a disciplinary point of view to want to apply what they knew. Little did I realize then that I was on the fringes of an issue which was to become hotter as time went on for this new breed of "cool cats," to be called also later "change agents." In this piece I began to formulate the personal qualifications that I thought such people should have. I think I would say about the same things now as I did then, except perhaps I would extend my remarks so as to apply to all organizations, not just to those of business, and I would conclude with the statement, "It's tougher and later than you think."

For those in the applied field in industry, I should like to raise a question that perplexes me a good deal. What have *we* learned, if anything, about how to apply what we know about matters of social organization to the solution of human relations problems in business? By "we" I shall refer to those of us who are in a field which bears many labels; "applied anthropology in industry," "industrial sociology," "group dynamics," "human relations in industry," and now the latest arrivals, "managerial sociology" and "cow sociology." Some of these labels we have chosen for ourselves; others have been thrust upon us. But we welcome all contributions.

I shall assume that what keeps us all together in spite of variations of labels, doctrines, and ideological leanings is (1) our common passionate desire to work in the field and to study men at first hand in their natural surroundings; (2) our interest in studying matters of social organization at all cost; (3) our common methods of interviewing and participant observation, and yet also our willingness to accept all methods, both qualitative and quantitative, which help us to describe, understand, and deal with the relations among individuals in their organizations; and (4) our unwillingness to accept methods or approaches, no matter how scientific or quantitative they may be, which do not tell us anything about the relations among individuals in concrete living groups or organizations. What also holds us together is (5) our interest in what George Homans calls "experiments of light" as well as in "experiments of proof,"[1] our concern with conceptual formulations which allow us to improve our skills of observation and listening as well as which help us to explain and verify the intuitive insights we have reached. Another binding factor is (6) our common conceptual framework of viewing man as a whole and of looking at organizations as a system of relationships.

But over and above these factors which have held us together, I also detect another, (7) our common desire to apply the little that we know to the practical problem of business. We have all, I believe, felt that we could and should try to learn by doing from the very start, as well as to seek that more distant goal of systematic knowledge, the principles of which we could apply later with more certainty. We felt not only that our methods and ideas were mutually consistent and part of a "grand strategy,"[2] appropriate to our stage of development for the effective accumulation of knowledge, but also that these very same ideas and methods were useful tools for application and practice here and now. This hand-in-hand development of both theory and practice was our "war cry" as I remember the early days of 1940. We felt that our ideas and methods had far-reaching implications for administrative practice, as well as for the integration of the social sciences.

This emphasis on the side of application appeared in an editorial statement of the first issue of *Applied Anthropology* in 1941. Let me quote some sentences from this editorial to remind you of this concern. "*Applied Anthropology* will publish only articles which contribute to the solution of practical problems" . . . "In all cases, the practical uses of the work must be clearly stated and a method outlined by which the results of the investigation could be applied" . . . "Before very long we hope to be able to publish a majority of articles in which an account is given of the way recommendations were arrived at and what the results were of putting them in operation" . . . "*Applied Anthropology* is designed not only for scientists but even more for those concerned with putting plans into operation, administrators, psychiatrists, social workers and all those who as part of their responsibility have to take action in problems of human relations."

I wonder if the subsequent issues of *Applied Anthropology* have quite lived up to this original statement. It is my impression that few articles have appeared in which the investigator showed how he put

1. See George C. Homans, "The Strategy of Industrial Sociology," *American Journal of Sociology*, Vol. LIV, No. 4 (January 1949), 333.
2. Ibid., 335.

his recommendations into effect and what the results were of putting them into operation. I make this observation not to be critical merely of *Applied Anthropology;* to the contrary, I think all of us have tended to "sluff off" with too facile verbal solutions the difficult problems of applying what we know. Also, I imagine that those of us who viewed ourselves "chiefly as 'plumbers,' mending the leaky pipes in human relations plumbing"[3] felt that our plight at this mundane level was not too well appreciated by our more research-minded colleagues. Somehow the problem did not quite come up as simply as the editorial statement suggests. Before we could determine the results of putting our recommendations into operation, we had to get someone willing to put them into effect. And this I suspect is the heart of the problem.

For the human relations expert who is also a practitioner, the distinction between making recommendations and getting them put into effect is only too real. It is one thing to diagnose what needs to be done; it is quite another matter to get people to do what needs to be done. It is one thing to want to help people with their problems; it is quite another matter to get them to accept and perceive you as a source of help.[4] The skills of diagnosing a human situation are not quite the same as those skills which are needed to secure the understanding of people involved in the situation. It is easier to tell people things than to help people recognize things for themselves; yet the results are rarely satisfactory.[5] To the "human relations plumber" these distinctions are not just theoretical; he can ignore them only at his peril. These distinctions bring up the difficult question of just what is the relation of the human relations expert to the organization he studies and to the executives in them who are responsible for taking action in problems of human relations. How does the expert establish a satisfactory relationship with them when so often the object of his endeavor is to change or modify their behavior? Is the human relations expert merely the repository of abstract knowledge or does he, too, have to practice a skill in getting his knowledge accepted?

Many of us have become quite skilled in being able to go into an organization and seeing what the problem is. With our point of view

3. See Douglas McGregor, "The Staff Function in Human Relations," *Journal of Social Issues,* Vol. IV, No. 3 (Summer 1948), 2.

4. Ibid., 14.

5. See Elliott Jaques, "Social Therapy: Technocracy or Collaboration," *Journal of Social Issues,* Vol. III, No. 2 (Spring 1947), 59. See also Carl R. Rogers, "Divergent Trends in Methods of Improving Adjustments," *Harvard Educational Review,* Vol. 18, No. 4 (Fall 1948), 209.

and methods we can easily distinguish the quality of the face-to-face relationships that exist in an organization from the verbal policies enunciated about them. We can see that the quality of these face-to-face relationships does not arise solely from the policies of management, that it arises from the nature of individuals and groups in organizations and how these dimensions are administered. We can readily see that individuals and groups are not responding to the same perceived realities, that what is important to one person or group is not important to another person or group whose positions in the structure are different. Because people respond to the reality as they perceive it and because all people in an organization do not share the same perceived reality, we can see why the problem of communication in an organization becomes difficult. We can see in certain organizations the friction that results when—because of the arrangement of their work—people of lower status originate action upon people of higher status. We can see how what happens in one part of the structure affects what happens in other parts of the structure, how the behavior of one group affects the behavior of another, and particularly how the behavior of the superior affects the behavior of the subordinate.

From these observations and insights we have come to have some ideas of those patterns of activities, interactions, and attitudes which will bring about harmonious and healthy human relations in an organization. Our literature on the applied side is flooded with such recommendations as "the need to educate in more favorable attitudes," "changing the pattern of human relations," "changing frames of reference," "introducing social skills in the supervisory or executive levels." But how do we do these things? To perform them successfully, it seems to me that our solutions always imply hopefully the introduction into the social system of some person aware of the effect of his behavior on others and with some skill in securing the understanding of others. Without such a person in the system, our recommendations become impotent; they only become meaningful and effective if they are put into operation by some person with some depth of understanding. Without such understanding on the part of some person, our recommendations are reduced to the state of manipulative techniques. And the results we get at this level are rarely satisfactory to ourselves or our clients.

Here is the dilemma. The expert in human relations is the first person introduced into the social system as a means of introducing social changes in it. He is the expert on the effects of introducing change. At the employee level he knows the effects certain technical changes have, the resistances they provoke if introduced too quickly or without understanding of their effects upon the relations of people. He realizes that differences in the way management introduced these changes would make an appreciable difference in the way employees responded to them. But how does he communicate these new ways of doing things to management, particularly when these changes involve important changes in management's own behavior? He knows from his experience in gaining the emotional acceptance of employees to change that telling them the need for the change is not enough. On what grounds can the expert then behave differently in relation to the executive—to gain his acceptance and understanding—from the way he is asking the executive to behave in relation to his subordinates so as to gain *their* acceptance and understanding? The expert who does behave differently creates in management the very anxieties and resistances which management by the same behavior in turn creates among its employees. This uniformity of response we have found time and time again in situation after situation, in organization after organization. It would be a sad state of affairs indeed if we could not apply to our own behavior as "experts" what we have found holds true in the behavior of others. It would be curious indeed if the expert in human relations refused to practice human relations in his face-to-face dealings with executives and policymakers.

So the conclusion I find myself reaching more and more is that our practical solutions of applying what we know to organizations depend upon introducing into the social system a self-aware person with skills of an unusually high order. Not only does he need skills of diagnosis; he also needs skills of communication, i.e., skills of securing the understanding of people. Above all, he has to be aware of himself and the effect of his behavior on others.

It is not enough that he has a capacity to assess the personal and social determinants in a concrete piece of behavior, which is what I mean by diagnostic skill. This kind of understanding gives insight only to the practitioner of the skill. In human situations his (the practitioner's) understanding is not enough; rather, the persons in the situation must have it. To develop such understanding requires another kind of skill. It is a skill which helps others secure understanding of the problems that affect them. In many human situations this is the

kind of skill that is needed. Without it all our diagnostic skills become
ineffectual or obsessively elaborated. We are trying to solve problems
from the "outside"; we are trying to superimpose our understanding on
the understanding of others. As a result we provoke anxiety, appre-
hension, resistance, and feelings of dependence upon the expert.

Although these two skills, capacity to understand situations and
capacity to help others develop understanding, are closely related, they
are not the same. Experience has repeatedly shown that a person who
is skilled in the first does not necessarily have skills in communicating
his understanding to those who need it. The brilliant diagnostician
whose insights cut directly to the heart of the problem often cannot
provide the patient step-by-step assistance that they need.

A common element in both skills is the capacity to understand one's
own relation to a situation. This development of self-awareness is
closely related to both these skills. Experience suggests that although
everyone has some capacity for it, in many it remains low. In others
their awareness becomes an inward elaboration of self-centered preoccupations that defeat effective action. But he who seeks to improve
his skills cannot escape the uncomfortable involvement and responsibility of his position. He must learn to accept the fact that all evaluations are human evaluations and that he has to make judgments and
decisions. Those who achieve a balanced awareness secure a deeper
understanding of the factors operating here and now in a given situation and a greater capacity for taking effective action in respect to it.
By itself, self-awareness can become an overriding, sometimes neurotic,
conviction of sin resulting in crises of indecision. But, in connection
with the practice of the skills we have described, it helps increase their
effectiveness. For most of us, however, this road to balanced awareness
is bound to be full of the frustrations and pains of growth.

What have we learned then about applying what we know to the
practical problems of business? As I see it, we have learned that just
as skills are needed to secure our data about organization, so skills are
needed to apply our understanding to organizations. Just as it is necessary for us to maintain good relations with our subjects over long
periods of time in order to secure the kind of data we want about the
relations of individuals in their groups and organizations, so must we
maintain good relations with the people in organizations who need our
help, so that they perceive us as a source of help rather than as a
threat to their feelings of personal integrity. This application of our

understanding of organization to the needs of people in organizations is a skill of an unusually high order. Without such a skill we are likely to do more harm than good; most of our knowledge remains ineffectual and sterile.

Neither as collectors of data nor as formulators or appliers of abstractions can we escape our total involvement in the human situations in which we do our research or apply what we know. We are inextricably part of the situations we study and try to help. We have to learn to accept this involvement; we cannot escape it by better abstractions or more measurements. We can only learn to deal with it more effectively through the development and application of better skills as well as better abstract knowledge.

George Homans[6] has said that as he watches us he thinks he sees that we "are beginning to discover in each new situation the same kinds of things over and over again," that we seem to find ourselves "beginning at the beginning every time." In trying to diagnose and recommend the way out of this cessation of growth and complication, he suggests the need to develop more quantitative methods and analytical concepts. With these suggestions there can be little quarrel. By all means, let us have better abstractions and more measurement so long as we measure things that we think are relevant to the understanding of the relations of individuals in organizations.[7] But let us not delude ourselves that by better abstractions or more measurements we can escape the problem I am trying to state. Nor are his recommendations the only next steps we can take in order to get us out of our compulsively repetitive discoveries. There is another great adventure which also lies ahead. Our ability to apply better what we know depends not only upon better abstract knowledge but also upon better and more skilled people. We need more research on how to obtain knowledge in the area of human relations. We need to understand better the nature of these skills of communication that I have been pointing to and how people can be trained in them. We need to learn better ways of dealing with matters of social organization in concrete face-to-face relationships where we are one of the uncomfortable parties.

At universities I find too little attention being given to this problem. At present the university-trained student in social science is much

6. George C. Homans, "The Strategy of Industrial Sociology," *American Journal of Sociology*, Vol. LIV, No. 4 (January 1949), 336.
7. See William F. Whyte, "The Social Structure of the Restaurant," *American Journal of Sociology*, Vol. LIV, No. 4 (January 1949), 310.

better equipped to handle complex logics than complex facts. He is much more likely to receive intensive training in laboratory methods of investigation than in clinical methods of exploring and diagnosing concrete situations. He is much better equipped to report others' opinions than to handle their feelings or even his own. Confronted with a concrete situation—an upset group, a person emotionally disturbed—he often exhibits extraordinary lack of insight and understanding. His theories leave him singularly naked and uncomfortable in the presence of the concrete, the complex, the unanticipated, and the disturbances of his own viscera.

If my analysis is correct, there are two roads of growth and complication we should take. One is in the direction of developing more analytic concepts and quantitative methods. The other is in the direction of developing better-trained people with those skills that are also necessary if we are to apply effectively the knowledge that our more analytical tools and quantitative methods can secure. To take one of these roads without the other would be disastrous. Let's not be inflexible and rigid of course, but let us also not desert our original clinical insights when the going gets tough. If we hold on now and learn to handle our own anxieties, we may prevent this premature leap or should I say escape into "objectivity." In learning to handle our own subjectivity through skill, we may not get our better abstractions so quickly, but we will in turn get more social scientists of more maturity who will be better able to handle those abstractions when they come.

8 The Human Equation in Employee Productivity

This piece originated as a talk to the National Retail Dry Goods Association on January 10, 1950, and was printed in their Personnel Group's publication *Supervising People*, January 1950. Later with some revisions I submitted it to the *Revue Suisse pour l'Organization Industrielle*, Zurich, Switzerland, and it was published by them (in English) in Vol. 19, No. 4, March 1950. With their permission it is this version that I am including here.

Here again it can be seen how I shift the problem of employee productivity from an individual to an organizational frame of reference and then make it a problem of administration. So upon reflection now I think a better title for this piece would have been "Employee Productivity: A Problem of Administration."

Most of us would agree that employee productivity cannot be conceived apart from employee satisfaction, needs, and attitudes. But just how these human factors are related to production is not so clear. Some of us are too prone to believe that the human factor is just one more of the many factors—such as light, heat, ventilation, pay, etc.—which need to be taken into account when thinking about employee productivity. Frankly, I do not find this way of thinking useful or fruitful. It oversimplifies and ultimately distorts the complex, concrete situations with which, as administrators, we have to deal. What is needed in these situations is a new way of thinking about the behavior of individuals at work. In this new framework the problem of employee productivity takes on a new dimension. It becomes no longer the sole problem of major concern to management; it becomes only one of the many interrelated problems of administering people at work.

TWO DIFFERENT CONCEPTS OF WORK

Let me begin by contrasting two radically different ways of conceiving the nature of work and the worker.

There is one class of ideas about work which runs something like this: Work is something requiring physical and mental effort basically unpleasant. It is something that is "taken out of" the worker, something that is primarily done in order to earn a living and as something that can be done either "efficiently or inefficiently." These constitute one family of related ideas about work.

In contrast to these conceptions we have those ideas which view work as an activity satisfying the needs of people and as a way of life. These ideas derive from quite a different frame of reference regarding the worker. They view the worker as a social creature primarily striving to satisfy his many needs through his association with people at work. His motivations, like the motivations of any human being, are thought of as complex.

I should like to discuss these two radically different views of men at work with two questions in mind: one, which one of them does least violence in representing the reality of work from the point of view of the worker? And, two, which one of them is it more useful and convenient for the supervisor of human beings at work to entertain? In short, which one gets the better over-all results?

Work and Effort

The conception of work as something basically unpleasant, I imagine, is as "old as the hills." Some people in all generations and in all cultures have entertained this idea at some time. But I doubt if it gained such widespread acceptance before the industrial revolution in our western civilization. In our present industrial civilization, it has become almost a self-evident proposition. It underlies the behavior and policies of both management and union leaders, and much business practice bases itself on this simple assumption, which economic theory also seems to justify. Work is basically unpleasant and, therefore, the hours of work should be as short as possible and the pay as high as possible. Only by such means can workers be attracted to this basically unpleasant activity. Closely associated with this belief is also the notion that work "takes something out of the worker." Hence, wages are paid the worker as a compensation for this vaguely conceived loss, sometimes referred to as "fatigue."

At this point, I can imagine some readers' objections. Wages, they will say, are not paid for what is "taken out of the worker" but for what the worker "puts out" on the job, for his productivity. This is what businessmen are interested in; this is what they pay for; this is what they want to increase. The question they want answered is how can human relations, the new touchstone in our industrial scene, help to increase employee productivity?

This way of viewing work exclusively in terms of productivity and rate of performance, it should be noted, is more important to management than to the worker. Under this conception, work is being evaluated in terms external to the worker. He does not view his work primarily in terms of his rate of output. It is the way other people appraise what he is doing. This is perhaps an obvious point but, nevertheless, from the point of view of human relations, a very important one, and I shall have more to say about it later.

It is not difficult to understand how this evaluation of work solely in terms of productivity has become increasingly important with the rise of mass production and how, coupled with the idea of work as something basically unpleasant, it has formed our modern concept of "efficiency." Of course, there are many people who still think of efficiency merely in terms of rate of performance. Such people assume that if the rate of output goes up, efficiency also increases. The engineers tell us, however, that this confusion between the rate of output and efficiency is serious. They point to the steam engine. The efficiency of a steam engine, they say, is not determined by output alone. Its efficiency is the ratio of output to input. To determine the efficiency of a machine it is necessary to know the proportion of the energy input of the machine that is recovered in useful work. A similar ratio, therefore, they feel, should be applied to the human organism.

From this point of view, the efficiency of the individual worker is to be viewed as a ratio of his output to the cost of this work to him in terms of energy and effort expended, fatigue suffered, and dissatisfactions incurred. In these terms, obviously, if the rate of output goes up, efficiency may go up or down or remain constant, depending upon the changes in the cost of work. For example, to determine the relative efficiency of two different methods of performing a task, it is not enough to know merely the differences in the rates of performance between these two tasks; it is also necessary to know whether under the new method the worker has had to exert himself more, whether he is more fatigued or "jittery" at the end of the day, whether it has impaired his appetite, his capacity to sleep, to enjoy leisure, and to get along with his wife and children, etc. Increases in these factors will lower the efficiency of the worker, make supervision more difficult, increase rates of turnover and absenteeism, and generally affect the overhead of the operation.

Obviously, these factors regarding the cost of work to the individual cannot be ignored and, as a result, a great deal of time has been given to them. These factors, however, are much more difficult to measure than the rate of performance of the worker. It is much easier to measure output than to measure the jitters, nervous exhaustion, and boredom. As a result, this measurement of efficiency of the human organism at work represents an ideal which is never quite reached in practice.

In practice, much cruder ideas or ideals prevail. In most cases, an increase in the rate of production is assumed to indicate an increase in over-all efficiency. Nevertheless, under this steam engine conception of work and the worker, the structure of modern business has been greatly altered. This development in the direction of improving productivity has generally taken one of three different forms.

One approach has been to try to improve the conditions surrounding work, to make them more pleasant and less distracting. Although it has been difficult to determine the effect upon efficiency or productivity of such specific factors as noise, light, temperature, ventilation, rest periods, etc., apart from the attitudes of workers toward them, nevertheless technicians have done much to improve these factors surrounding the work itself with the hope that such improvements in and by themselves would create a physical environment favorable to increased productivity apart from the workers' "will to work."

Another very important approach has been in the direction of improved work methods. This approach tries to find the best way of doing a task, to find those methods which will involve the least effort in doing a job so that production can be increased at no additional cost to the worker. There is little question that the aim of these "methods engineers" is to improve efficiency as well as productivity, and much fruitful work has been done in this direction.

A third approach is directed more to the workers themselves. This approach tries to stimulate directly by incentives the level of effort that workers themselves put into the job. In this approach, however, more than in the other two, the steam engine analogy tends to break down because the complex problem of human motivation, with which one does not need to be concerned when considering steam engines, now rears its ugly head in a most unfortunate way. In order to make the analogy hold even slightly and in a somewhat attenuated form, one has to conceive of the worker's motivation as being exceedingly simple. The worker has to be viewed as being primarily interested in the pursuit of pleasure and economic gain and as pursuing these ends in an essentially logical manner. In short, he has to be conceived as either a pleasure machine, an egotist, or an economic man—or all of them together. In spite of the fact that many simple observations about the behavior of workers give little support to this notion, it nevertheless remains deeply rooted in the minds of men.

I shall not belabor any further this steam engine concept of work and the worker. Personally, I feel that the idea is bankrupt. It has guided us some distance in the direction of understanding some of our problems in business and industry. Much useful work has been done in the past under this conceptual framework, but as the principal guiding hypothesis for the future it seems to me no longer useful. We have explored the permutations and combinations of this old idea *ad nauseam*. The time has come for a Copernican revolution in the field of industrial relations, a new way of thinking about our problems.

Work as Satisfaction of Needs

The steam engine conception of work and the worker is not entirely "wrong"; work can be usefully conceived of in this way for certain purposes. But its uses for supervision are limited because it fails to include one very important observation about employee behavior, very important to supervisors when seeking the cooperation of their people. In the thousands of interviews my colleagues and I have had with workers, we have never heard one single statement suggesting that the worker conceived of himself or his work as a steam engine. Nor can I find any other investigator having recorded such an observation. If there is one common reaction, heard over and over again from workers and stated in no uncertain terms, it is to the effect that they do not like or want to be treated as machines.

This is a most interesting state of affairs, and from it I can draw only one conclusion, namely, our steam engine analogy of work does not represent the reality of work as the worker himself views that reality. In fact, it seems to be a way of thinking which does violence to everything he considers holy and important to him about it.

If we listen to workers talk about themselves and their work and the satisfactions and dissatisfactions they obtain from it, the picture we get is something quite different. From such evidence we find that people at work are not so different from people in any other aspects of life. They are not entirely creatures of logic; they, too, have feelings. They like to feel important and to have their work recognized as important. Although they are interested in the size of their pay envelopes, this is not the only matter of their concern. Sometimes they are more interested in having their pay reflect accurately the relative social importance to them of the different jobs they do. Sometimes even still more important to them than the maintenance of socially accepted wage differentials is the way their immediate superiors treat them. They like to feel secure in their relations with their superiors. They like to work in an "atmosphere of approval." They like to be praised rather than blamed. They do not like to have to admit their mistakes —at least, not publicly. They like to know what is expected of them and where they stand in relation to their bosses' expectations. They like to have some warning of the changes that may affect them. They also like to feel independent in their relations to their superiors. They like to be able to express their feelings to them without being misunderstood. They like to be listened to and have their feelings and points of view taken into account. They like to be consulted about and participate in the actions that will personally affect them. In short, employees, like most people, want to be treated as belonging to and being an integral part of some group.

From the point of view of the workers themselves, then, the picture we get of them and their jobs is quite different from that of the steam engine. From them we see the worker as a social creature, who has personal and social as well as economic needs, whose willingness to cooperate is dependent upon the satisfaction of his social as well as his economic needs, who does not want to be paid merely for doing what he is told, but who also wants to satisfy through his work his needs for security, independence, participation, and growth. We see that work provides him with a way of life as well as a means of livelihood.

EMPLOYEE PRODUCTIVITY: A PROBLEM
OF HUMAN ADMINISTRATION

This, then, is the meaning of work to workers, which anyone who takes time to listen to them can obtain. Not only does this conception represent better the reality of work to employees but, curiously enough, it also provides a much more useful and fruitful view for management. It provides management with a much more comprehensive picture of the job situation. It allows supervision to do a better job. It is particularly useful to management and supervision in their face-to-face dealings with people when trying to secure their understanding of and cooperation toward the goals of the organization. It provides management with a more useful way of thinking about employee productivity. Let me amplify these points very briefly.

This view of work as a social activity satisfying the needs of people forces management to look at the employee and his job not only in terms of the specific factors affecting his productivity but also in terms of the kinds of relationships which the employee has developed or can develop with his bosses and his co-workers, as well as with other people and groups in the organization. It forces management to look at the opportunity for social development and for the satisfaction of needs these relationships afford. And particularly it forces management to look at the behavior and attitudes of the employee's immediate superior as one of the primary determinants of job satisfaction.

According to this conception, employee productivity is merely one of the many facets of employee behavior and cannot be treated as an entity separable from the intricate web of human relationships of which it is a part. All the evidence we have from recent studies would seem to indicate that supervisors who administer their people in terms of their total social and economic needs get better results than those supervisors who supervise their people exclusively in terms of their productivity. And they get better results not only in terms of better morale and employee satisfaction but, curiously enough, in terms of employee productivity, too.

This state of affairs is not so curious as it may appear. It merely means that, in the last analysis, business is an organization of people. In order to secure their cooperation, one has to see and understand what is important to them from their point of view. People are curious in that they do not like to be treated as means to someone else's ends; they like to be treated as ends in themselves. To be exclusively concerned with their productivity is treat them as means to management's ends. All the tools which management uses to cut costs and improve efficiency—job evaluation, time and motion study, work simplifications, monetary incentives, employee testing, etc.—can have this meaning to employees if improperly used. These tools in and by themselves can never supplant sound human relations. Without the cooperative attitudes of employees these tools become worthless. They merely provoke feelings of being misunderstood, of being pushed around, and workers resist them. Only as they are administered with some understanding of the needs of people can they be made to work. And these needs are primarily satisfied through their relationships with other individuals and groups of individuals at work.

In these terms, the problem of employee productivity is not solely a matter of technical contrivance; it becomes primarily a problem of management leadership. It becomes a problem of balanced operation, of maintaining in an organization both efficient operation and sound human relations. This conflict between efficient operation and the cooperative attitudes of employees is inevitable, if we persist in thinking about work and the worker in our old ways. Only under a new conception can we gain insights and find new methods of dealing with our problems. In this new conception, employee productivity cannot be the sole end in terms of which management administers its human organization. It becomes only one of the many values of which account has to be taken by management when administering its complex human institutions.

9 Training Supervisors in Human Relations

This was originally given as a talk to the Training Directors of America (now the American Society of Training Directors) in Philadelphia on March 16, 1951, and was published by them in the *Proceedings* of their Seventh Annual Conference. It was also published with minor revisions in the *Harvard Business Review*, September 1951, and it is this version I have used here. Permission to reproduce the paper has been granted by both the American Society of Training Directors and the *Harvard Business Review*.

The "human relations movement" started as a research activity. It emerged in part from the Hawthorne studies reported by me and William J. Dickson in *Management and the Worker* (Harvard University Press, 1939). By 1951, however, "human relations" had become primarily associated with a training activity confined mostly to the supervisory level. To those for whom the word "human" in "human relations" was the important word, it had become the road to "salvation"; to those for whom "relations" was the important word, it remained still only the road to "competence." In this piece I was trying hard to steer it in the second direction and hoping that the supervisors' supervisors, called "executives," might also get the point.

In the past decade heavy stress has been placed on the need for a better understanding of human relations on the part of supervisors—foremen, office managers, or others whose role it is to supervise men and women at work. As a result, training programs designed to teach supervisors how to deal with people at work have become increasingly popular. These programs have run the gamut from those that try to teach general principles of human behavior to those that are organized at the "how to do it" level, such as how to handle grievances or how to induct new workers.

In view of the increasing importance and popularity of these programs, it would seem timely to ask ourselves some questions. How successful have they been? On what assumptions are they based? How can they be improved? In this article I should like to try my hand at answering these questions. If I speak feelingly about some of these matters, let me remind the reader that it is because they are very important to me and because it is one good way of being "objective."

HOW SUCCESSFUL?

For some time now I have been impressed by how ineffective and unrealistic many of these programs are. They do not accomplish what they are designed to do, that is, to help supervisors with the human aspects of their jobs. Many of them raise "loaded" questions, give facile answers, indulge in platitudes, present principles that cannot be applied to concrete situations, and discuss unreal situations—situations that never have existed except in someone's imagination. In many of them the conference leader is armed with the points that the trainees are supposed to make. He is allotted so much time to draw these points out, and should the trainees fail to respond, he is instructed to make them himself.

In many of these programs supervisors are instructed in "why employees behave as employees." Very few have much to say as to why supervisors behave as supervisors." Most of them *tell* the supervisor how he should behave. This *telling* may be done directly or indirectly, tactfully or not so tactfully, in terms of facts or principles or by sentimental appeals, persuasion, and "pep talks." But no matter how thin you slice it (just like baloney), it still remains *telling*.

What so often astonishes me is how docilely supervisors go through these verbal hoops and how readily they learn the proper verbal responses with which to please their conference leader. Every supervisor in the country knows by now that he should have "all the facts" before he acts, and that when all is said and done about these problems of human relationship, "it is just a simple matter of applying the golden rule."

What are we trying to do? Surely we must hope that what goes on in these training sessions will make some difference in the way the trainees will behave in the future, in the shop or office. But when the trainee goes back to the shop or office, he is under particular pressures, both internal and external, which determine his behavior there far more than anything which has gone on in the training meetings. Very little is done about these matters in our training sessions.

Rather, we apparently prefer to spin out our good intentions and beliefs, mostly erroneous, about an ideal supervisor—a little tin god on wheels—that never existed at any place or any time; a man who is always "objective," who gets all the facts before he acts, who never loses his temper, who is always courteous and kind and, above all, fair, who treats people the way he would like to be treated, who now can tell an introvert from an extrovert, who knows about the private lives of all his employees and just what is troubling them, who now knows the four methods of resolving conflict, while of course at the same time he gets out the work and maintains cost and quality. What a guy!

BASED ON WHAT ASSUMPTIONS?

Because we do not know in a very clear way what we are after in our programs, we underestimate the difficulty of the job. We bring to our training sessions an odd assortment of beliefs and assumptions not only about what a supervisor should be and how he should behave but also about the way he learns, grows, and changes and the time it takes to accomplish these things. So long as these beliefs and assumptions persist, we cannot improve upon what we are doing. One of the most persistent of these assumptions is the belief that learning from experience is a simple process.

Learning from Experience

From childhood we have all heard that we learn from experience and that experience is the best teacher. All of us would agree that what a supervisor learns from his personal experience is likely to be more important to him than what he gets from any training meetings. Yet often we seem to be asking supervisors to apply to their problems rules and principles that ignore or deny their personal experiences.

Let us explore more carefully this idea of learning from experience. One of the interesting things about experience is how personalized it becomes, how important to each of us our own personal experience is, and how difficult it is to communicate this importance to others. What does this personal experience teach us? Astonishingly enough, personal experience seems to teach different people quite different lessons. It often teaches the "wrong" as well as the "right" lesson. The school of hard knocks makes criminals as well as businessmen.

In talking to supervisors I have found that personal experience has taught them a number of things, if we can take the beliefs that they express at their face value. For example, it has taught them that women are more easily upset by unimportant things, that you have to let employees know who the boss is to gain their respect, and that "it's not what you know but who you know" that counts in getting ahead in most organizations. Such statements and many others like them can be frequently heard.

These beliefs are not entirely unfounded. For the people who hold them, such beliefs reside in personal and social experiences they have had. Some of them can be traced to certain experiences that particular supervisors have had with particular employees, bosses, and organizations. Some of them have been picked up as part of the collective beliefs of certain social groups of which supervisors have been members. But these are not very adequate generalizations from experience; if applied too rigidly, they may get the supervisor into trouble, and perhaps even more important, they may prevent him from learning any new lessons from experience. More often than not, instead of helping supervisors to do better jobs, the function of such beliefs is to allow supervisors to maintain their self-respect in the face of their inadequacies.

Once such beliefs have been built up, it is astonishing how they persist and how experience has a way of confirming them. For those of us who believe the world is essentially a hostile place, experience has a curious way of fulfilling our expectations. People with chips on their shoulders are more likely to find other people with chips on their shoulders. This is because we are constantly selecting from experience those aspects which prove our point and also because our attitudes toward other people are likely to determine their attitudes toward us. There are always enough instances of poor women drivers to reinforce our conviction that women drivers are always poorer than men. There are always a sufficient number of people talking about us to confirm our suspicions that we are being talked about, particularly if this belief that we are being talked about makes our behavior sufficiently peculiar to provoke comment. Just as attitudes of hostility and suspicion tend to provoke similar attitudes from others, so do attitudes of friendliness tend to provoke attitudes of friendliness in return.

If my analysis is correct, it would seem to follow that learning from experience is not the simple process we so often assume it to be. On the contrary, it is a rather difficult achievement to learn the valid and useful lessons experience can teach us. Our limited backgrounds, let me emphasize, often tend to produce inadequate generalizations, beliefs, and attitudes. Hell or high water, logic or evidence to the contrary, they tend to persist.

Assumptions versus Facts

It would also seem to follow from my brief analysis that if we are to learn the useful lessons new experience can teach us, we have to question and re-explore continuously the assumptions and attitudes we bring to it. And this for most of us is a difficult business. It is much more comforting to believe that women are peculiar beings than to face up to the uncomfortable feelings of inadequacy we have when trying to relate ourselves to them in a work situation. If this be so, the difficult task, then, which faces most training directors is not how to tell supervisors what they do not know about human behavior; it is how to get supervisors to "unlearn" what they believe about people that is not true. As someone has so aptly said, it is not people's ignorance but "what they know that ain't so" that gets them into trouble.

However, when trainers teach "what they know that ain't so" to supervisors who are equally convinced of "what they know that ain't so," the confusion is confounded and compounded. We have a veritable Tower of Babel. Take, for example, the precept that the supervisor should have all the facts before he acts. How often have I heard this said in one course or another? Why do we persist in telling supervisors to do what is not only difficult but impossible to do? No supervisor, or executive, for that matter, has ever acted or ever will act in terms of all the facts, let alone all the relevant facts, in a situation. All action is based on certain assumptions about the unknown and even the unknowable. By the kind of assumptions we make about these matters the wise man is differentiated from the fool.

Moreover, in this precept we gloss over the difficulty of getting even some of the relevant facts in any human situation. We talk of "facts" as if they were crystal-clear, simple entities which any fool can observe and find and which will also be considered "facts" by all other observers. In the human relations area, I find nothing more elusive and difficult to determine and to find than the "facts." Moreover, as has been said, "facts do not speak for themselves; they have to be interpreted for their meaning."

That we teach supervisors such "untruths" does not bother me so much. I realize there are some important and useful "half-truths." What does bother me is that this kind of nonesense goes on in the name of common sense, realism, and practicality—and that the grim, earnest, and serious discussion of these silly little points is not even helpful. It takes all the adventure out of learning. It is the best way I know of losing not only your mind but also your sense of humor. And from what I hear, the supervisor does not enjoy it or learn much from it either.

Perhaps we need a more concrete example. Let me record for you an actual discussion that took place in a particular training session between a conference leader and his trainees.[1] The topic under discus-

1. These selections have been taken from a study by Abraham Zaleznik, *Foreman Training in a Growing Enterprise* (Boston: Division of Research, Harvard Business School, 1951).

sion was "emotions." The conference leader was asking for comments on whether or not the various emotions listed in the training manual were good or bad. Included in the list was the word "loyalty." The discussion I shall record starts here.

1. CONFERENCE LEADER: How about loyalty?

2. TRAINEE: Good, you have to have it.

3. CONFERENCE LEADER: Is it ever bad?

4. TRAINEE: When the company gives you a raw deal, you can't be loyal.

5. CONFERENCE LEADER: Well, then you'd quit.

6. TRAINEE: Well I don't know.

7. CONFERENCE LEADER: Here we have an emotion that is unequivocally good. To whom do we have to be loyal? First to the company— to all executives and to all workers.

With this pronouncement the discussion about loyalty ceased. Somewhat later the group discussed the emotion of "ambition." Let us listen in to the conversation as the conference leader is again speaking.

8. CONFERENCE LEADER: Now take ambition. Is it important in a group like this? Damned right! We all want to give the impression of success to outsiders as well as to our inner self. Suppose you were put in the vice president's office to copy the encyclopedia at a salary of $10,000 a year. How long would you be happy?

9. TRAINEE: All my life. [Laughs]

10. CONFERENCE LEADER: He doesn't want a cinch. He wants to do something. And $10,000 is not enough to keep you satisfied. What about fellows who don't have ambition, are they executive timber?

11. TRAINEE: No.

12. CONFERENCE LEADER: You want to shoot for the boss's job. All right. But ambition has a twist. Can it have a bad effect?

13. TRAINEE: If a guy has a swell head.

14. ANOTHER TRAINEE: If you try to chop down smaller guys, that's bad.

15. CONFERENCE LEADER: Ambition might drive a man to underhand tactics. That's completely undesirable. Ambition drives him. Ambition is like fire—it's essential, but when uncontrolled, it's dangerous.

16. TRAINEE: Is a man without ambition useless?

17. CONFERENCE LEADER: If he is an executive, yes.

18. TRAINEE: Suppose a supervisor gets to be an assistant general manager, and he is satisfied and does a wonderful job?

19. CONFERENCE LEADER: That's not good. He can't continue to do a wonderful job.

As I see it, many of our training programs fall short in the area of human relations because (1) they are oriented more to words and techniques than to the understanding of situations; (2) they ignore the feelings and attitudes which supervisors bring to these training sessions; (3) they "misevaluate" the complexity of the learning process; and hence (4) they substitute good intentions and wheezes for intelligent reflection about experience. As a result, it is not surprising that supervisors often leave these meetings little changed except perhaps for having acquired a slightly enlarged vocabulary and a few tricks.

HOW SECURE IMPROVEMENT?

This evaluation of our training efforts shows the need of more realistic objectives. For our aims I feel we should choose nothing short of the highest. What may sound idealistic is also common sense and practical.

Educated People

What industry and business must have in their supervisory and executive groups is more educated people—not more trained seals. I realize the word "educated" may prove a stumbling block; so let me say what I mean. I am not saying that supervisors should necessarily be college or university graduates. Lord forbid! By an "educated" person I mean a person (1) who knows what he does not know; (2) who has an honest perplexity and curiosity about his personal experience; (3) who has a stop, look, and listen attitude toward his own experience so that he is capable of re-evaluating it and learning from it; and (4) who has some skills in the direction of being able to receive communications from others.

In short, my picture of an educated person is a person with those mental attitudes which allow him to grow from his experience in the direction of learning how to live better with himself and others. We can find such people in all walks of life and with varying degrees of formal education. I find little evidence to confirm the belief that only universities turn out such people. In fact there is some slight evidence that in such institutions one is least likely to find them.

Be that as it may, please note that my picture of an "educated person" is a far cry from a person (1) who has all the answers; (2) who knows clearly right from wrong and what the "proper attitude" of people should be; (3) who accepts the maxims of others as a substitute for reflection and re-examination of what experience can tell him about himself and others; and (4) who is insensitive to the opinions, feelings, and attitudes of the people with whom he works. Recent studies[2] would seem to indicate, moreover, that supervisors who have the attitudes toward experience I call "educated" are also the supervisors who seem to be better able to secure the cooperation of others.

If this be so, it would seem as if the aims of "real education" are consistent with the kind of person we would like our supervisor to be. With these aims in mind we are now in a better position to state more clearly what our role as trainer in these training sessions should be.

Facilitating Self-Learning

I shall start negatively. We should stop giving supervisors "the word." This I imagine is going to be difficult for some of us. "Do you mean," I can hear someone ask, "that we can no longer tell supervisors anything?" Let there be no mistake about it; I mean just that. We have to stop telling supervisors how they should behave and what their attitudes should be. We have to stop trying to change their personalities. We have to stop talking down to supervisors, lecturing them, giving them pep talks and little sermonettes. We have to give up our precepts, maxims, wheezes, and even the more dignified manifestations called "principles."

Why must we stop these things? For the simple reason that once and for all we are going to take seriously the idea that supervisors learn by themselves from their own experience, and what we can do most effectively is to help them in this process. Let us remember that our new objective is to assist people in learning from their own experience. We are no longer trying to change them; we are giving them the opportunity to change themselves, if they wish, by reflecting upon and re-evaluating their own experience.

2. See William F. Whyte, *Human Relations in the Restaurant Industry* (New York: McGraw-Hill, 1948); and Daniel Katz, Nathan Maccoby, and Nancy C. Morse, *Productivity, Supervision and Morale in an Office Situation* (Ann Arbor: Institute for Social Research, University of Michigan, 1950).

This last point may need to be underlined. We are not interpreting their own experience *for them;* we are not telling them *our* personal experience. Instead *we are allowing them to examine and re-evaluate their own experience.* Let us not confuse these quite different phenomena, as I fear too many people do.

So let us be clear. We are not even going to tell supervisors what they should have learned from their own experience. They are going to have to learn the hard way. No more spoon feeding, no more ten commandments. They are big boys now, and "poppa" is no longer there to provide them with the answers. Each supervisor is going to have to work out his own salvation, to find the particular answer which best fits himself and his own situation.

Under this new objective, therefore, what we do is to set the conditions which will facilitate this process of self-learning. What are these conditions? In considering this question I shall have to go back to my analyses of how and what we learn from experience. Regarding personal experience I made several assertions; let me repeat them:

1. Personal experience has a way of being very important to the person whose experience it is.

2. Not only is each person's personal experience extremely important to him, but he is an authority on the subject. Nobody else knows more about it than he.

3. Different people learn different lessons from experience, sometimes useful, sometimes not.

These facts—and I shall call them that—make our problem both difficult and intriguing. They make us realize that learning the valid and useful lessons which experience can teach us is a very complex process. It means that there is no such thing as uninterpreted experience. Experience is constantly being evaluated. And lest we forget, please remember that each one of us is doing the evaluation. Sometimes we may interpret from too limited experience. Because of certain attitudes we bring to experience, we may misevaluate it and fail to see its significance. Therefore, before we can learn some things, we have to unlearn "many things that ain't so."

But this is difficult because of the reality to each of us of his own interpretations, no matter how limited and "screwy" they may be. Try to tell the supervisor whose experience has taught him to beware of redheads that not all redheads are volatile and explosive, and you will see what I mean. How does one get out of this impasse? I shall enumerate three ways that I find helpful:

(1) One can help people to recognize the feelings and attitudes which they bring to experience. For most of us these feelings and attitudes are implicit or unconscious; often we do not realize we have them. Nevertheless they determine in good part what we see and hear. They underlie our beliefs and conceptions. They provide the frame of reference for our interpretations. They function as ill-defined and vague questions. Until we recognize more clearly some of these feelings and attitudes, there is no way of correcting them. We do not see how they distort the meanings we assign to our experience.

(2) If experience does not speak for itself, if we have to keep asking questions of it in order to elicit its useful meaning, we can be helped to ask "better" questions of experience. By "better" I mean clear and answerable questions. There is no clear answer to a vague question, but perhaps still more important to realize is that there is no answer to an unanswerable question. It is astonishing how often we ask and continue to persist in asking of experience questions which experience cannot answer. Scientists no longer feel frustrated because experience cannot tell them how many angels can sit on the point of a needle; they have given up asking such questions. But in human affairs we have not progressed that far; we continue to ask unanswerable questions and feel frustrated because we cannot answer them.

The most common questions we ask in matters of human affairs are: "Who is to blame?" "Who is the villain?" "What is the cause of all our woes and miseries?" That the mutually interconnected, interrelated, and interdependent character of experience makes these questions unanswerable does not bother us. This hunt for the "spherical sonovabitch"—and by that I mean a sonovabitch from every point of view—goes on. I do not need to remind you that the search for this person or entity is rampant in the world today, and that for short periods in history we think we have found him or it. In our wishful thinking there must be such an entity, and in spite of our repeated disillusionments the quest continues.

(3) Not only can we help persons to recognize the feelings they bring to experience and to ask better questions of experience; we can also help them to be better observers of experience. We can provide them with a useful way of thinking about experience, which will allow them to make their own observations. Not until they can make better observations do they have something concrete against which to check their questions and to revise their beliefs and assumptions. It is futile,

for example, to ask supervisors to address themselves to the feelings of employees when they are not yet able to recognize a feeling when it is expressed to them. If people have no capacity to observe the effect of their behavior upon others, it is of little use to tell them to "listen." So many of our precepts, maxims, and principles fall by the wayside because of this limitation. The practice of a precept can be no better than the observations in the concrete territory to which the precept is applied.

THE CASE METHOD APPROACH

The time has come to raise the $64 question which by now I feel may be lurking in the back of many readers' minds. Let me try to state it: "We accept the propositions that the process of self-learning is facilitated (1) by helping people to recognize the attitudes they bring to experience; (2) by helping people to ask better questions of experience; and (3) by providing them with a *useful way* of thinking about matters of human behavior so that they can make better observations about themselves and their relations to others. This is all very fine, but please don't leave us hanging in the air. Get out of your ivory tower and become concrete. Just how can this be done?"

At this point I shall have to become extremely personal. I cannot tell you how you should do it; I can only tell you how I try to do it. The approach I take represents my own personal understanding and adaptation of the case method of instruction as used at the Harvard Business School. For this understanding I am greatly indebted to my colleagues there, so that what I have to say is far from original. Nevertheless I shall continue to talk in personal terms so as to avoid any possible embarrassment to my colleagues for any shortcomings in my understanding. Moreover, I am only speaking of the case method as applied to the area of "human relations," since it is to this area alone that my experience has been limited.

Setting Up the Discussion

In the first place, because learning begins with concretions and not abstractions, my procedure is to choose a description of a concrete case for discussion—not an "armchair case," but a description of a real situation, of something that actually happened, of what actual people said, felt, did, and thought in a particular situation. This description does not contain all the facts, but rather some of the facts that some of the people involved in the situation have or that are available to them. I have the students or trainees (students or trainees—it does not matter) read and prepare this case before the discussion. This description may involve as little as two or as many as twenty pages of reading matter.[3]

In discussing such a case, I ask the students or trainees what they would do in such a situation if they were in a position of responsibility. I generally choose for this position of responsibility one of the minor characters in the situation, let us say a department head or foreman rather than a president of the company. I do this because it allows me very soon to ask them not only what they would do but also how they would do it. Most students are much more articulate with "what to do" than "how to do it." This is much truer when they are assuming the role of a foreman than when they are assuming the role of the president. I am always interested in how many supervisors think the president is a "free agent" and can do anything. I sometimes wonder how complimented presidents would be if they realized what prodigious feats their supervisors thought they were capable of accomplishing.

By stressing not only what needs to be done but also how to go about doing it, I help the student to realize the difference, for example, between "being tactful" in general and what the particular tactful remark in a particular situation would be. By this device I hope the students will realize how often their solutions are merely verbal. Notice I am not telling them anything. After they tell me that they would be "tactful," I merely ask them to tell me what they would say in particular to this particular person in this particular situation. The sweating, fumbling, silence, exasperation, or sheepishness which generally follows this question is more meaningful to them than anything I can say.

Helping Them to Recognize Their Attitudes

There are several different assumptions and attitudes that students or trainees are likely to bring to bear on a case:

(1) While they are discussing and "solving" the case, I usually observe them "hunting for the villain." There is never complete agreement on just who in particular the villain is, but that there is one and

---

3. For examples of the kind of cases I mean, see John D. Glover and Ralph M. Hower, *The Administrator: Cases on Human Relations in Business* (Chicago: Richard D. Irwin, 1949).

that he should be exterminated is almost always assumed. "A" wants to fire Joe Blow, "B" wants to fire the foreman, "C" wants to fire the department head, and "D" may even want to fire the president. By the time every villain has been exterminated in some fashion or other and there is no one left in the situation to do any work, I call the group's attention to this interesting "solution" and ask for any further comments. In my best wolf-in-sheep's-clothing manner, I perhaps mutter something to the effect that it does seem odd to me that we can only correct this condition by firing everybody in it.

(2) During the discussion I observe not only the "hunt for the villain," but also the "hunt for perfection." After their energies in the direction of exterminating villains have worn a bit thin, students often like to play God. With a flip of the wrist they change the personalities of the characters in the case. They make them objective, calm, dispassionate people who see all, know all, and hear all. I give this God-playing tendency full reign. Generally during this phase I am merely muttering such phrases as "How interesting!" "You don't say?" "Bless my soul!" "Really?" "Extraordinary!" "I wouldn't have believed it," and equally innocuous remarks.

(3) Concurrent with the hunt for the villain and the hunt for perfection there frequently occurs also the "hunt for authority." This game is a favorite pastime of people in staff positions. The reason why they cannot get certain things accomplished, these people claim, is that they do not have "authority." Without it they are impotent; with it they could issue orders and injunctions which would be immediately obeyed. Their underlying assumption is that they lack authority, never that they lack understanding or skills. The solution therefore is to put themselves in a position as close to the president as possible, so that they will have the authority to get their plans and schemes accepted by the people below them.

During this period in which they are elevating themselves to higher and higher positions in order to get things done, I merely ask them how they would get there and, assuming they did get there, how and in what way, if at all, their behavior would change. Do they see any difference between the "authority" which is earned and recognized by the bottom and the "authority" which is conferred from the top?

(4) By this time the group becomes restless. The teacher does not seem to be approving of their behavior, although let me assure the reader that I am deeply interested. I am neither approving nor disap-

proving. I am just observing and reflecting my observations; but this is not the way the stereotype of a professor should behave. So by this time the group becomes a bit "aggressive." They begin to complain, "You haven't told us all the facts. How can I tell how to do it when I don't know if Joe Blow is an introvert or an extrovert? You haven't told us." I readily confess my guilt and then ask, "Let us assume that Joe Blow is an introvert. Just what difference, if any, would it make with regard to what you would do and how you would do it?" Sometimes I ask, "O.K., you don't know, but how would you find out if Joe Blow is an introvert or extrovert?" I wouldn't quite say that these questions have a soothing effect on the class, but, to put it crudely, it does set them "back on their heels." They have to think again for themselves, and that is disagreeable.

(5) Now the class is filled with tension. The students have exterminated villains; they have played God; they have sought for a mystical authority; they have asked for more "facts"; and still the professor or leader does not seem to be satisfied. At this point their attitude is likely to be, "We've worked hard enough. You tell us. You give us the answer." Here is the toughest nut to crack. Being human and having a nervous system, I would like to tell them "the solution." But so long as I am not too fatigued to hold out against them, I generally say, "The discussion has been very interesting. I'm not sure I know just what should be done or how it should be done. I can tell you what I would do and how I would go about it. But that would not be *the* answer. It would be *my* answer. Perhaps we should discuss another case next time."

Note that I am not telling the students or trainees what to do. I am merely pointing out to them the assumptions they are making and the attitudes they are bringing to the problem. I am trying to help them to recognize these attitudes so that they can question and re-examine them. I do not force them to re-examine their assumptions. My attitude is permissive but questioning. "So you like to exterminate villains? So you like to play God? So you like to be given the facts, the authority, and the answer? How human, how interesting, but how come? Are we engaged here in an exercise of wishful thinking, or are we realists and men of practical affairs?"

Please do not think that there is not a very difficult problem of "timing" the innocuous and perhaps facetious remarks I make, but then I cannot give you all my "secrets." Also please do not think that these hunts for the villain, perfection, authority, the facts, and the answer are the only attitudes that students or trainees bring to these case situations. I have only mentioned some of the most common ones for purposes of illustration.

Helping Them to Ask "Better" Questions

Before considering this step, let me emphasize the importance of helping students to recognize the feelings and attitudes they bring to experience. This phase of the case discussion is very important. It is by far the most difficult to learn for those who are beginning to teach by the case method. It is time consuming; it requires the patience of Job; it plays real havoc upon the nervous system of the case discussion leader. Moreover, it involves that aspect of the learning process which is most ignored—that we have to unlearn some things experience has taught us before we can learn some of its more fruitful and helpful lessons. Until this is realized by the learner—even if only in an intuitive way—knowledge in the area of human relations remains sterile.

In matters of human affairs I often find it more helpful to ask "What is going on here?" than "Why are things the way they are?" The former question often helps us to sharpen our observations about what is going on right under our noses; the latter question frequently leads to idle speculation. The clinician, for example, has to be able to diagnose "a case of measles" before he can help the patient to get well. Moreover, the diagnostic skill of being able to recognize that "this is a case of measles" is as important to the physician and the patient as to try to answer the question of how the patient got the measles. In fact, in medicine the recognition of a syndrome precedes any explanation of its etiology. The skill of the clinician is his capacity to identify what is before him here and now.

When we instruct in the human relations area, this fact is often ignored. We talk as if there were no such equivalent diagnostic skill based upon an intuitive familiarity with the way people behave. We try to solve problems intellectually, abstractly, and analytically instead of trying to identify and recognize what is taking place here and now. When Joe Blow comes up to complain to us, instead of trying to listen to the feelings he is expressing to us here and now, we are wondering about how his wife treats him, whether his mother rejected him as a child, whether he has an "inferiority complex." So we observe nothing and hear nothing. We do not even hear or observe ourselves responding to our speculations rather than to the feelings of Joe.

So in the discussion of cases, instead of encouraging students to speculate as to why people behave the way they do, I try to turn their attention to the way a particular person in a particular situation is behaving and the effect of this behavior upon others. "Tell me," I ask, "do you see what this particular person is doing, what he is saying, what feelings he is expressing, here and now? Can you see in this particular case that the foreman is doing all the talking; can you see how this prevents Joe Blow from talking; can you identify some of the feelings Joe Blow expressed in the few moments he was allowed to talk? Can you see whether or not the foreman responded to these feelings of Joe or to his own preoccupation? Can you see what effect upon Joe the foreman's particular response had?"

Notice that the new questions I am raising are questions which can be answered by observation here and now. I am hoping that when the supervisors go back to the shop or office, they will ask similar questions of their present situation. In this way I hope to encourage them to make better observations, which will allow them to learn from their present experience.

Helping Them to be "Better" Observers

In discussing the previous point I have already discussed in part this one. I defined a "better" question as one which can be answered approximately by experience. Experience, if it is to be useful, requires more precise observation. Observation occurs in the present—not in the past or future. By "better" observation I therefore mean the recognition and identification of what is taking place here and now.

Before we can observe skillfully, we need a useful way of thinking about the phenomena we are observing. Because most of us do not have a very clear way of thinking about what is happening when two people are talking together, we do not observe very clearly what is occurring. As a result, we are likely to pay more attention to what is being said than to the person saying it. In human relations we are observing events which involve the relationships of people. By relationships I do not mean logical relationships. I mean *the activities* which bring people together or separate them from one another. I mean *the sentiments and feelings* they do or do not share. I mean *the interactions* they have, how often or how few. Note that *activities, sentiments, and interactions* are referring to things that can be seen and heard. They are elements to be found in any human relationship.

For the human relations observer, this need for a conceptual scheme —for a way of thinking about human relationships—is paramount. Without such a conceptual scheme, his observations become dissipated. Let me try to illustrate what I mean in terms of the conversations I recorded earlier between a conference leader and his trainees in a training session. What did you (the reader) observe or hear in them?

Were you preoccupied with such questions and observations as the following:

1. What is loyalty anyway?

2. Did the conference leader answer the questions of the trainee correctly?

3. The trainee is right when he says, "You can't be loyal when the company gives you a raw deal."

4. The conference leader does not seem to be too bright.

5. The trainees do not seem to be too bright.

6. The conference leader should have said this or that, etc.

Or did you see and hear the following activities, interactions, and sentiments and their interrelations, and did you consider the following questions:

1. The conference leader began and ended each conversation.

2. The one conference leader used more words than the several trainees put together and spoke more often (ten times to their nine).

3. The conference leader was frequently expressing how people should feel.

4. When they had a chance, the trainees were expressing how they felt.

5. The conference leader did not address himself to the trainees' feelings and thus did not seem to encourage the trainees to speak.

6. The feelings of the trainees acted upon the feelings of the conference leader and vice versa.

7. The discussion was about "words" rather than about "situations."

8. The conference leader assumed that words meant something— not that people meant something. As a result, the "words" discussed provoked more heat (feelings) than light (exploration).

9. The trainee in statement no. 4 might have been talking about a previous personal experience.

10. What is likely to be the trainee's feeling when the conference leader responds to his statement (no. 6) with statement no. 7?

11. What is the trainee in statement no. 16 trying to say?
12. Did the conference leader help him to say it? Etc. . . .

It is my contention that if you (the reader) made the latter kind of observation and raised the latter kind of questions, you had a more useful way of thinking about these conversations. You were thinking of man as a creature living and learning in and through a network of relationships. You were thinking of what purposes are secured and what needs are satisfied in these relationships. You were thinking that what man brings to his experience in terms of assumptions and feelings determines in part what he perceives (sees and hears). You were thinking that what takes place in a conversation when two or more people are talking together is more likely to be an interaction of sentiments and feelings than a strictly logical phenomenon.

Therefore you were sensitive to the feelings which the trainees were trying to express. Therefore you were sensitive to the possible effect of the conference leader's feelings upon the feelings of the trainees and vice versa. Therefore you were curious about "what the hell" was going on there. In short, you had a way of thinking which allowed you to observe what could be observed instead of indulging in idle analysis and speculation.

Accordingly, in helping students to be better observers, I try to provide a useful frame in which they may observe what is occurring in a concrete situation and in which they may think and operate on the facts. Such a way of thinking not only assists the observer to make certain observations; it also helps him to see certain uniformities in the facts—certain recurring phenomena. To cite some very simple cases, he can begin to see that persons are likely to talk more freely to him about matters that are of importance to them if he tries to understand what they are saying from their point of view rather than from his own. He can begin to see how persons resist changes that do too much violence to their customary ways of behavior. These uniformities in the territory he can observe over and over again. Once they can be recognized and identified, he can begin to take them into account in his behavior and the behavior of others.

Not until the student reaches this stage of being able to recognize some of the brute and stubborn facts of human behavior does "human relations" become something more than words, good intentions, rituals, and techniques.

Helping Them to Make "Better" Decisions and to Behave Responsibly

It is my belief that in the area of human relations making better decisions is dependent on the three points already discussed; i.e., that better decisions will only follow from better observations, better questions, and more self-awareness. I assume that the conscious decision-making process in the area of human relations is only a very, very small part of the evaluational process which is constantly going on at various levels of consciousness in the minds of people in positions of responsibility. The supervisor or executive is "evaluating" every minute of the day (and night too, sometimes). These evaluations determine what he assumes, sees, hears, feels, and does in the many interactions he has each day with superiors, subordinates, and colleagues. These evaluations enter very strongly into his more conscious deliberations and decisions. To treat "decision-making" apart from the personal and social evaluations of persons in which it is deeply imbedded would be a grave error—a form of "misplaced concreteness."

For these reasons I allow my students to make up their own minds, to reach their own decisions. I only try to make them more aware of what they are assuming, feeling, perceiving, doing, and saying and of how these processes are interdependent. By such a process of self-awareness I assume they not only will make "better" decisions but also will act more responsibly. Responsible behavior is acting with awareness of the effect upon oneself and others of what one is doing. Without such an awareness, good intentions are not enough. Without a capacity for observation, awareness cannot be achieved.

CONCLUSION

In conclusion I should like to make four comments:

(1) I know I have treated a very serious and difficult problem in a very cavalier fashion. Articles or books, for that matter, could be written on each of the last four points I have been considering. My only excuse for my oversimplified treatment is that my purpose has been to intrigue the reader with a point of view rather than to expound it systematically.[4]

4. For those readers who are interested in more scholarly presentations of useful ways of thinking about matters of human relationships, I should like to recommend George C. Homans, *The Human Group* (New York: Harcourt, Brace, 1950); Carl Rogers, *Client-Centered Therapy* (Boston: Houghton Mifflin, 1951); and William F. Whyte, *Pattern for Industrial Peace* (New York: Harper & Brothers, 1951).

(2) What I have been trying to say is a matter of deep concern to me. My plea in this article has been for more spontaneity and humility in the teaching of human relations. The teaching of human relations can be a great adventure, a great challenge, and a great hope. Let's not make it a farce.

(3) In the many human relations programs in business and industry, I see an opportunity for the recovery of spontaneity, a sense of perspective, as well as a sense of humor. Too often in each of his many courses the supervisor is too much concerned with the grim, earnest, and often humorless discussion of some specialization, so that nowhere does he get a sense of perspective with regard to the nature of his job as a totality. In my opinion, the human relations area offers an ideal opportunity to regain this lost sense of proportion about matters of supervision. It is the one place where the supervisor can be himself— without having to pretend to be an expert on all matters. Let's keep it that way.

(4) I realize that what I have been talking about is not so simple to do as my remarks may have seemed to indicate. The skills of teaching by the case method cannot be learned in three easy lessons. Nevertheless, in spite of this handicap, the case method of instruction should not remain unexplored by business. It is realistic, down-to-earth; it provides an ideal medium for helping self-learning to take place. Moreover, particularly in an institution like business which is unhampered by academic tradition it could really grow and develop.

10 The Role of the Administrator in Our Modern Society

This was given as a talk to the Third Midwestern Conference of the Harvard Business School in Chicago, March 29, 1952. It was published in the *Harvard Business School Bulletin,* Summer 1952, and is reproduced here with the School's permission.

Although this piece is addressed to "bigger shots" than I was talking to in the last chapter, I was not discriminating between big and little "shots" at this stage of my career. Any person in a position of formal responsibility for evaluating the performance of others was grist for my mill. I called him an "administrator" instead of an "executive" because when I made verbs of these nouns, although I thought the verb "execute" fitted better his stereotypical image, the verb "administer" fitted better, it seemed to me, what the total situation demanded that he should be doing. Anyway in this piece I was not trying to create a new image for this executioner of business so that the public would feel more kindly toward him. I really thought I was stating a role that would represent more closely what he was up to, and that he would realize this if he would just stop acting for a while and begin to think big about it.

It is perhaps a truism to say that a man will behave in the way he evaluates the situations he meets. It is also a commonplace to say that some evaluations are more mature and discriminating than others, and lead to more effective action. What constitutes a more proper evaluation of immediate experience? I realize this is a question of a rather large order to raise; nevertheless, since it is so closely related to certain observations I wish to make, I will consider it briefly. Of the many misevaluations man can make, I should like to differentiate two classes.

One class of misevaluations can be called "errors of judgment." For want of some of the relevant facts in the situation, a person may reach a wrong conclusion. This overlooking of the facts to which we are all liable on occasions is very common. With this class of misevaluations I shall not be much concerned, because within them lies the possibility of self-correction. Given the new facts, or seeing the false assumptions made, the person is capable of correcting his judgment. Such errors of judgment are just temporary departures from good sense under the influence of strong feelings, poor observations, etc.

There is another class of misevaluations of quite a different order. These misevaluations are not so easily corrected. Experience does not so easily disprove them. In fact, experience often seems to verify them.

Because I shall be concerned primarily with misevaluations of this sort and because what I wish to say depends upon an understanding of them, let me give you an example of what I mean.

A foreman sees a worker coming late to his job. He assumes that lateness is an indication of an improper respect toward him and the rules of the company. The foreman feels angry, and therefore he reprimands the worker with some such statement as, "You better learn to come on the job on time or else." Note that given this assumption of disrespect to him and the company, anger must follow, and this anger will determine his evaluation of the late worker. The foreman does not separate out of his perception from his assumption and feeling. From his point of view it is a unitary experience perhaps better described by the statement that he perceives the worker as rude and as intentionally flouting his (the foreman's) authority. It is to this total evaluation that he responds by reprimanding him (the worker). The foreman thinks he perceives a rude worker. He would call this a fact. He would not see that what he perceived was a late worker and that his assumption and anger is what makes the worker "rude."

Let us take another example. Again a foreman sees a late worker. Because he knows this worker has a sick child, he assumes that the worker has been up most of the night taking care of the child. Therefore he feels sorry. He responds to this total situation by saying, "How's the kid today?" Note again that feeling sorry is related to what he assumes and perceives. He perceives or thinks he perceives the worker who has been up half the night taking care of a sick child and he is sympathetic. He therefore inquires about the child's health. This foreman also does not separate out his perception from his feeling or his assumption. The foreman thinks he sees a tired worker. He does not see that what he perceived was a late worker and that his assumption and feelings of sympathy make the worker "tired," regardless of whether or not in fact this be so.

To some of you my examples may seem to illustrate the point that "proper evaluation" depends upon whether or not the foreman assumes correctly what is so. They may appear to be demonstrating that the first foreman made the wrong assumption and the second foreman the right assumption about the late worker. Let me be clear. My examples are not intended to illustrate either of these points. Rather, they are intended to show that even if the foreman makes the correct assumption, he may still be misevaluating. I grant that more effective behavior will follow if the foreman makes the right rather than the wrong assumption, but if he is not aware that he is assuming, how can he correct his evaluation if it is wrong? He is not too different from that little girl who "when she was good, she was very, very good, but when she was bad, she was horrid." Let's see what happens if the assumption of my first foreman is wrong. When he tells the worker, "You better learn to come on time or else," will he find it out? Not likely, because what is more likely to happen is that the worker will respond, "Says who?" In short, the foreman's assumption of a rude worker is verified. The foreman has made his wrong assumption come true. Can't we hear him say, "Didn't I tell you he is disrespectful and rude?"

Perhaps now I can make what seems to be the real distinction between proper and misevaluation of immediate experience. By "proper evaluation" *I mean an awareness or understanding of the possibility of misevaluation so that a better evaluation is possible.* By "misevaluation" *I mean those evaluations in which the seed for self-correction is not present.* This kind of misevaluation arises because we do not know we are evaluating. As a result we confuse what we see with what we assume and feel. We treat our inferences as if they were facts.[1] Within this realm of misevaluation, our particular assumptions may be right or wrong, but there is no skill or method of finding out whether they are or are not. Within this realm, good or bad judgment becomes a matter of chance with no skill or method or point of view to guide it. In this realm we often make our assumptive worlds come true. Not so in the realm of "proper evaluation." Here we can make mistakes, errors of judgment. But from them we can learn. We can find the facts we fail to observe, and we can re-examine and correct the assumption we made.

A COMMON MISEVALUATION OF THE EXECUTIVE'S FUNCTION

In the last twenty-five years, since I've been concerned with the human problems of administration, I have been very interested in what seems to me a basic misunderstanding and misevaluation of the executive's job. It crops up in many forms and guises and has a persistence that astonishes me. Like the many-headed Hydra of mythology, you lop off one head only to have two more take its place. Although

1. See Irving J. Lee, *How to Talk With People* (New York: Harper & Brothers, 1952).

the misconception still exists to this day, it does not seem to me to flourish with the same persistence and acceptance it once had. It no longer is the only guiding hypothesis for administrative action, and in this I see the possibility for change.

To explore this misconception thoroughly would require a book; so I hope you will forgive me if in my attempt to be brief my version may sound like a caricature and travesty of it. When I first started doing research in business, some twenty-five years ago, the popular but not too illuminating slogan was "Business is business." Under this slogan, management was busily engaged in trying to make its assumptive world come true—although, be it said, with some difficulty. Should a worker be found singing on his job, the current attitude was, "Hey, you, we're running a business around here, not a glee club." It took an intrepid investigator indeed who could find in business anything but business—i.e., anything short of logical, purposive behavior. By definition all monkey business was ruled out. A strike wasn't business. Singing on the job wasn't business. Restriction of output wasn't business. Feelings of insecurity weren't business. All noneconomic motives were not business, and, as you will remember, coffee-drinking and management wives had not as yet become legitimately business. In those days there were only people with very simple needs and wants indeed. Stockholders merely wanted good profits, employees merely wanted good wages, customers merely wanted good goods at a low price. The function of management was merely to see that all these simple wants of people were satisfied. As all this could best be accomplished by keeping costs low, this then was the major function of management— to minimize costs so as to maximize markets and profits so as to pay good wages.

It is this evaluation of the executive's job that I want to explore. Is it useful? Does it help the executive to do a better job? Does it represent correctly the territory the executive administers? That it contains some of the important economic factors in a business organization in our present economic system goes without question. But is it equally a good blueprint for securing the cooperation of people? And if not, does it contain the seed for self-correction? And if not, why not?

To answer these questions we will have to look at how this evaluation works out in day-to-day operations. We will have to look at the assumptions it makes, the perceptions and feelings it engenders, and as a result the behavior it dictates. In turn, we will have to see the effect of this behavior upon others as well as the effect of this effect again upon the perceptions, feelings, and assumptions of management. By this time I hope you will get the "ring-around-a-rosey" effect I want you to get.

In the first place, what does this evaluation assume? I shall consider only a few of the assumptions. You will note that the evaluation equates exclusively the functions of the executive with the economic purposes of the organization and therefore assumes that management alone is concerned with, interested in, and responsible for securing them. Moreover, it assumes that if management is only allowed to do its job, the needs and interests of all the other contributors to the purpose of the organization not only will be, but should be, automatically satisfied. Under such assumptions it follows that the function of management is to secure the best policies, the best methods, the best systems, as well as, of course, the best people to carry them out, so that the purposes of the organization in turn will be best secured. That under these assumptions the intentions of management are also of the best is guaranteed by the economist. Everybody will be or (should I say) should be happy—profits and wages will be high and prices will be low. Under these assumptions, management, like poppa, knows best not only what is best but should be best for everyone.

The perceptions and feelings which are likely to be aroused by these assumptions (or should I say arrogance?) should not be too difficult to imagine. For, working under the best policies, the best methods, the best system, as well as the best intentions, people should be happy, but as a matter of fact, they aren't. Supervisors have a hard time carrying them out; workers have a hard time understanding and accepting them, too. But management cannot see this, for under their assumptions this is not possible. When the facts of discontent become so blatant that they can no longer be overlooked, how must they be perceived? If the assumptions cannot be questioned, these facts can only be seen in one light. Workers can only be perceived as being economically illiterate and therefore not knowing their own best self-interest. Supervisors in turn can only be perceived as not knowing enough to educate them. The behavior that must follow such perceptions is obvious. Workers and supervisors must be educated, i.e., taught the ABC's of economics and shown wherein their own best interest lies.

Let's look a minute at the effect of such behavior upon the feelings and perceptions of workers and supervisors: When someone is told not only that he should not feel the way he does feel, but also why he should not feel the way he does—no matter h: w good the reasons may be—he is likely to feel misunderstood. It is denying what for him must be the reality, namely his own feelings. Such communications from management therefore are likely to produce more heat than light. People who feel angry and misunderstood are not likely to be cool, dispassionate, reasonable, and logical. When workers and supervisors feel this way they are not likely to see the good intentions of management. They are more likely to see management—shall we say—as "bastards." The behavior that must follow such a perception is also clear. Workers and supervisors must become more articulate about what conditions must obtain if their lives are to be more tolerable, even if in the process they may "cut off their noses to spite their faces."

The effect of this behavior upon the perceptions and feelings of management in turn is also interesting. Workers who do not accept as "good" the "good" intentions of management must become in the eyes of management "ungrateful." Moreover, workers who are seen as tampering or interfering with the objectives of management (which, by definition are "good") must become (by definition) "bad." They must be seen as flouting management's "authority" and interfering with management's "prerogatives." Under such feelings workers not only become "bad," but "vicious." However, when management perceives its workers as "ungrateful," "bad," and "vicious," they can only behave in ways which accentuate the very behavior they dislike. In this way the vicious cycle as well as the vicious behavior becomes complete. What management does not see is that it has produced this behavior just as in my previous example the foreman made the worker "rude." It sees these properties either as being in the worker or as resulting from some outside bad influence.

This self-perpetuating misevaluation I have tried to describe here only too briefly reached its peak, it seems to me, somewhere around 1936. At that time at our assembly lines, conveyor belts, and work benches, as well as at our double-pedestal desks, we were turning out "s.o.b.'s" of high quality at about the same rate as we were turning out goods of high quality at low cost. The "system of best policies, best methods, and best intentions" seemed to be producing one just as well as the other. Management and workers perceived the "s.o.b.'s" all right, but each did not perceive the other as his handiwork. Managers had their eyes so fixed on their good intentions that they could not see the effect of their behavior upon workers. Workers had their attention so fixed upon their feelings of injured personal integrity that they could not see the effect of their behavior upon management.

A MORE PROPER EVALUATION OF THE
EXECUTIVES FUNCTION

I should like to think that somewhere around 1936 something began to come to an end. An old but no longer useful way of thinking began to die and in its wake a new, much more exciting, much more adventurous and much more fruitful way of thinking was born. Amidst all the clatter of recriminations some still small voice must have asked, "What the hell is going on here?" In that awful moment of silence a new orientation—a more scientific one, I may say—was born. This orientation did not spring from the need to justify or defend, to praise or to blame. Rather, it sprang from a desire to learn and to find out what is taking place when people are working together. With this new willingness to learn, a new role for the administrator emerged. What is this new and more professional role of the administrator which is beginning to emerge and to be revealed by research? It is on this more constructive question and I hope more optimistic note I should like to conclude.

As I have said before, executives will behave in accordance with the way they perceive the situations they meet. Any fundamental change in behavior, therefore, must involve a fundamental change in perception. If this change in the role of the executive is as fundamental as I think it is and not merely the product of my wishful thinking, it should involve a new way of perceiving things. For the executive it must follow from a new way of perceiving the organization he administers and his relationship to it. Let me try to indicate briefly these new perceptions.

How does our new administrator perceive the organization he serves? No longer does he think of it as merely the product of certain impersonal economic forces. More and more he is coming to regard it as "a system of consciously coordinated activities of two or more persons."[2] This system contains, first and foremost, persons. These persons have relationships with one another. Some of these relationships are formal and more directly related to the securing of purpose; some of

2. Chester I. Barnard, *The Functions of the Executive* (Cambridge: Harvard University Press, 1938), p. 72.

them are informal and more directly related to the satisfaction of needs. Nevertheless, through this intricate web of interpersonal relationships, people contribute their services and satisfy their needs, and by contributing their services secure the purposes of the organization they serve. Under this conception please note that the personal needs of each contributor to the organization—worker, superior, and executive—are differentiated from the purposes of the total enterprise. The purposes of the organization, under this conception, are a property of the total system and not the exclusive concern or property of any one group. Each person and subgroup makes his own unique contributions to them.

Under this conception the executive must perceive his function differently. To keep his organization alive and productive, he not only must satisfy economic needs but also must satisfy those very basic human needs which make people willing to contribute their services. Unless he achieves the economic purpose his organization dies; but equally so unless he secures willing and cooperative contributors his organization also dies. One is as important as the other. As we may not immediately see the tremendous alterations in the executive's perception of his function that this new way of thinking brings about, let me spell some of them out in terms of vivid contrasts.

Under this new conception the executive becomes no longer the *prime mover,* the *prime doer,* and the *prime actor.* No longer can he be chiefly concerned with formulating policies, setting standards, and making decisions that others should implement and carry out. He begins to perceive that more important than this is to formulate policies, set standards, and make decisions in such a manner that other people *can and are willing to implement them and carry them out.*

Under this conception the executive becomes less interested in what's right and more interested in what works. This may sound strange, but what I mean is that he becomes less interested in his "good intentions" and more concerned with the effects of his behavior upon others. He becomes less concerned with his "authority" and prerogatives. No longer does he assume he knows what is right and best for everyone. His previous assumptions of arrogance become liquidated. As a result he begins to perceive values different from his own. He learns to accept them and to live with them. No longer does he feel obliged to make coal miners think like coal operators nor does he assume that cooperation can only be secured if this millennium is reached. He begins to enjoy differences in the values of individuals as well as in the values of groups, and he perceives that it is through this kind of human stuff he must learn to secure understanding and cooperation. And to do this he perceives that his major function is not to be the chief *evaluator* of performance, to which others must conform. He must also be an *acceptor* of people as they are and not as they ideally should be.

If the executive is not the prime mover, the prime doer, the prime actor, the prime evaluator, the prime watchdog and the prime exponent of what's right and best (and if the notion of all these "primes" makes him to his work force, as we have seen, only one prime s.o.b.), what is he? Is his new function to be the prime dispenser of happiness and security? This I'm sure is what some of you think I am leading up to; so let me shatter this belief quickly. This conception would be just one more assumption of arrogance and does not follow from the new way of thinking I propose. Our new executive perceives that he cannot dispense security and happiness any more than he can dispense pills, nostrums, or any other forms of Utopia. He can only help people to become productive and not merely producers.

Under this new conception, as I see it, the executive becomes the chief *maintainer, balancer,* and *facilitator* of a set of conditions which allow a number of desirable processes to emerge. He becomes interested in setting those conditions which help people to belong and to grow, as well as to contribute and to cooperate. To set these conditions and to keep them in balance is not easy; this is no swivel chair job; it requires "blood, sweat and tears." It requires that the executive become an interactor more than an actor, a receiver as well as a giver of communications, an acceptor more than a judge of people. Above all, it requires a faith in people—a faith that under certain conditions people have the capacity and desire for independence, growth, and for becoming essentially mature.

If in the brave new world of the future we want free, independent and mature people as well as a standard of living twice as high, should we not operate under these new assumptions, perceptions, and feelings about people? What is our alternative? The alternative, as we have seen, produces s.o.b.'s as well as a high standard of living. In the years to come let us try to achieve not only a higher standard of living but also a higher standard of development for people. This as I see it is the new role for the administrator.

11   Barriers to Communication between Men

This paper was presented on October 11, 1951, in a panel discussion at Northwestern University's Centennial Conference on Communications, and appeared in the periodical *Northwestern University Information*, April 21, 1952. It was reprinted by the *Harvard Business Review*, July–August 1952, and that is the text I am reproducing here. (The *Review* printed the paper with one by Carl R. Rogers under the single title "Barriers and Gateways to Communication.") Both the Northwestern Publication Office and the *Harvard Business Review* have granted permission to include my essay in this book.

Although I was a strong advocate of listening, the reader by now may get the impression that in relation to management I was not practicing what I preached; namely, I was telling 'em instead of listening to them. But really it was Aristotle and his logic (according to Alfred Korzybski) and Gutenberg and his printing press (according to Marshall McLuhan) and a long-standing tradition (according to academia) that got me into this "hot" fixation. When not making speeches I really was a "cool baby"; that is, I listened, if you know what I mean by that by now.

When I think about the many barriers to personal communication, particularly those that are due to differences of background, experience, and motivation, it seems to me extraordinary that any two persons can ever understand each other. Such reflections provoke the question of how communication is possible when people do not see and assume the same things and share the same values.[1]

On this question there are two schools of thought. One school assumes that communication between A and B, for example, has failed when B does not accept what A has to say as being fact, true, or valid, and that the goal of communication is to get B to agree with A's opinions, ideas, facts, or information.

The position of the other school of thought is quite different. It assumes that communication has failed when B does not feel free to express his feelings to A because B fears they will not be accepted by A. Communication is facilitated when on the part of A or B or both there is a willingness to express and accept differences.

As these are quite divergent conceptions, let us explore them further with an example. Bill, an employee, is talking with his boss in the boss's office. The boss says, "I think, Bill, that this is the best way to do your job." Bill says, "Oh yeah?"

1. For the concepts I use to present my material I am greatly indebted to some very interesting conversations I had with my friend, Irving Lee.

According to the first school of thought, this reply would be a sign of poor communication. Bill does not understand the best way of doing his work. To improve communication, therefore, it is up to the boss to explain to Bill why his way is the best.

From the point of view of the second school of thought, Bill's reply is a sign neither of good nor of bad communication. Bill's response is indeterminate. But the boss has an opportunity to find out what Bill means if he so desires. Let us assume that this is what he chooses to do, i.e., find out what Bill means. So this boss tries to get Bill to talk more about his job while he (the boss) listens.

For purposes of simplification, I shall call the boss representing the first school of thought *"Smith"* and the boss representing the second school of thought *"Jones."* In the presence of the so-called same stimulus each behaves differently. Smith chooses to *explain;* Jones chooses to *listen.* In my experience Jones's response works better than Smith's. It works better because Jones is making a more proper evaluation of what is taking place between him and Bill than Smith is. Let us test this hypothesis by continuing with our example.

WHAT SMITH ASSUMES, SEES, AND FEELS

Smith assumes that he understands what Bill means when Bill says, "Oh yeah?"—so there is no need to find out. Smith is sure that Bill does not understand why this is the best way to do his job; so Smith has to tell him. In this process let us assume Smith is logical, lucid, and clear. He presents his facts and evidence well. But, alas, Bill remains unconvinced. What does Smith do? Operating under the assumption that what is taking place between him and Bill is something essentially logical, Smith can draw only one of two conclusions: either (1) he has not been clear enough, or (2) Bill is too damned stupid to understand. So he either has to "spell out" his case in words of fewer and fewer syllables or give up. Smith is reluctant to do the latter; so he continues to explain. What happens?

If Bill still does not accept Smith's explanation of why this is the best way for him to do his job, a pattern of interacting feelings is produced of which Smith is often unaware. The more Smith cannot get Bill to understand him, the more frustrated Smith becomes and the more Bill becomes a threat to his logical capacity. Since Smith sees himself as a fairly reasonable and logical chap, this is a difficult feeling to accept. It is much easier for him to perceive Bill as uncooperative or stupid. This perception, however, will affect what Smith says and does. Under these pressures Bill comes to be evaluated more and more in terms of Smith's values. By this process Smith tends to treat Bill's values as unimportant. He tends to deny Bill's uniqueness and difference. He treats Bill as if he had little capacity for self-direction.

Let us be clear. Smith does not see that he is doing these things. When he is feverishly scratching hieroglyphics on the back of an envelope, trying to explain to Bill why this is the best way to do his job, Smith is trying to be helpful. He is a man of goodwill, and he wants to set Bill straight. This is the way Smith sees himself and his behavior. But it is for this very reason that Bill's "Oh yeah" is getting under Smith's skin.

"How dumb can a guy be?" is Smith's attitude, and unfortunately Bill will hear that more than Smith's good intentions. Bill will feel misunderstood. He will not see Smith as a man of goodwill trying to be helpful. Rather he will perceive him as a threat to his self-esteem and personal integrity. Against this threat Bill will feel the need to defend himself at all cost. Not being so logically articulate as Smith, Bill expresses this need, again, by saying, "Oh yeah!"

WHAT JONES ASSUMES, SEES, AND FEELS

Let us leave this sad scene between Smith and Bill, which I fear is going to terminate by Bill's either leaving in a huff or being kicked out of Smith's office. Let us turn for a moment to Jones and see what he is assuming, seeing, hearing, feeling, doing, and saying when he interacts with Bill.

Jones, it will be remembered, does not assume that he knows what Bill means when he says "Oh yeah"; so he has to find out. Moreover, he assumes that when Bill said this, he had not exhausted his vocabulary or his feelings. Bill may not necessarily mean one thing; he may mean several different things. So Jones decides to listen.

In this process Jones is not under any illusion that what will take place will be eventually logical. Rather he is assuming that what will take place will be primarily in interaction of feelings. Therefore, he cannot ignore the feelings of Bill, the effect of Bill's feelings on him, or the effect of his feelings on Bill. In other words, he cannot ignore his relationship to Bill; he cannot assume that it will make no difference to what Bill will hear or accept. Therefore, Jones will be paying strict attention to all of the things Smith has ignored. He will be addressing himself to Bill's feelings, his own, and the interactions between them.

Jones will therefore realize that he has ruffed Bill's feelings with his comment, "I think, Bill, this is the best way to do your job." So instead of trying to get Bill to understand him, he decides to try to understand Bill. He does this by encouraging Bill to speak. Instead of telling Bill how he should feel or think, he asks Bill such questions as, "Is this what you feel?" "Is this what you see?" "Is this what you assume?" Instead of ignoring Bill's evaluations as irrelevant, not valid, inconsequential, or false, he tries to understand Bill's reality as he feels it, perceives it, and assumes it to be. As Bill begins to open up, Jones's curiosity is piqued by this process.

"Bill isn't so dumb; he's quite an interesting guy" becomes Jones's attitude. And that is what Bill hears. Therefore Bill feels understood and accepted as a person. He becomes less defensive. He is in a better frame of mind to explore and re-examine his own perceptions, feelings, and assumptions. In this process he perceives Jones as a source of help. Bill feels free to express his differences. He feels that Jones has some respect for his capacity for self-direction. These positive feelings toward Jones make Bill more inclined to say, "Well, Jones, I don't quite agree with you that this is the best way to do my job, but I'll tell you what I'll do. I'll try to do it that way for a few days, and then I'll tell you what I think."

CONCLUSION

I grant that my two orientations do not work themselves out in practice in quite so simple or neat a fashion as I have been able to work them out on paper. There are many other ways in which Bill could have responded to Smith in the first place. He might even have said, "O.K., boss, I agree that your way of doing my job is better." But Smith still would not have known how Bill felt when he made this statement or whether Bill was actually going to do his job differently. Likewise, Bill could have responded to Jones in a way different from my example. In spite of Jones's attitude, Bill might still be reluctant to express himself freely to his boss.

The purpose of my examples has not been to demonstrate the right or wrong way of communicating. My purpose has been simply to provide something concrete to point to when I make the following generalizations:

(1) Smith represents to me a very common pattern of misunderstanding. The misunderstanding does not arise because Smith is not clear enough in expressing himself. It arises because of Smith's misevaluation of what is taking place when two people are talking together.

(2) Smith's misevaluation of the process of personal communication consists of certain very common assumptions, e.g., (a) that what is taking place is something essentially logical; (b) that words in themselves apart from the people involved mean something; and (c) that the purpose of the interaction is to get Bill to see things from Smith's point of view.

(3) Because of these assumptions, a chain reaction of perceptions and negative feelings is engendered which blocks communication. By ignoring Bill's feelings and by rationalizing his own, Smith ignores his relationship to Bill as one of the most important determinants of the communication. As a result, Bill hears Smith's attitude more clearly than the logical content of Smith's words. Bill feels that his individual uniqueness is being denied. His personal integrity being at stake, he becomes defensive and belligerent. As a result, Smith feels frustrated. He perceives Bill as stupid. So he says and does things which only provoke more defensiveness on the part of Bill.

(4) In the case of Jones, I have tried to show what might possibly happen if we made a different evaluation of what is taking place when two people are talking together. Jones makes a different set of assumptions. He assumes (a) that what is taking place between him and Bill is an interaction of sentiments; (b) that Bill—not his words in themselves—means something; (c) that the object of the interaction is to give Bill an opportunity to express freely his differences.

(5) Because of these assumptions, a psychological chain reaction of reinforcing feelings and perceptions is set up which facilitates communication between Bill and him. When Jones addresses himself to Bill's feelings and perceptions from Bill's point of view, Bill feels understood and accepted as a person; he feels free to express his differences. Bill sees Jones as a source of help; Jones sees Bill as an interesting person. Bill in turn becomes more cooperative.

(6) If I have identified correctly these very common patterns of personal communication, then some interesting hypotheses can be stated:

(a) Jones's method works better than Smith's, not because of any magic, but because Jones has a better map than Smith of the process of personal communication.

(b) The practice of Jones's method, however, is not merely an intellectual exercise. It depends on Jones's capacity and willingness to see and accept points of view different from his own, and to practice this orientation in a face-to-face relationship. This practice involves an emotional as well as an intellectual achievement. It depends in part on Jones's awareness of himself, in part on the practice of a skill.

(c) Although our colleges and universities try to get students to appreciate intellectually points of view different from their own, very little is done to help them to implement this general intellectual appreciation in a simple face-to-face relationship—at the level of a skill. Most educational institutions train their students to be logical, lucid, and clear. Very little is done to help them to listen more skillfully. As a result, our educated world contains too many Smiths and too few Joneses.

(d) The biggest block to personal communication is man's inability to listen intelligently, understandingly, and skillfully to another person. This deficiency in the modern world is widespread and appalling. In our universities as well as elsewhere, too little is being done about it.

(7) In conclusion, let me apologize for acting toward you the way Smith acted. But who am I to violate a long-standing academic tradition!

12 The Administrator's Skill: Communication

This paper was given as the Alfred Korzybski Memorial Lecture in New York, April 24, 1953, under the auspices of the Institute of General Semantics, and published in their *General Semantics Bulletin*, Winter–Spring 1954, under the title "Human Relations in Industry: A Problem of Communication." It also appeared in the *Harvard Business Review*, November–December 1953, as "The Administrator's Skill: Communication," and that is the text being used below. Permission has been granted by both journals.

In this piece I am still concerned with the fateful encounter between A and B in the superior–subordinate setting, but this time I explore the different ways of conceptualizing what is going on in such an encounter and what differences to A or B or both it might make if A thought of it one way instead of the other.

For some time I have been deeply interested in the process of interpersonal communication within the administrative setting. What is taking place when two people engaged in a common task interact? What do the actors involved perceive is taking place? What is a useful way for the executive to think about these interpersonal proceedings in which he is engaged, and what skills can he practice which will make him more effective as an administrator of people?

In this article I want to discuss these questions in terms of a specific, down-to-earth case in an industrial plant[1]—a case of misunderstanding between two people, a worker and a foreman. (It is not important that they happen to be foreman and worker; to all intents and purposes they might as well be superintendent and foreman or, for that matter, controller and accountant.) A brief review of the case should be useful in providing us with a point of departure as well as a point of return for our questions. And it should make it possible for us to discuss the practical application of some of the recent findings of general semantics and human relations.

A CASE OF MISUNDERSTANDING

In a department of a large industrial organization there were seven workers (four men and three women) engaged in testing and inspecting panels of electronic equipment. In this department one of the workers,

1. This case (names and places disguised) is adapted from a case in the files of the Harvard Graduate School of Business Administration.

Bing, was having trouble with his immediate supervisor, Hart, who had formerly been a worker in the department.

Had we been observers in this department we would have seen Bing carrying two or three panels at a time from the racks where they were stored to the bench where he inspected them together. For this activity we would have seen him charging double or triple setup time. We would have heard him occasionally singing at work. Also we would have seen him usually leaving his work position a few minutes early to go to lunch, and noticed that other employees sometimes accompanied him. And had we been present at one specific occasion, we would have heard Hart telling Bing that he disapproved of these activities and that he wanted Bing to stop doing them.

However, not being present to hear the actual verbal exchange that took place in this interaction, let us note what Bing and Hart each said to a personnel representative.

What Bing Said

In talking about his practice of charging double or triple setup time for panels which he inspected all at one time, Bing said:

"This is a perfectly legal thing to do. We've always been doing it. Mr. Hart, the supervisor, has other ideas about it, though; he claims it's cheating the company. He came over to the bench a day or two ago and let me know just how he felt about the matter. Boy, did we go at it! It wasn't so much the fact that he called me down on it, but more the way in which he did it. He's a sarcastic bastard. I've never seen anyone like him. He's not content just to say in a manlike way what's on his mind, but he prefers to do it in a way that makes you want to crawl inside a crack on the floor. What a guy! I don't mind being called down by a supervisor, but I like to be treated like a man, and not humiliated like a school teacher does a naughty kid. He's been pulling this stuff ever since he's been a supervisor. I knew him when he was just one of us, but since he's been promoted, he's lost his friendly way and seems to be having some difficulty in knowing how to manage us employees. He's a changed man over what he used to be like when he was a worker on the bench with us several years ago.

"When he pulled this kind of stuff on me the other day, I got so damn mad I called in the union representative. I knew that the thing I was doing was permitted by the contract, but I was intent on making some trouble for Mr. Hart, just because he persists in this sarcastic way of handling me. I am about fed up with the whole damn situation.

I'm trying every means I can to get myself transferred out of his group. If I don't succeed and I'm forced to stay on here, I'm going to screw him in every way I can. He's not going to pull this kind of kid stuff any longer on me. When the union representative questioned him on the case, he finally had to back down, because according to the contract an employee can use any time-saving method or device in order to speed up the process as long as the quality standards of the job are met.

"You see, he knows that I do professional singing on the outside. He hears me singing here on the job, and he hears people talking about my career in music. I guess he figures I can be so cocky because I have another means of earning some money. Actually, the employees here enjoy having me sing while we work, but he thinks I'm disturbing them and causing them to 'goof-off' from their work. Occasionally, I leave the job a few minutes early and go down to the washroom to wash up before lunch. Sometimes several others in the group will accompany me, and so Mr. Hart automatically thinks I'm the leader and usually bawls me out for the whole thing.

"So, you can see, I'm a marked man around here. He keeps watching me like a hawk. Naturally, this makes me very uncomfortable. That's why I'm sure a transfer would be the best thing. I've asked him for it, but he didn't give me any satisfaction at the time. While I remain here, I'm going to keep my nose clean, but whenever I get the chance, I'm going to slip it to him, but good."

What Hart Said

Here, on the other hand, is what Hart told the personnel representative:

"Say, I think you should be in on this. My dear little friend Bing is heading himself into a showdown with me. Recently it was brought to my attention that Bing has been taking double and triple setup time for panels which he is actually inspecting at one time. In effect, that's cheating, and I've called him down on it several times before. A few days ago it was brought to my attention again, and so this time I really let him have it in no uncertain terms. He's been getting away with this for too long and I'm going to put an end to it once and for all. I know he didn't like my calling him on it because a few hours later he had the union representative breathing down my back. Well, anyway, I let them both know I'll not tolerate the practice any longer, and I let Bing know that if he continues to do this kind of thing, I'm going to take official action with my boss to have the guy fired or penalized somehow. This kind of thing has to be curbed. Actually, I'm inclined to think the guy's mentally deficient, because talking to him has actually no meaning to him whatsoever. I've tried just about every approach to jar some sense into that guy's head, and I've just about given it up as a bad deal.

"I don't know what it is about the guy, but I think he's harboring some deep feelings against me. For what, I don't know, because I've tried to handle that bird with kid gloves. But his whole attitude around here on the job is one of indifference, and he certainly isn't a good influence on the rest of my group. Frankly, I think he purposely tries to agitate them against me at times, too. It seems to me he may be suffering from illusions of grandeur, because all he does all day long is sit over there and croon his fool head off. Thinks he's a Frank Sinatra! No kidding! I understand he takes singing lessons and he's working with some of the local bands in the city. All of which is O.K. by me; but when his outside interests start interfering with his efficiency on the job, then I've got to start paying closer attention to the situation. For this reason I've been keeping my eye on that bird and if he steps out of line any more, he and I are going to part ways.

"You know there's an old saying, 'You can't make a purse out of a sow's ear.' The guy is simply unscrupulous. He feels no obligation to do a real day's work. Yet I know the guy can do a good job, because for a long time he did. But in recent months he's slipped, for some reason, and his whole attitude on the job has changed. Why, it's even getting to the point now where I think he's inducing other employees to 'goof off' a few minutes before the lunch whistle and go down to the washroom and clean up on company time. I've called him on it several times, but words just don't seem to make any lasting impression on him. Well, if he keeps it up much longer, he's going to find himself on the way out. He's asked me for a transfer, so I know he wants to go. But I didn't give him an answer when he asked me, because I was steaming mad at the time, and I may have told him to go somewhere else."

VIEWS OF MISUNDERSTANDING

So much for the case. Let me start with the simplest but the toughest question first: "What is going on here?" I think most of us would agree that what seems to be going on is some misunderstanding between Hart and Bing. But no sooner do we try to represent to ourselves the nature of this misunderstanding than a flood of different theories appear. Let me discuss briefly five very common ways of representing this misunderstanding: (1) as a difference of opinion resolvable by common sense, by simply referring to the facts; (2) as a clash of personalities; (3) as a conflict of social roles; (4) as a struggle for power; and (5) as a breakdown in communication. There are, of course, other theories too —for example, those of the interactionists, the field theory of Kurt Lewin, and even the widely held views of Adam Smith or Karl Marx. But for our purposes here the five I have mentioned will suffice.

Common Sense

For the advocates of common sense—the first theory, though most of them would not call it that—the situation resolves itself quickly:

Either Hart is right or Bing is right. Since both parties cannot be right, it follows that if Hart is right, then Bing is wrong; or if Bing is right, then Hart is wrong. Either Bing should or should not be singing on the job, carrying two or three panels at a time and charging double or triple setup time, and so on.

"Let us get these facts settled first," say the common-sense advocates. "Once they are ascertained, the problem is easily settled. Once we know who is doing what he should not be doing, then all we have to do is to get this person to do what he should be doing. It's as simple as that."

But is it? Let us look again at our case. Let us note that there are no differences of opinion between Hart and Bing about some matters. For example, both would agree that Bing is taking double or triple setup time when he carries his panels two or three at a time to his bench for inspection. Both would agree that Bing sings on the job and occasionally leaves his work place a bit early for lunch.

Where they differ is in the way each *perceives* these activities. Hart perceives Bing's activities as "cheating," "suffering from illusions of grandeur," "thinking he is Frank Sinatra," "interfering with Bing's efficiency as well as the efficiency of other workers," "disturbing the other workers," "inducing them to goof off," and "influencing them against [Hart]." To Bing, on the other hand, these activities are "perfectly legal," "something we've always been doing," "something that is not disturbing the other workers," and so forth.

Among these many different conflicting claims and different perceptions, what are the facts? Many of these evaluations refer to personal and social standards of conduct for which the company has no explicit rules. Even in the case of taking double and triple setup time, there are probably no clear rules, because when the industrial engineer set the standards for the job, he did not envisage the possibility of a worker's doing that which Bing is now doing and which, according to Bing, is a time-saving device.

But we can waste effort on this question. For, even if it were clear that Hart is not exploring the situation, that he is not getting these important facts or rules which would settle who is right and who is wrong, it would still be true that, so far as Hart is concerned, he *knows* who is right and who is wrong. And because he *knows*, he has no reason to question the assumptions he is making about Bing's behavior.

Now this is very likely to happen in the case of advocates of the common-sense theory. Significantly, Hart himself is a good advocate of it. Does this have anything to do with the fact that he is not being very successful in getting Bing to do what he should be doing? Let us postpone this question for future consideration.

Clash of Personalities

For the second school of thought, what is going on between Hart and Bing can be viewed essentially as a clash of personalities—an inter-action between two particular personality structures. According to this view, what is going on cannot be known in detail until much more information about these different personality structures is secured. Hence we can only speculate that what is going on may be something of this order:

Neither Hart nor Bing feels sure of himself, and each seems to be suffering from feelings of inadequacy or inferiority. Being unable to recognize, admit, or accept these feelings, however, each one perceives the behavior of the other as a personal attack upon himself. When a person feels he is being attacked, he feels strongly the need to defend himself. This, then, is essentially what is taking place between Hart and Bing. Because of his feelings of inferiority, each one is defending himself against what he perceives to be an attack upon himself as a person. In psychology, the feelings of each man are conceived as being rooted somehow in his "personality."

That this theory is pointing to some very important phenomena can hardly be questioned. Certainly I will not argue its validity. I am only concerned with what it is telling us and what follows from it. As I understand it, this theory says that neither Hart nor Bing is aware of his own feelings of inadequacy and defense mechanism. These are the important facts that each is ignoring. From this it follows that there is little hope of correcting the misunderstanding without helping Bing and Hart to become aware of these feelings and of their need to defend against them. Short of this, the solution lies in transferring Bing to a supervisor whose personality will be more compatible with Bing's, and in giving Hart a worker whose personality will be more compatible with Hart's.

Conflict of Social Roles

Let us look at the third explanation. Instead of viewing the misunderstanding as an interaction between two individual personality units, it can also be viewed as an interaction between two social roles:

With the promotion of Hart to the position of a supervisor of a group in which he had been formerly a worker, a system of reciprocal expectancies has been disturbed. Bing is expecting Hart to behave toward him in the same way Hart did when Hart was a worker; but by telling Bing to stop "crooning his fool head off," for example, Hart is not behaving in accordance with the role of a friend. Similarly, Hart, as the newly appointed supervisor, is expecting that Bing should do what he tells Bing to do, but by singing Bing is not behaving in accordance with the customary role of the worker.

According to this theory, as any recent textbook on sociology will explain, when two actors in a relationship reach differing definitions of the situation, misunderstanding is likely to arise. Presumably this is what is happening between Hart and Bing. The role-expectation pattern has been disturbed. Bing views his singing as variant but permissive; Hart views it as deviant. From these differing definitions of what each other's role should be, misunderstanding results. According to this view, it will take time for their new relationship to work out. In time Bing will learn what to expect from Hart now that Hart is his supervisor. Also in time Hart will define better his role vis-à-vis Bing.

Struggle for Power

The fourth way of representing what is going on between Hart and Bing would be in terms of such abstractions as "authority" and "power":

When Bing refuses to stop singing on the job when Hart tells him to, Bing is being disobedient to the commands or orders of a holder of power. When this occurs, Hart, who according to this theory is a "power holder," has the right to exercise or apply sanctions, such as dismissal or transfer. But the threat to exercise these sanctions does not seem to be too effective in getting Bing to stop, because Bing is a member of the union, which also has power and the right to apply sanctions. By going to his union representative, Bing can bring this power structure into play.

In other words, what is going on in the case is not merely an interaction between two individual or social personalities; it is also a struggle between two kinds of institutionalized power. It is an issue between the management and the union which may even precipitate a strike. Management will charge that it cannot have workers in the plant who are disobedient to the orders of their foremen. The union will charge that Bing is merely introducing a labor-saving device which the foreman has not enough sense to recognize. To avoid things getting to this stage, the struggle-for-power theory would recommend that if Hart and Bing between them cannot settle their differences, they should refer them to the grievance machinery set up for this purpose by union and management.

According to this theory, Hart got into trouble not because he had authority but because when he tried to exercise it and was unsuccessful, he lost it. Authority ceases to exist when it cannot be exercised successfully.[2]

Breakdown in Communication

The fifth way of stating what is going on would be to say that Hart and Bing think they are talking about the same things when in fact they are not:

Hart assumes he understands what Bing is doing and saying; Bing assumes he understands what Hart is doing and saying. In fact, neither assumption holds. From this "uncritical assumption of understanding," misunderstanding arises.

Thus, when Hart tells Bing to stop "crooning his fool head off," Bing assumes that Hart is talking about Bing's singing when Hart

2. For an elaboration of this view see Robert Bierstedt, "An Analysis of Social Power," *American Sociological Review* (December 1950).

may in fact be talking about his difficulties in maintaining his position as formal leader of the group. Hart assumes that Bing is singing deliberately to flaunt his authority, whereas in Bing's mind singing may be a way of relating himself to people and of maintaining his conceptions of himself.[3]

According to this theory, Hart and Bing are not on the same wave length, and as a result communication bypassing occurs. Each is behaving in accordance with the reality as he perceives it to be, but neither is aware of the assumptions that underlie his perceptions. Their misunderstandings arise as a result.

This theory strikes a new note that I should like to explore further.

ROOTS OF MISUNDERSTANDING

So far our theories have explained well why there is misunderstanding and conflict; they have not shown so clearly how any new behavior patterns on the part of Hart or Bing or both can emerge or be encouraged to emerge from the present ones. In them we have found no responsible actor, no learner, and no practitioner of a skill.

Could it be that what is going on between Hart and Bing results also in part from the fact that nobody is taking any responsibility for what is going on? May we not assume that people can learn through experience how to determine their relationships with each other as well as be determined by them? Let us therefore look at these interpersonal proceedings from the point of view of a person who is responsibly involved in them and who may be capable of learning something from them. I shall start with Hart and raise the questions: (1) "What is Hart doing to contribute to misunderstanding?" (2) "What, if anything, might he learn to do differently to minimize this effect?"

From now on I shall be chiefly concerned with Hart, not because I think Hart is any more or less guilty than Bing of creating misunderstanding, but because I wish to develop a useful way of thinking for persons in a position of responsibility like Hart. This way of thinking, I hope, will not be in conflict with our other theories. It will merely spell out what a supervisor must learn if he is to take into account the significant processes which these other theories say have been going on.

So, instead of viewing Hart in his dealings with Bing as a supervisor

3. For an analysis of this theory, see Wendell Johnson, "The Fateful Process of Mr. A Talking to Mr. B," *Harvard Business Review* (January–February 1953), 49.

expressing his personality, playing a social role, or exercising power, let us view him as a practitioner of a skill of communication. Let us see what skills, if any, he is using. And if we find, as I fear we may, that he has not been very skillful, let us see if he can learn to become a more skillful practitioner, and how this can be done.

Hart's Trouble

When we ask ourselves what Hart is doing to facilitate misunderstanding, we meet again a number of different theories. Although I am not sure that these theories are pointing to different things, each uses a slightly different terminology, so I shall state them separately:

1. *Hart is making value judgments.*—According to one view, the biggest block to personal communication arises from the fact that Hart is making value judgments of Bing from Hart's point of view. Hart's tendency to evaluate is what gets him into trouble. Not only is he evaluating Bing, but he is trying to get Bing to accept his evaluation as the only and proper one. It is this orientation that angers Bing and makes him feel misunderstood.[4]

2. *Hart is not listening.*—According to another and not very different view, Hart gets into trouble because he is not listening to Bing's feelings. Because he is not paying attention to Bing's feelings, he is not responding to them as such. Instead, we find him responding to the effect of Bing's feelings upon his own. Not only is he ignoring Bing's feelings, but also he is ignoring the effect of what he is saying upon them. This kind of behavior also leads to Bing's feelings of being misunderstood.[5]

3. *Hart is assuming things that may not be so.*—Still another point of view says that Hart is getting into trouble because he is making assumptions about Bing's behavior that may not be so. Hart is confusing what he sees with what he assumes and feels.

When Hart sees Bing leaving early for lunch, for example, he assumes that Bing is doing this deliberately, intentionally, and personally to discredit him and to test his authority. Because of this assumption he feels angry and his feelings of anger reinforce his assumption. Now if Bing's going to lunch a few minutes early is such an

---

4. See Carl R. Rogers and F. J. Roethlisberger, "Barriers and Gateways to Communication," *Harvard Business Review* (July–August 1952). [My part of this double article appears in the present volume as Chapter 11.]

5. Ibid., 50–52.

attempt to discredit him, then Hart's anger and his attempt to retaliate make sense. But if he starts with this assumption and makes no attempt to check it, then his anger makes less sense. Hart may be assuming something that is not so.

Again, Hart shows he may be making assumptions that are not so by the way he talks in trying to get Bing to stop singing at work or to stop inspecting panels two or three at a time. When he uses phrases like "crooning your fool head off" and "cheating the company," is he not assuming that Bing should feel about these activities in the same way that he himself does? And if Bing does not feel this way, then obviously, in Hart's view, Bing must be a "fool," "defective," or a "sow's ear." To Hart, Bing *is* a sow's ear. And how does one feel toward a sow's ear? Toward such an entity one must feel (by definition) helpless and hopeless. Note that Hart's assumptions, perceptions, and feelings are of a piece; each reinforces the other to make one total evaluation.

In short, all of Hart's evaluations are suspect because he confuses what he sees with what he assumes and feels. As a result, there is no way for Hart to take another look at the situation. How can Hart check his evaluations when he is not aware that he is making them? When he treats inferences as facts, there is no way for him to explore the assumptions, feelings, and perceptions that underlie his evaluations.[6] For Hart, Bing *is* the way he perceives Bing to be. There is no way for him to say that "because of the assumptions I make and because of the way I feel, I perceive Bing in this way."

4. *Hart is making his false assumptions come true.*—A fourth theory emphasizes still another point. This theory says that the very kind of misevaluations which our last theory says Hart is guilty of must provoke *ipso facto* the very kind of behavior on the part of Bing of which Hart disapproves.[7] In other words, Hart is getting into trouble because, by his behavior, he is making his assumptive world come true.

Let us examine this theory first by looking at the effect of Hart's behavior on Bing. Very clearly Bing does not like it. Bing tells us that when Hart behaves in the way Hart does, he feels misunderstood, humiliated, and treated like a child. These feelings give grounds to his

6. For a fuller explanation see Irving J. Lee, *How to Talk With People* (New York: Harper & Brothers, 1952).

7. For example, see Hadley Cantril, *The Why of Man's Experience* (New York: Macmillan, 1950).

perception of Hart as "a sarcastic bastard," "a school teacher" pulling "kid stuff" on him. These perceptions in turn will tend to make Bing behave in the way that will coincide more and more with Hart's original untested assumptions about Bing's behavior. Feeling like a "marked man," Bing will behave more and more like a "sow's ear." Although he will try to "keep his nose clean," he will "slip it to [Hart], but good" whenever he gets the chance.

That this kind of misevaluation on the part of Hart will tend to produce this kind of behavior on the part of Bing is, according to this view, a fact of common experience. To explain it one does not have to assume any peculiar personality structure on the part of Bing—an undue sensitivity to criticism, defensiveness, or feeling of inferiority. All one has to assume is an individual personality with a need to maintain its individuality. Therefore, any attempts on the part of Hart which will be perceived by Bing as an attempt to deny his individual differences will be resisted. What Hart says about Bing is, from Bing's point of view, exactly what he is *not*. Bing *is* what he is from his own frame of reference and from the point of view of his own feelings, background, and situation. Bing *is* what he assumes, feels, and perceives himself to be. And this is just what Hart's behavior is denying.

In spite of the different terminology and emphasis of these theories, they all seem to point to certain uniformities in the interpersonal proceedings of Hart and Bing which should be taken into account regardless of the actors' particular personalities or social roles. For the misunderstandings that arise, Hart and Bing are not to blame; the trouble resides in the process of interpersonal communication itself.

ADMINISTRATIVE SKILLS

Let us turn now to the second question: What might Hart learn to do differently in order to minimize the misunderstandings between him and Bing? I also want to consider briefly the question of what difference to Bing a slight difference in the behavior of Hart might make.

So far it would seem as if we had made Hart the villain in the piece. But let us remember that although Hart has been intellectually and emotionally involved in what has been going on, he has not been aware of this involvement. All of our theories have implied this. Hart's ego has been involved; his actual group memberships have been involved; his reference groups have been involved; his feelings, assumptions, and perceptions have been involved—but Hart is not aware of it. If any new behavior on the part of Hart is to emerge—and *all* our theories would agree to this—Hart must in some sense become aware of and recognize this involvement. Without such an awareness there can be no reevaluation and no change in perception. And without such a change no learning can take place.

How can this change be accomplished? Some theories would seem to imply that misunderstanding will be minimized only when Hart *logically understands* the nature of his involvement with Bing. Hart will learn to evaluate Bing more properly only when he understands better the personality structures of himself and Bing and the social system of which they are a part. Only by the logical understanding and critical probing of his and Bing's feelings of inadequacy and defense mechanisms can he make a proper evaluation and bring about any real change in his behavior.

But there is another view. It holds that logical understanding is not of the first importance. Rather, misunderstanding will be minimized when Hart learns to *recognize and accept* responsibility for his involvement. Better understanding will be achieved when Hart learns to recognize and accept his own and Bing's individual differences, when he learns to recognize and accept Bing's feelings as being different from his own, and when as a result he can allow Bing to express his feelings and differences and listen to them.[8]

Let me explore this second theory further, for it suggests that Hart might possibly learn to do a better job without having to become a professional social scientist or be psychoanalyzed. Moreover, it coincides with some facts of common experience.

Some administrators have achieved the insights of the second theory through the school of "hard knocks" rather than through the help of books or by being psychoanalyzed. So should there not be simple skills which Hart can be taught, which he can learn and practice, and which would help him to recognize and accept his involvement and to deal with it better?

Now it may be that Hart, because of certain personal deficiencies, is not able to recognize or accept his own feelings—let alone Bing's. That this holds for some supervisors goes without question. But does it apply to all? I do not think so, nor do I think it applies to Hart. Is it

8. For a fuller explanation see Carl R. Rogers, *Client-Centered Therapy* (Boston: Houghton Mifflin, 1953).

not possible that some supervisors may not be able to do these things because they have never learned how to do them? .

The fact is, if our analysis up to this point is sound, that Hart does not get into trouble because he feels hopeless and helpless in the face of a worker who sings on the job, leaves early for lunch, and so on, and who refuses to stop doing these things when Hart tells him to. Any one of us who has had to deal with a worker behaving like Bing will recognize and remember feelings of inadequacy like Hart's only too well. We do not need to have very peculiar or special personality structures to have such feelings. Rather, Hart's trouble is that he assumes, and no doubt has been told too often, that he should *not* have feelings of inadequacy. It resides in the fact that he has not developed or been given a method or skill for dealing with them. As a result, these feelings are denied and appear in the form of an attribute of Bing—"a sow's ear."

In other words, I am suggesting that Hart gets into trouble partly because no one has assured him that it is normal and natural—in fact, inevitable—that he should have some feelings of inadequacy, that he cannot and *should* not try to escape from them. No one has helped him to develop a method of dealing with his own feelings and the feelings of Bing. No one has listened to him or helped him to learn to listen to others. No one has helped him to recognize the effect of his behavior on others. No one has helped him to become aware of his assumptions and feelings and how they affect the evaluations he makes.

Instead, too many training courses have told Hart what an ideal supervisor should be and how an ideal supervisor should behave. Both explicit and implicit in most of the instruction he receives is the assumption that an ideal supervisor should not become emotionally involved in his dealings with people. He should remain aloof, be objective, and deny or get rid of his feelings. But this goes against the facts of his immediate experience; it goes against everything upon which, according to our theories, his growth and development depend. Indeed, to "behave responsibly" and be "mature" in the way he is instructed to, without becoming emotionally committed, would be, to use the *New Yorker's* phrase, "the trick of the week."

Is it any wonder, therefore, that Hart remains immature—socially, intellectually, and emotionally? He gets no understanding of how these frustrations and misunderstandings must inevitably arise from his dealings with others; he gets no help on how to deal with them when they do arise. He probably has had many training courses which told him how to recognize and deal with workers who are sow's ears. He probably has had no training course which helped him to see how his assumptions and feelings would tend to produce sow's ears by the bushel. He has not been helped to see how this surplus of sow's ears in modern industry might be diminished through the conscious practice of a skill. Thus he has not even been allowed to become intellectually involved and intrigued in the most important problem of his job. Yet there *are* training courses designed for just such a purpose, and they have worked successfully.[9]

CONCLUSION

Am I indulging in wishful thinking when I believe that there are some simple skills of communication that can be taught, learned, and practiced which might help to diminish misunderstanding? To me it is this possibility which the recent findings of general semantics and human relations are suggesting. They suggest that although man is determined by the complex relationships of which he is a part, nevertheless he is also in some small part a determiner of these relationships. Once he learns what he cannot do, he is ready to learn what little he can do. And what a tremendous difference to himself and to others the little that he can do—listening with understanding, for example—can make!

Once he can accept his limitations and the limitations of others, he can begin to learn to behave more skillfully with regard to the milieu in which he finds himself. He can begin to learn that misunderstanding can be diminished—not banished—by the slow, patient, laborious practice of a skill.

But we expect too much from this possibility, so let me conclude by sounding two notes of caution:

(1) Although these skills of communication of which I am speaking deal in part with words, they are not in themselves words, nor is the territory to which they apply made up of words. It follows, then, that no verbal statement about these skills, however accurate, can act as a

9. See Kenneth R. Andrews, "Executive Training by the Case Method," and F. J. Roethlisberger, "Training Supervisors in Human Relations," *Harvard Business Review* (September 1951). [This article by me is reprinted as Chapter 9 in the present volume.]

substitute for them. They are not truly articulate and never can be. Although transmissible to other persons, they are but slowly so and, even then, only with practice.

(2) Let us remember that these interpersonal proceedings between Hart and Bing, or A and B whoever they may be, are extremely complex. So far as I know, there exists no single body of concepts which as yet describes systematically and completely all the important processes that our separate theories have said are taking place and how they relate to each other. Let us therefore accept gracefully and not contentiously that these interpersonal proceedings, unlike the atom, have not been as yet "cracked" by social science. Only then can we as students of human behavior live up to our responsibility for making our knowledge fruitful in practice.

13 How to Develop Controllers

This is my contribution to the 23rd National Business Conference of the Harvard Business School Association, June 13, 1953. It was published that same year in a book entitled *How to Increase Executive Effectiveness* (the theme of the conference). Edward C. Bursk was the editor of the volume and Harvard University Press the publisher.

Thus far my talks had been addressed to persons in production, marketing, engineering, and personnel. As I did not wish to discriminate against any of the functions of business, I thought the time had now come to deliver my message to the controllers. If it has a slightly monotonic character, this is because at that time the conceptions of "control" held by controllers and executives were not very different. And I thought that a clearer differentiation needed to be made between the "control of costs" and the "control of behavior" if a more effective integration between the two was to result. About this need for differentiation between them, I have not changed my mind. But as to how they might become better integrated by the solutions I proposed, particularly the last one in this paper, I have now some doubts. I will comment about this in a postscript.

What I know about the technical activities of controllers is practically zero. About the consequences of their behavior for other people in the organization, however, I have heard a great deal. Therefore, I shall attempt to develop this point. I believe it has a close bearing on how to develop controllers.

According to theory, the purpose of the controller is to serve the people in line management by providing them with information that will allow them to do a better job. This being so, how does it so often happen that the people in the controller's office are regarded by the people in the line management (particularly those at lower levels) as a source of interference rather than as a source of help? This is the question I should like to consider.[1]

Let me start by looking briefly first at the way controllers view their activities and then at how factory supervisors view these same activities.

Quite properly controllers believe that they serve very important functions. They constitute "the eyes and ears of the plant." They provide those figures which set the goals of the organization. They also

---

1. In preparing this statement I have borrowed very freely from the findings presented in *The Impact of Budgets on People*, prepared for the Controllership Foundation, Inc., by Chris Argyris and published by the School of Business and Public Administration, Cornell University, 1952.

provide those figures which show whether or not the goals have been met. In terms of these variances between actual and standard, they keep line management informed about where it stands. As controllers see it, these figures furnish not only a goal but also a challenge to factory people. They are the vehicle for improvement and change, for increased productivity and efficiency. Inconsistencies, errors, and weaknesses can be quickly located; improvements can be quickly made. As a result, factory people are "kept on their toes" and are motivated to do a better job.

Most controllers are aware that their outlook on these matters is not shared by the operating people. But this difference they explain by saying that factory supervisors tend to look at things from the short-run rather than from the long-run point of view. Unlike them, operating people have not been trained to think logically and analytically and to see things objectively and as they are. Hence controllers perceive their problems with operating people as being due to lack of education, lack of information, or lack of understanding about what controllers are up to. Their solution, therefore, runs in the direction of educating and training factory supervisors with regard to the use and need of cost standards, how these standards are constructed, and so on.

Now let us look at the same activities from the point of view of shop supervisors. How do they talk and feel and think about these same activities? They find that these figures which controllers provide, far from presenting the "cold pictures" of why things are the way they are, show them instead why things are not the way they have been or should be. To them this is a "horse of a different color." Such pictures are fraught with emotion and feeling. They can arouse—and more often than not do arouse—fear, resentment, hostility, and aggression instead of encouragement, stimulation, and good cheer.

To the factory supervisor the living and important reality is today—not yesterday or tomorrow. The controller, emphasizing past and/or future performance, ignores the present. But he uses the past or the future to measure the present. And to most supervisors this is unrealistic. Is it any wonder, then, that the supervisor so often perceives the activities of the controller as "perpetual needling," "shots in the arm," or "hammers waiting to hit you on the head"? Moreover, that he needs such stimulation and would be lost without it is an insult to his integrity. Instead of spurring him on, such activities often tend to anger him.

Because shop supervisors see these standards which controllers provide as unrealistic, rigid, and failing to take into account the concrete realities of their situations, their solution to this problem of misunderstanding is also clear. In the language of the shop, the solution lies in giving these "sarcastic bastards" who have a too-exalted opinion of their importance a "taste of factory life." They should be taught that their figures are not final, and how to see the other person's point of view. They also should be "untaught" a few things—for example, (1) that everyone besides themselves is lazy and wants to do as little work as possible; (2) that the best way to raise production is through pressure; and (3) that they are superior to factory people.

Granted that I have oversimplified the picture a great deal, I have done this purposely to make vivid the two quite different frames of reference from which the activities of the controller can be viewed. What from one frame of reference is helpful and challenging becomes from another frame of reference interfering and enervating. Now the question I want to consider is: How can we think and talk about these differences of perception constructively?

To me the most futile of all questions to raise is: Which one of these perceptions is right or wrong? In my experience the quest for the answer to this question only leads to more and more misunderstanding. It leads to trying to get factory people to think like controllers or to get controllers to think like factory people. But this is a hopeless goal. Nothing that we know about the behavior of people in an organized human activity allows us to make the assumption that such a goal is either possible, desirable, or necessary for the achievement of purpose. Part of these differences of perception is written into the social organization of any factory. They are inevitable. They are just as brute and stubborn facts of life and living as any figures the controller can produce. To deny them is just as foolhardy as to deny the economic realities to which the controllers point.

For me, then, the solution does not lie in trying to deny or obliterate these differences. It lies in the way these differences are administered. They have to be administered so that they are not maximized to the point where they make for real trouble. When is this point reached? When factory supervisors really think that the activities of the controller are carried on deliberately and intentionally to discredit and humiliate them is one such point. When controllers really believe that factory supervisors are deliberately and intentionally trying to sabotage their efforts is another such point.

In both these instances the secondary complication of these differences becomes harmful to the efforts of the total organization. In such cases a new dimension is introduced which causes bitterness. This secondary complication, however, is not inevitable. It can be prevented by wise administration of those differences of outlook which must inevitably occur in any organization. Let us note that these harmful secondary effects occur because the reality of the differences in perception is being denied.

Perhaps I can make my meaning clear by looking at five possible solutions to this problem which have been tried, including two I have already considered:

1. An attempt to train supervisors to understand the need for and use of cost standards;

2. An attempt to train accounting people in the ways of the shop;

3. Group discussions with supervisors in which the latter are allowed to participate in the setting of the standard;

4. Group discussions with supervisors in which the latter are allowed to express freely their feelings, attitudes, and differences as the first step in gaining their emotional acceptance of the standard; and

5. An attempt to train controllers in human relations.

Let me state briefly some of the merits and demerits of these five approaches.

The first solution—training supervisors in the need for and use of standards—seems to me to miss the important point of the problem. It assumes that the primary difficulty is due to a failure in understanding logically the need and use of standards, when more often than not it is due to an unwillingness and incapacity to accept emotionally the standard. Under these conditions *telling* people how they should think and feel is the poorest way of obtaining their emotional acceptance.

The second solution—training accounting people in the ways of the factory—would be an expensive and lengthy job. Moreover, it assumes that experience *per se* without a pair of glasses through which to look at that experience will produce the desired results. Too often an accountant in the shop, because of his previous training, will be provided with ample ammunition to reinforce his own attitudes and preconceptions about shop people. As a result he often will not learn from this approach the lesson he is supposed to learn.

The third solution—allowing supervisors to participate in the setting of standards—is workable if done with sincerity, skill, and understanding. Before going into this approach, however, controllers should be sure that their definition of the situation as covered by the word "participation" agrees with that of the supervisors. "Participation" is a good idea and one which in general we are all for, but in my experience it is a concept difficult to implement in behavior. Too often rituals of participation are substituted for the genuine article; and, when this occurs, supervisors do not like it.

The fourth solution—bringing supervisors together in small face-to-face groups in which ample opportunity is given them to ventilate their old attitudes and feelings as a first step in the process of "unfreezing" them—is an approach which for me has a great deal of merit. It addresses itself directly to what I consider the central problem of getting people's acceptance to change. It is dealing directly with those variables which are controlling in the situation—the attitudes, feelings, and values of people. It recognizes and accepts differences of perception. The weakness in this approach is that it requires understanding, skill, and patience on the part of the person who leads such discussions. In my experience the results to be obtained can go no further than the understanding and skill of the discussion leader.

For this reason I should like to recommend a fifth approach to go hand-in-hand with the fourth. This would be to give training to controllers in human relations. Such training should be focused on getting the controllers to see, feel, and understand the consequences of their behavior for others. Until this problem is seen and felt in its full depth and complexity, controllers can never understand why their control systems can never work automatically and impersonally and why they will always have to be *administered* in terms of people and their relationships to each other.

In these last two suggestions I see the trend which the development of controllers might take. In such a development controllers would have to learn to see themselves more as *administrators* than as *technical specialists*. They would have to learn to become better listeners and to practice the art of appreciating and accepting points of view different from their own. They would have to learn to become better discussion leaders. In this way they would become gradually oriented to the administrative point of view. In my opinion, the technical specialist has to face up to and accept responsibility for only *some* of the consequences of his behavior, generally only the good ones. The administrator, on the other hand, has to face up to and accept responsibility for *all* the consequences of his behavior. This is what makes his job tough, but also a real challenge.

Postscript, 1968

What bothers me about my proposal in the last paragraph of this paper is that I think it may be just as futile to try and make technical specialists into administrators as to make administrators into technical specialists. In the process one may succeed only in making each one less competent in his own expertise and in achieving a pseudo harmony between the two. It is more important for each one to have respect for the competence of the other than for each to become an expert in the other's domain.

Although I was not unmindful of this point when I wrote the last paragraph, I think now that I did not state the position clearly enough. Too often the human relations approach sounds as if it is advocating a harmony of less differentiated parts, that is, a state where everyone thinks more and more alike and where differences become less and less. I just want to make it clear now that this is not the kind of harmony or integration I was advocating. For me A and B can only become better integrated if and when differences are clearly recognized and not blurred. So my position is neither asserting that (1) east is east and west is west and ne'er the twain shall meet nor (2) we should try to make the east like the west or the west like the east, but (3) the more the east and west recognize their differences the more likely a better integration may occur.

I tried to make this point in Chapter 1 when I considered the "false dichotomy." I will do so again in Chapter 26. But it is an elusive point; it tends to get lost in the shuffle of words and under the influence of the strong sentiments which I had when I wrote the foregoing piece.

14 The Territory and Skill of the Administrator

This essay was presented on April 26, 1954, at a conference on industrial relations sponsored in Detroit by the Bureau of Industrial Relations of the University of Michigan, and was first published by the *Michigan Business Review* in November 1954. That periodical has permitted me to reprint it.

Here I tried again to take "human relations" out of the realm of gimmickery and put it in a framework of thought leading to the development of professional competence on the part of the modern manager. When I wrote this piece the term "human relations" was on the road to becoming a dirty word in academic circles. In a few more years new and more respectable words were going to be coined for the area I was talking about. But in 1954 this semantic upgrading of the area had not as yet occurred. Academic respectability was still just around the corner.

There are three curious things that I notice when I listen to executives in industry talk about their problems and when I read books by management experts on how these problems should be solved.

First, I find many important problems being ignored because there is no useful language in terms of which to talk about them. When businessmen talk to me about costs, wages, materials, machines, standards, and matters of this sort, they are articulate and intelligible; their words sound positive and convincing. But when they talk about matters of personality, of attitude, of evaluation, or of feeling, their articulateness vanishes, their stance becomes wobbly, and they sound as if they were standing on a "bushel of eels."

This is all the more curious since so many executives tell me that their major job is the administration of people—and all the human problems I know are manifestations of these matters about which they have so much difficulty speaking.

Second, I find ever so many executives who in spite of the fact that they "know" just how everyone else should behave, still have difficulty in getting the other person to behave the way he should. For example, personnel people often say they know how workers, foremen, other staff people, middle and top management people should behave; but in spite of this knowledge, they cannot get these different groups to do what they should. Moreover, personnel people themselves have difficulty in behaving the way experts tell them they should!

This, too, is a very curious state when so many men of practical affairs cannot apply what they know. As a result, it seems to me that many people in business are suffering from an excessive burden of guilt, as one might expect from people who are surfeited with knowledge they cannot use.

Third, there is the way executives describe the tools they use to do their jobs. They usually say, in effect, that they get their work done by securing facts or information and by applying or implementing policies, standards, and principles of management. But very seldom do they describe the skill they use to secure the relevant facts or information they need, or more important still, to gain the understanding of people about the policies they formulate, the standards they set, or the principles of management they apply.

What makes this so curious, once again, is that executives commonly practice (some more expertly than others) a skill of communication that they are so reticent about—and all the human problems I know are manifestations in one form or another of breakdowns in communication.

Let me repeat my three curious findings: One: Although the executive tells me he is primarily administering people, I find that he has no useful language in terms of which to talk about himself and his relation to the people he administers. Two: Instead of administering people, I find him administering policies and standards. Through these standards he knows how people ought to behave and yet in spite of this knowledge (or should I say because of it?) he has great difficulty in getting people to behave in the way they should. And three: I find him practicing—admittedly often in a rudimentary form—a skill of communication which he does not profess to have or even need.

It will not be easy for me to make sense out of these three observations, but I want to try. For me these observations raise three important but too little discussed questions: (1) What is the administrator administering? (2) What is his relation to what he administers? and (3) What skill, if any, does he practice in dealing with the situations in which he finds himself? Let me start with the first question.

WHAT IS THE ADMINISTRATOR ADMINISTERING?

This simple question, like so many simple questions, has a way of becoming embarrassingly complex. It poses a difficult problem of where and how to begin describing an organic whole. The best method I have found is to jump in somewhere and try like hell to get back to the place from which I started.

Let me begin, therefore, with the problems that administrators say they have in their dealings with people. What problems are they referring to? As I see it, they are talking about the problems they have in getting people to do what they are supposed to do. They are talking about the difficulties they have in securing the understanding of people about the need to meet standards, the need to be "cost conscious," "quality conscious," and "safety conscious," and the need to cooperate with other people. Why are all these matters necessary? From management's point of view the answer is simple. Only by such intelligent, understanding behavior will the organization survive.

System of Coordinated Activities

In other words, the administrator is not administering people as separate and discrete individuals, but he is administering "the consciously coordinated activities of persons."[1] These coordinated activities are directed toward the achievement of purpose. If the organization is to survive in its competitive environment, these purposes of the organization have to be attained. Therefore management must give considerable attention to the logical coordination and efficient operation of its separate activities. Job evaluation, wage administration, time and motion study, methods analysis, work simplification, monetary incentives, the setting of standards—all these and many others with which you are all only too familiar—are directed toward the best and most efficient ways of securing the organizational goals.

Unfortunately, it happens that between the organizational purposes and the most efficient and logical means of obtaining them there are a number of intervening variables. Were the relation between the ends to be sought and the means by which they are reached a simple, direct, and logical one, as some administrators would have us believe, there would be no problem. But the fact remains that the best methods, the best policies, and the best standards do not always produce the best results. Sometimes they produce poor attitudes, poor morale, and poor communication. This happens because of certain intervening variables. So let us look at some of them.

Social Systems

Most difficult to deal with are certain elements of the behavior of persons other than their activities which are being coordinated.

1. See Chester Barnard, *The Functions of the Executive* (Cambridge: Harvard University Press, 1938), p. 73.

First, there are the required *interactions* that must take place between the persons whose activities are being coordinated. Second, there are the *feelings* that the persons bring to and develop from these interactions.

For example, from the logical division of labor certain people are brought together more frequently than others. They interact with one another in certain prescribed ways. From these prescribed and frequent interactions, certain feelings appear. Persons who interact frequently with one another, it has been observed, tend to like one another. Moreover, it can be observed that these very sentiments lead in turn to further interactions and activities, over and above those required by the purposes of coordination. Workers who are brought together by their work, for example, frequently eat lunch together, converse together, drink together, and go to parties together.

From such processes of interaction small groups and other phenomena appear. Moreover, ideas begin to develop among the members of these small groups as to what they or others should do and are expected to do under given circumstances. Workers, for example, develop ideas as to how much work they should do, what constitutes a day's work, and so forth. Such ideas of expected behavior, the sociologists call "norms." They are not behavior itself, but the ideas which govern behavior.

In terms of these norms, the activities of persons are evaluated. Some jobs are considered better or worse than others. Such sentiments elaborate in turn to all the activities of the members of groups holding certain kinds of jobs. What workers holding higher-ranking jobs do in their games, in their conversations, in their lives in and outside of the factory, is considered superior to what workers holding lower-ranking jobs do. And the more nearly all of the activities of a person conform to these norms of the group, the higher is his rank within the group. From these processes informal leaders appear who in turn produce new activities, interactions, sentiments, norms, and evaluations.

These continuing processes by which the activities, interactions, and feelings of people tend to develop and form an "organized whole" do not lend themselves to orderly description and discussion. With them we are all intuitively familiar. No administrator can ignore them; yet these phenomena, so important to the administrator, are difficult to talk about.

Just to fix our attention upon them I shall use the term "social system."[2] By a "social system" I shall mean the interconnected character of the elements in the social behavior of the members of small groups. I am referring to the fact that people who come to work bring with them into the work situation certain sentiments. They are asked to perform certain jobs; these jobs link them into relation with certain other people. From these given sentiments that they bring to work, from these given activities that they are supposed to perform, certain patterns of relationship develop. On the foundation of these initial relationships, new ones spontaneously emerge. New sentiments, new activities, new interactions appear. These new elements in turn are linked together and form themselves into a pattern, an "organized whole," a system.

From these processes norms of behavior are adopted; ideas of what is expected are developed. In terms of these norms, evaluations are made and the behavior of people is controlled. And finally these very processes feed back upon and affect—sometimes favorably, more often adversely—those very initial relationships set up by management for logical coordination and efficient operation.

Personality Systems

Thus these "social systems" make the administrator's job difficult. They are closely related to many of his most perplexing problems: maintaining discipline, establishing "control," introducing change, and so forth. Were these the only phenomena with which he had to deal, his problem would be difficult enough. But unfortunately, another set of intervening variables comes in to plague him. Some people do not like to conform to the norms of the group. The particular emotional needs they bring to work are not satisfied by the social systems of which they are members. Their particular conceptions of themselves, as developed from their past personal experience, are threatened rather than enhanced by their associations at work.

What I am pointing to here is the fact that the feelings which people bring to work have already combined themselves with other elements in the person to form another kind of "organized whole" or "system." I shall refer to such an "organized whole" as a "personality system." I

2. For a much better statement of these processes, see George Homans, *The Human Group* (New York: Harcourt, Brace, 1950). In this statement about "social systems" I have borrowed freely from this book.

am using this mouthful of words rather than the one word "personality" not to be highbrow, but to emphasize that what I am referring to is a dynamic whole made up of mutually dependent parts. Let us look briefly at the make-up of a "personality system."

The feelings and sentiments people have and the values and assumptions they hold tend to affect the way they see things about them. Hence, they do not perceive the world in the same way. For instance, what is important to one person or group is not important to another. By the same token, matters that are of importance to management are not of the same importance to employees. Older-service employees do not share the same values as younger-service employees.

I realize I should not belabor this commonplace observation. All of us have had enough experience to realize that we do not perceive the reality quite in the same way as our parents, our teachers, our bosses, our wives, or our children. And yet it is curious how in the heat of controversy we seem to forget this fact when it is important for us to remember it.

As unique individuals we also hold different beliefs about ourselves. On the basis of these different beliefs we evaluate what happens to us. Just as we find comfortable and reassuring those happenings that tend to reinforce the cherished pictures of ourselves, we find disturbing and threatening those happenings that challenge them. Thus, a young supervisor will be upset when his employees do not do cheerfully and quickly what he tells them to do. In such behavior he will perceive a threat to his conception of himself as a capable supervisor.

Again I realize I should not belabor this commonplace observation. All of us have had enough experience to realize that we have pictures of ourselves that we need to maintain and defend at all cost. Not only do we have to learn to live with others; we also have to be true to ourselves. And yet again it is curious how when it is most important for us to remember this, we have a way of forgetting it. Between these two forces—the need to adjust and the need to be true to ourselves—many of us find the going pretty rough and the administrator finds many of his most stubborn and baffling problems.

Again let me remind you that people respond to the reality as they perceive it to be and not as it actually is (or, more accurately, as other people generally think it is).

Let us never forget that we do not respond to the facts as such; we respond to the facts as we perceive them. What most of us call "facts" are actually an interrelated set of feelings, assumptions, and perceptions. For example, a boss sees two workers in the same office going out to coffee together. Because this behavior arouses in him certain feelings of anger and because of certain assumptions he makes about how workers should behave, he sees these two workers as "irresponsible." Often he would call that a fact. He does not just *see* two workers going out to coffee together. He perceives two *irresponsible* workers doing this. And he acts accordingly—sometimes, upon later reflection, to his regret.

Likewise two workers may perceive their common boss in quite different ways. If worker A perceives his boss as a domineering person, he will respond in terms of that perception; if worker B perceives the same boss as a rather pathetic, insecure person, he will respond to that perception. These two different perceptions arise from different sets of assumptions and feelings that constitute the personality systems of these two workers. A and B do not realize they are doing any evaluations of their own. For A the boss *is* domineering. For B the boss *is* a "sorry figure." Such perceptions are brute and stubborn phenomena, as anyone who has tried to change them by argument or persuasion soon finds out.

Three Different but Interrelated Dimensions

It is unfortunate that the territory of the administrator is exceedingly complex. But it is not his fault, any more than it is mine or yours. I am sure that we would all prefer it to be simpler. But let us be stubborn realists and in spite of the queasy feelings it may cause, let us look at the facts (or should I say the assumptions, feelings, and perceptions that underlie them?). In light of our foregoing discussion, these facts appear to comprise three dimensions.

The first dimension comprises the initial activities that people must perform and the initial relationships that they must have in order that the purpose of the organization be achieved. It also includes ideas as to how these activities should be efficiently performed and logically coordinated. These ideas, stemming from science and technology, govern what the behavior and relationships of people should be—if only matters were ideally coordinated. As they do not coincide with behavior itself, I shall call them "the logics of management." These "logics," to put it briefly, include the best policies, the best methods, the best standards, the best controls, the best systems, and of course the best behavior to carry them out. It covers what is found in most books on personnel administration. This is the most articulate part of business and many personnel people have contributed to its articulation. Were this the only dimension and were this all there was present, personnel people would soon be able to close up shop because all their problems would be solved—eventually, if not now. But I fear their jobs will persist, because there are some further thorny facts.

The second dimension arises from the fact that in any organized human activities the persons whose activities are being coordinated happen to be social as well as logical. Now it may be very poor luck for all personnel administrators that the situation is rigged like this. But it can't be helped.

This second dimension arises from man's loneliness, from his desire for intimate association with his fellow men. As a result, man is literally forced to elaborate, proliferate, and expand those initial activities, interactions, and relationships which the logical coordination of the business provides him. By so doing, he provides himself with those satisfactions that no benevolent administrator, public or private, personnel or line, can give him. He elaborates his *own* social systems and through them develops his *own* norms in terms of which he controls his *own* behavior, and as a result he runs smack into what management perceives as one of its prerogatives.

And finally, the third dimension arises from the fact that even in business, the persons whose activities are being coordinated bring with them to work their *own* "personality systems" as well as develop at work their own "social systems." Through this third dimension the social contexts in which people live their lives are internalized, and they respond to the happenings about them as they perceive them, assume them, and feel them to be.

These three dimensions, although quite different, are interrelated. Technical standards of performance affect and are affected by norms of behavior. Norms of behavior affect and are affected by people's conceptions of themselves. It is the interrelation of these three dimensions that constitutes the "total pattern" of business which is what the administrator is administering. He is administering a system of coordinated activities which are in a relation of mutual dependence to both an external and internal environment.

More specifically, on the one hand he is concerned with those external changes required for the competitive survival of the social system in its environment. On the other hand he is concerned with how these changes required for survival are initiated, administered, and assimilated by this system so that the internal needs for stability are also maintained and so that the needs of the individual personality systems are also satisfied. In dealing with these processes, he is concerned with evaluations of people (i.e., their feelings, perceptions, and assumptions) to this changing and dynamic "organized whole."

THE ADMINISTRATOR'S RELATION TO WHAT
HE IS ADMINISTERING

We come now to the second major question: "What is the relation of the administrator to what he is administering?" Let me begin with this observation: the administrator is part of the social system he administers. From this involvement there is no escape. He cannot treat the social system which he administers as something apart from himself. He both affects it and is affected by it.

Remember, too, that the executive has a nervous system and a personality system. As a result he, like those he administers, responds to what he assumes, feels, and perceives things to be. His behavior also is no better or no worse than what he perceives or fails to perceive. It too can be altered only by changing his perceptions.

In the process of maintaining stability, the administrator plays an important role. As he leads his group to a new goal, his own behavior can facilitate or put into jeopardy the stability of the social system. And yet curiously enough the very people who administer or initiate changes in the activities of others very often do not see themselves as being a part of and working with a social system. This seems to be the "blind spot" of many supervisors and executives.

But one point should be clear: Supervisors and executives do not miss these things because they are stupid or because they willfully ignore them. They miss them because they do not have a way of thinking that allows them to see them. In most business organizations executives have much more adequate ways of thinking about the tools and products of technology than about social systems. As a result they do not see that the phenomena I have been talking about are part and parcel of the work situation. They *feel* these phenomena as something annoying, but they do not see them in any explicit or systematic sense.

Only by being aware of his own involvement with the social system he administers and of the feelings which such an involvement is bound to produce can the executive perform his functions skillfully. On the part of some executives this involvement is a blind subjectivity—a complete incapacity to see the situation except from their own point of view. What they feel is for them the reality. Other executives try to maintain their "objectivity" by denying their feelings and by refusing to admit any emotional involvement. They give the facts of logic and reason priority; they try to relegate their feelings and the feelings of others to the trivial and inconsequential. And so what they end up by doing is projecting their denied feelings as "facts" into the external environment.

In my experience the administrator who can accept gracefully and handle with some skill his own personal involvement in the situations he administers is likely to do a better job. Such a supervisor or executive does not deny his feelings. He accepts them and his responsibility for them. He does not identify his feelings with the feelings of others. He recognizes his own feelings but does not give them priority. As a result, he "latches on" to the *processes* underlying human discord rather than to the problems in which they become manifested. Through this awareness of his own subjectivity he becomes more objective.

THE ADMINISTRATOR'S SKILL

This leads me to my third question. In dealing with this involvement (his own as well as that of others) what skill does the administrator practice? In view of the nature of the situation in which he is involved, it should be clear that his primary tool must be a skill of communication. He must be able to communicate with many groups with different points of view, with many unique individuals whose perceptions of the situation are different, as he administers not only the situation as he sees it but the many different perceptions of it.

And how does he do this? Too often, I fear, he tries to do this by trying to get all the groups and individuals to feel alike and to share *his* point of view and perceptions. He tries to tell the many different people how they should feel and what they should see and assume. And sometimes this takes the form of trying to get employees and supervisors to think, feel, and perceive things exactly like top management.

But this is not in the cards. It goes against all we know about individual and social behavior. The administrator has to recognize *all* of the varying values of all the social system he administers, not just those of one segment. He has to learn to respond to many different perceptions and values, not just a selected few. Above all he has to learn to accept and appreciate points of view different from his own.

It is the practice of this orientation that I call the skill of human relations. By this skill I mean the capacity of an individual to communicate his feelings and ideas to another, as well as his capacity to respond to the feelings and ideas of others in such a fashion as to promote cooperation and congenial participation in a common task.[3] And since the administrator is emotionally involved in the social system he administers, he must learn to deal with his own feelings as well as the feelings of others. For the seasoned supervisor or executive, self-knowledge is paramount.

In my opinion this human relations skill is the most misunderstood, the most ignored, and the most underestimated part of the executive's job. Compared with the more articulate, elaborate, and tangible "controls" with which the executive is provided, this skill, when talked about, may sound silly and superficial to some, difficult and intangible to others. Nevertheless, I shall insist that it is the most important part of the executive's job. All the problems of securing the understanding and cooperation of people depend upon it. Without it the best methods, policies, and standards that management can devise become mere exercises in futility; and the executive's job becomes mere dust and ashes—a ceremonial ritual at best, a "ballet of bloodless categories" at worst.

SUMMARY—THE SIGNIFICANCE OF THE OBVIOUS

Let me summarize what I have been saying in a slightly different form. So far I have made three obvious and commonplace observations:

1. The administrator is dealing with an evolving "organized whole," surviving in an environment.

2. He is emotionally involved in this organic whole he administers, and

3. If he is to do a better job, he has to learn to deal more skillfully with his involvement as well as the involvement of others in this organic whole. The skill of dealing with these involvements is the skill of human relations.

3. See Elton Mayo, *The Social Problems of an Industrial Civilization* (Boston: Division of Research, Harvard Business School, 1945), pp. 13–22.

Let me assure you that my intent has not been to lull you to sleep with the obvious. Rather, I want to excite you with its significance. Because if what I have been saying is so obvious, then many personnel administrators must fail to see its significance.

The trouble that most of us have with the obvious is that we do not see its importance; hence we tend to relegate it to the trivial and inconsequential. Yet, contrary to popular belief, some of our greatest advances in knowledge have come from the systematic exploitation of the obvious. So let me conclude, therefore, by spelling out what I believe to be the significance of these commonplace observations for personnel administration.

From my analysis it would follow that the chief function of the personnel administrator would be to help people to change their behavior in the direction of becoming more competent and skillful in dealing with the changing, organic wholes of which they are a part. His chief job would be that of a trainer and multiplier of human relations skill in the organizations he serves. He would act as a multiplier of competence in human relations skill at all levels of the organization —employee, supervisory, and executive.

If this were his major function, it would follow then that the personnel administrator no longer would be preoccupied exclusively with the logical coordination of activities and those ideas—the logics of management—which express this important dimension of business. He would not be exclusively concerned with the creation and maintenance of systems and standards of performance. He would not be solely an instrument of change in the activities of people. Rather he would be primarily concerned with facilitating changes in the total behavior of people that would help them to deal more effectively with the total situations in which they find themselves. In so doing, he would be trying to create and maintain changes in the behavior of persons that are quite different from those changes that are concerned primarily with improving methods, costs, output, quality, and other unidimensional factors of this sort.

Let me illustrate this difference by looking at modern standard shops and the sorts of changes that have been introduced in them. In some shops there have been introduced not only new machines, tools, materials, activities, and methods of work but also new standards of all kinds which say what the performance of people should be in terms of time, quantity, quality, cost, and so forth. It has often been assumed by the people who have introduced them that such standards will make the job of the supervisor easier. Because everyone will know clearly what is expected of him, the supervisor of such a shop, it has been alleged, will require less social skill or perhaps none at all.

But is this what we find? I, for one, do not. Instead, I find that the supervisor of the modern shop requires more and not less human relations skill. Where the supervisor is still using the old-fashioned social skill of the know-how shop, I find trouble, discontent, and low morale.

But is this result so strange? According to my conceptual framework, it is obvious. In the process of developing the standard shop, a new kind of social system has been created for which no parallel in history exists. These new social systems require new understanding on the part of the people who administer them. For their successful administration, more and not less explicit and expert human relations skill is required.

How to improve in the behavior of persons the new understanding and skill that these organizations require seems to me to be the most important problem of our industrial civilization. How to introduce such understanding and skill in the organizations they serve is the formidable task which personnel people face. Let us not minimize the difficulty of the task. It is extremely complex.

If my analysis of the administrator's situation is correct, it follows that he needs a multidimensional tool to deal with the multidimensional situation in which he is involved; no unidimensional tool will suffice. Yet the history of personnel work seems to reveal the development of one unidimensional tool after another—job evaluation, merit rating, work simplification, teaching workers the A B C's of economics, Job Instruction Training, Job Methods Training, and Job Relations Training. No sooner is one found wanting than another rears its head. But with the introduction of each of these new tools, the need for a way of thinking that will keep them related becomes greater, not less.

This multidimensional tool that the administrator needs, I call "human relations." It is designed to help persons to deal with the concrete situations in which they are involved. It provides them with a useful way of thinking about such situations. It provides them with a skill of diagnosing such situations. It helps them to understand, to become more sensitive about, and then to respond more skillfully to what is taking place when they interact with people in face-to-face relations and as members or leaders of a group. In particular it helps them to see the effect of their behavior upon others and vice versa. Thus it helps them to learn to accept their own feelings as well as the feelings of others.

Human relations is quite different from all other tools with which management is provided. All the other tools for the administrator are predicated upon the assumption that he should be certain, perfect, and consistent. Yet the multidimensional situations with which he has to deal involve him in uncertainty, imperfection, and inconsistency. Thus, none of these tools tell him anything about the most real aspect of his workaday world—how to learn to accept and deal with the uncertainties, imperfections, and contradictions in which his involvements with the concrete place him. Human relations is predicated upon the premise that from this uncomfortable predicament arising from his involvment, there is no escape. Unlike all the other tools which are trying to help the executive to escape from his involvement, human relations is trying to help him to learn to accept and cope more skillfully with it.

Among all the butterfly chasers in the modern industrial arena, the advocates of human relations seem to be the only brute, stubborn realists left.

15 Learning in and Training for a Multidimensional World

For this piece I have selected excerpts from a report I made on a Program for Advanced Training and Research in Human Relations subsidized by a grant from the Ford Foundation and conducted by me at the Harvard Business School from 1951 to 1954. This report, entitled *Training for Human Relations,* was written with the assistance and collaboration of George F. F. Lombard and Harriet O. Ronken (now Mrs. Rolf P. Lynton). It was published as a monograph in 1954 by the Division of Research of the Harvard Business School. The Director of Research has granted me permission to reproduce Chapters VIII and IX, entitled "Learning in a Multidimensional World" and "Training for a Multidimensional World." It was in these two chapters that I tried to say what the three-year experience had taught us about training for human relations. I have condensed the chapters quite a bit but have not intentionally altered the original meaning and have introduced no new thoughts.

Before giving the excerpts I had better explain the nature of the training program; otherwise the excerpts would not be fully understandable.

The program, which in time came to be called the "human relations clinic," was addressed to the training of what I then called "second-level practitioners," that is, persons who would some day be in positions of responsibility for improving the competence of human relations practitioners at the first level. These first-level practitioners in turn were those persons who by the nature of their jobs had some responsibility for securing the understanding and cooperation of others in order to get their own jobs done. So my first-level practitioner could be an administrator at any level in any kind of organization, and my "second-level practitioner" bore some resemblance to those persons who later came to be called "change agents," but I thought of them as agents acting from within—instead of outside—the system of relationships which they were trying to improve.

Our program was designed to attract those students who wanted to be where the action was and to utilize their knowledge there. So the students—we called them "trainees"—were young men with career objectives somewhat different from those of students in a conventional doctoral program. There were nine of them in all. Although some were doctoral candidates in business or one of the behavioral sciences, they were not sure that upon graduation they wished to go into academic teaching and research. And then there were those who definitely did not wish to do this and felt no need of a doctoral degree. Both kinds of students were early manifestations of "drop-outs" from academia, which at that time no one was paying much attention to.

Perhaps a clearer picture of the kind of students we had can be seen from the way some of their careers developed. One, for example, set up a school in Mysore, India, for community workers in rural areas. Later he was engaged in a similar activity in Hyderabad, and is now helping to develop a human-relations-type program at a southern university in this country. A second student went into educational administration and is now vice-chancellor of a large midwestern university after having been first the dean of its business school; I suspect that he is engaged in trying to relate his university to the modern world. A third became a director of a non-university-affiliated research and training organization in the behavioral sciences in California. A fourth, after having become a professor of human relations in a Canadian university, has been working with management development programs sponsored by the Ford Foundation in developing countries, first in Egypt and now in Colombia. A fifth became a director of alumni relations in a large eastern business school and now is Director for Executive Development in a private educational institution. And so on—six, seven, eight, and nine.

It may seem strange that not one of the trainees went into a business organization, and that none of them strayed far from the fields of education—although they were not necessarily teaching an established discipline.

But in this program I was concerned not only with the careers of my trainees but also with experimenting on what the training for such persons should be, that is, what the training should consist of for those who wanted to act as multipliers of competence in matters of human relations. It seemed to me the difficulty of this job was being underestimated in many quarters, and for this reason human relations was coming to have a bad name. It tended either to remain at a superficial level or degenerate into a cult. So the "training design"—to use a highfalutin term—of this program was to try to break through this barrier. The program was not highly structured; it had no required courses and seminars. It was experimental through and through, not in the sense of a "controlled experiment" where I was able to evaluate one training method against another, but in the sense that both the trainees and trainers participated in the training method that gradually evolved.

At that time human relations training in this country had become for some persons the road to salvation; indeed, in certain quarters it was on the way to becoming "big business." But the findings of this program gave little comfort to those who were going in such directions. Instead they showed that human relations training as a road to competence was no superhighway on which one could reach his destination in a few days or weeks. Instead the road was badly lit and badly paved; it had few directional signs, some awful bumps and detours, and even some clover-leaf intersections that were hard to get out of.

Now we should like to evaluate our experiences in terms of what they meant to us (the staff) for the design, administration, and continuation of the program. What have we learned about human relations training?

PROBLEMS OF CULTISM

Time and again, in implementing our program, we came up against a set of difficulties we are calling the "problems of cultism." These difficulties were not new; they had been met before, but in the past they had been dealt with primarily at a name-calling level. Our critics have been prone to see in us the cults of "Mayo," the "small group," "cooperation," the "concrete," and the "practical." They saw us housed in the citadel of "capitalism," "free enterprise," and "embryonic executives," and thereby wittingly or unwittingly providing actual or would-be executives with the tools and skills of "manipulation." In turn, we have been prone to see in the activities of others the "cult of efficiency" and the "cult of science." These have been only too often the target of our attacks.

What lies beneath all this excitement? Among ourselves we have often speculated about these matters; each time we have come to the conclusion that to continue debate at this level of discourse would continue to produce more heat than light. We have never felt it would help matters to say to our accusers, "When you use those words, you'd better smile, Pardner." The recipients of our attacks have also been kind enough to allow us to "stew in our own juice" and await the outcome of our follies.

Had matters stayed at this level of "understanding," we would have decided to agree to disagree and let it go at that. But in our program during the past three years this problem of cultism manifested itself among our own trainees with a persistence that seemed to us at times formidable. This forced us to raise some embarrassing questions, such as, are we guilty of the same conduct as our accusers? Is it easier to see someone else's cult than one's own? Or perhaps is this problem of cultism not just an exhibition of "projection," "stereotyping," or "bad manners" but also something more basic to the problem of human relations training?

These questions, as we have said, arose first in relation to our own trainees. Probably their most recurring problem was to face up to the contradictions they felt in dealing with the multidimensional character of the situations in which they found themselves in our program. Over and over again they wished to reduce all human relations to one dimension and then became most unhappy with the contradictions into which this attempt led them. A few examples will help to make this problem more meaningful.

In the beginning, for example, some of our trainees became enamored of the "nondirective" approach (an approach that addresses itself to the feelings of people rather than to the logical content of what they say). Using it indiscriminately, they tried to reflect the feelings of people at all times, places, and occasions, and then were startled to find that these attempts often were not perceived by these people in the way they intended. To change their own behavior, they felt, would be inconsistent with their understanding of how they ought to behave (i.e., being nondirective); on the other hand, not to change their behavior would be inconsistent with another principle of behavior (i.e., being scientific in the sense of looking at the facts). As a result, there was much anguish, pain, and stewing. That they might not have been very skillful in reflecting the actual feelings of the person they were listening to; that they might have tried it in a situation where it was not appropriate (i.e., contrary to the norms of the group); that any tool has its limits—these were not for them the first matters to be considered. Instead, they held rigidly to the position that either *it* (unspecified) works or *it* doesn't.

Other trainees became enamored of being group-centered. They shrank from exercising any leadership or from contributing any ideas that would seem to be imposing their will on the group. The group must decide everything by itself and of course there must be unanimity. Often beginners further assume that such groups are wholly self-contained and that there is no external environment to which they have to relate. Operating under these assumptions, again the beginner finds that often certain things happen which are not mentioned in the books about being "group-centered." The members of the group become confused and frustrated. The leader becomes immobilized. The accomplishment of the goals is in jeopardy. Negative rather than positive feelings between members of the group arise. Here again the beginner finds himself in conflict. Should he remain true to his "principles of group-centeredness" and hope that from all this confusion and frustration learning will result, or should he do something and risk the possibility of being "autocratic"?

For our trainees these problems were highlighted whenever they were in situations and groups, as members, leaders, or interviewers, where they were involved in *talking with* people. When they were just among themselves (and for the moment, at least, not concerned with their own interpersonal relations) and primarily *talking about* other people, their concepts and words seemed adequate and illuminating. They could describe well the evaluations and misevaluations, the perceptions and misperceptions of others; they could see the values and norms of behavior that the persons did or did not share, the interactions they did or did not have, the feelings they expressed or implied in their verbal and overt behavior. They even were somewhat capable of seeing these different dimensions as an "organized whole." They saw

the consequences for employees of the "autocratic" or laissez-faire behavior of supervisors or executives. They saw the consequences for
employees of having to accommodate to too-rapid technological
changes required by the environment—changes that failed to take into
account their feelings and sentiments. But when they took these diagnostic insights into situations where they were involved in *talking
with* people, something happened.

When they acted as observers or interviewers, the going was not
especially rough. But when they acted as members or leaders of groups
these insights became increasingly difficult to practice. Up reared the
multidimensional character of the territory with all its conflicting
feelings for them and others. Should they be "nondirective" and risk
the chance of being regarded as "screwballs," or should they behave
in accordance with the norms of the group and risk the chance of
facilitating merely the expression of "superficial" feelings? Should they
intrude their own opinions and feelings and risk the chance of not
facilitating the "true" expression of opinions and feelings of others, or
should they refrain from the expression of all feelings and opinions
and arouse the suspicions (what-the-hell-is-going-on-here feeling) of
others? Should they be "permissive" and how "permissive" can you be?
Should they be group-centered and how group-centered can you get?
And when the people who are being given permission to express their
feelings and make their own decisions and formulate their own purposes do not appreciate this permissiveness but instead become bewildered, confused, angry, and will not make decisions, what then?
How can this be? Why do they not appreciate our good intention? our
permissiveness? The books are "screwy"; the books are not "screwy."
All diagnosis is bad; no diagnosis is bad. So goes the see-saw.

At these moments books are not very helpful, primarily because the
books on how to be permissive and group-centered do not go into these
matters. They only tell you how *to be* these things, without saying
much about what happens to people who try to be these things.

As we looked around us, however, we found that we were not the
only ones having these problems. In many places persons in positions
of responsibility were trying hard to be *client-centered, employee-cen-
tered, group-centered, subordinate-centered,* and *person-centered* when
they were in situations where they had to be also *organizationally-
centered, production-centered, superior-centered, decision-centered,*
and *task-centered*. In business and industry we had seen, to be sure,

many examples of production-centered supervisors, efficiency-centered executives, and autocratic behavior. But in our reaction against these matters, were we not guilty in our training of going in the direction of another excess and oversimplification?

It was not that we thought the insights to which these different kinds of "centeredness" (i.e., the "good" ones) referred were not of the greatest importance and significance. What bothered us was the lack of skill with which these insights were being practiced in groups and in face-to-face relationships. In looking at our trainees, ourselves, and others, we were appalled at the way these insights were being applied. It seemed at times as if we had lost the native intelligence with which God had endowed us as well as the elementary social skill that our parents and society had taught us. We were immersed in a sea of cults, some of which we had helped to create—the cult of the personality, the cult of the group, the cult of efficiency, and the cult of science. In trying so hard to be person-centered, democratic, purpose-centered, or scientific, we had ceased to be competent.

Why then is skillful behavior in the area of human relations so difficult to learn? Why is it so easy to impede this development by escaping into cults? Were there some brute and stubborn factors which we were ignoring and which made the development of cultism almost inescapable in the area of human relations? All our experiences were forcing us to raise this question: Why is it so difficult to learn?

PROBLEMS OF LEARNING

Let us start by looking more carefully at the milieu with which the practitioner is dealing, i.e., *an organized human activity*.[1] What are some of the common elements of this milieu?

Norms of Behavior. In any organized human activity, the human relations practitioner is faced with five quite different orders of phenomena, of which one is *norms of behavior*. In any group there are certain prescribed and customary ways of doing things. These norms are the ideas that develop in a group of how its members are expected to behave under given circumstances. Norms are not behavior itself

---

1. The remarks that follow will not be restricted to those organizations whose purposes are strictly economic, but by virtue of our background and experience we will often have such organizations in mind.

but the ideas that govern behavior of people in groups. In terms of them, the activities of persons are evaluated. Certain activities are considered better or worse than others.

The human relations practitioner cannot ignore this dimension of human behavior. Yet his skill cannot be drawn entirely from it. To do so would be to reduce social skill to the Emily Post school of thought—an elaborate set of rules of etiquette for different occasions. It would make human relations the cult of conformity—a charge which has often been made against it.

The human relations practitioner improves along this dimension when he recognizes how his own behavior is determined by the norms of his group and when he can learn to differentiate the norms of behavior of his own group from the norms of behavior of other groups.

Ideals of Behavior. Closely allied to norms but yet of a somewhat different dimension are the *ideals of behavior* which individuals bring to work from the wider culture of which they are a part. These are the "absolute logics" of our society, our unstated assumptions, our most sacred and cherished beliefs. In our families, schools, and churches these ideals are inculcated as premises for conduct—they are what behavior ought to be regardless of time, place, and circumstances. To the members of a particular culture they are matters so obvious that they do not require explicit formulation or proof. Everyone in the society admits and accepts them even if in his daily conduct he does not act upon them.

To the human relations practitioner these ideals also cannot be ignored. Frequently and most often (unless he is dealing with a culture entirely different from his own) he holds these values in common with the people with whom he is dealing. They are his absolutes too. Again, it was our belief that in spite of the importance of these ideals and the need for certain groups in our society to keep reminding us of them, the skill of the human relations practitioner could not be derived from them alone. Human relations is not stating these ideal patterns of behavior. It would take our practitioner out of the realm of day-to-day practice and the imperfect world with which he has to deal. And this is just where we want to keep him.

Our human relations practitioner, like any ordinary individual, improves along this dimension when he learns to differentiate these ideals of behavior from behavior itself, when he learns to develop these ideals in relation to and not apart from the other dimensions of the milieu in which he finds himself, when he realizes the contradictions in which they sometimes lead him and when he refuses to dogmatize about them. He is quite willing to accept that these ideals of behavior may vary from culture to culture. He is quite willing to accept that there may be some ideals which are universal and apply to all people regardless of differences of culture. About these matters his mind is open because in his day-to-day activities he does not need to close it.

Personality. Still another important dimension is the individual personalities of the members of the groups with which the practitioner has to deal and, of course, his own personality too. Each person brings to work his own more personal feelings, assumptions, and perceptions of himself as developed from his past experiences and associations with other groups. These personal feelings, assumptions, and perceptions of himself constitute an organized dynamic whole—"a personality system." In terms of this conception about himself, he assimilates the happenings about him. He finds enhancing those things that tend to reinforce the pictures about himself he cherishes and likes to hold. He finds disturbing those happenings that challenge them. For example, a young supervisor may be upset when his employees do not do cheerfully and quickly what he tells them to do. He perceives in such behavior a threat to his conception of himself as a capable supervisor.

In the past fifty years since the work of Freud no dimension of human behavior has been given more attention and studied more than these "personality systems" of individuals. They have been almost the exclusive concern of psychiatrists and clinical and social psychologists. Their studies have contributed valuable and important insights to human relations practice. Yet again, in spite of its importance it seems to us unwarranted to reduce all human relations practice to this single dimension of "personality." To do so would reduce human relations to practices involving the modification of "personality" alone. Again we felt there were other groups more competent to do these things than we. Moreover, alone it would fail to throw light on some of the most important problems of the human relations practitioner.

How does our human relations practitioner improve along this dimension? There is little question that he needs to know something about the personality structures of others; but above all he needs to know himself. Improvement along this dimension occurs when he can distinguish between his own needs and the needs of others and when he can learn that the satisfaction of his own personality needs are not *ipso facto* satisfying the needs of others. This requires self-control as well as self-understanding. And this is one of the most difficult lessons to learn. Too often we prefer to express our feelings rather than listen to the feelings of others; we prefer to maintain our pictures of ourselves even to the extent of behavior that is threatening to the self-concepts of others (e.g., bawling out a person in the presence of others).

Purpose. There is still another dimension which the human relations practitioner has to take into account. In his multidimensional territory there exist not only norms and ideals of behavior and unique personalities but also *the consciously coordinated activities of persons.* These coordinated activities have as their goal the achievement of a purpose. If the organization is to survive in its competitive environment, these purposes have to be attained. If these purposes are to be secured, the activities of persons have to be coordinated and operated efficiently toward these ends. It is for this reason that the leaders of any organized human activity must give considerable attention to the logical coordination and efficient operation of its separate job activities. From this concern ideas develop which say how matters should stand if these purposes are to be realized by rational processes alone. These ideas, stemming from science and technology, govern what the behavior and relationships of people should be, were matters ideally coordinated. As they do not coincide with behavior itself, we have called them "the logics of management."

In the past fifty years since the works of Frederick Taylor, the father of "scientific management," this dimension has also been given considerable attention and study. To it "big business" has given almost exclusive attention. It is the most articulate part of business, and many specialists have contributed to its articulation. Again the human relations practitioner can ignore this dimension only at his peril. It exists as a dominant variable in any organized human activity, big or little, articulated or not. It exists because any organized human activity has to survive in a larger environment. It comprises those essential activities that people must perform and the essential relationships that they must have in order that the purposes of the organization be secured. Yet again all human relations cannot be reduced to this dimension alone. To do so would be to reduce skill to the search for the best policies, the best methods, the best standards, the best controls, the best systems, and of course the best behavior to carry them out. It reduces human relations to the "cult of efficiency."

How does the human relations practitioner develop along this dimension? As we have pointed out again and again, this dimension has to be developed in relation to and not apart from these other dimensions that we have mentioned. The practitioner has to differentiate these "logics of management" from behavior itself. He has to learn to see that in any organized human activity the persons whose activities are being coordinated happen to be human and social as well as logical.

Science. We have tried to show that human relations practice cannot be deduced from the principles of any one of those dimensions alone. The attempt to apply the principles of any one of these dimensions alone to the concrete human situation becomes a "cult." Each dimension can be fruitfully studied alone, but the minute the "knowledge" derived from such study is directly applied to a concrete situation, another dimension of equal importance rears its head.

As a result, the protagonist of any one of these dimensions before engaging in combat with the enemy (i.e., the concrete) often seeks alliances with other dimensions for support. Probably the most popular alliance in the world today is the one with "science." From such alliances new combinations called "schools of thought" appear such as, for example, "industrial sociology," "personality psychology," and "scientific management." Again let us remember that this dimension is not behavior itself but a dominant idea which governs what the behavior of people should be if certain things are to be accomplished. It is concerned with those ideas which state what the behavior of a person should be if verifiable knowledge about the world (things and people) is to be acquired. These ideas are often referred to by different names such as, for instance, the "scientific method," the "experimental method," the "canons of induction," and "problem-solving."

There is little question that this dimension has gained increasing attention since the seventeenth century. Since this period no other ideas have so come to dominate the minds of men; no other ideas have so completely revolutionized our world.

Yet again in spite of the importance of this dimension, all human relations cannot be reduced to it alone. It would identify too quickly the practices of human relations with the practices by means of which scientific knowledge is acquired. It would identify one dimension of behavior with behavior itself. In spite of its extreme importance, we wish to keep it separate from behavior itself. Otherwise, it would reduce human relations to the "cult of science."

For our ordinary human relations practitioners improvement along this dimension, like all the others, is a slow, arduous, and painful route. Through this dimension he learns to see the consequences of his behavior and why "the road to hell is paved with good intentions." He learns to listen better to others. He learns to observe better his own behavior in relation to the behavior of others. He tries to improve it —not drastically but slowly. He is searching for those *ideas which state what the behavior of a person should be if he is to continue to learn to live with himself and others in the society in which willy-nilly he has been born and has to work and live.* In this search he checks his observations and ideas with the observations and ideas of others. As in the other dimensions, he tries to develop this dimension of "science" not apart from but in relation to the other dimensions. Through dimension one (norms of behavior) he learns what others expect from him as well as what he can expect from others, but he becomes no slave to conformity. Through dimension two (ideals of behavior) he learns the cherished beliefs of his society but realizes without bitterness that they often conflict and that they tell him little of what he should do in particular instances. Through dimension three (personality) he learns why he and others need to be true to themselves but why to do this alone would take them into mental hospitals. Through dimension four (purpose) he learns that he is determined in part by a system of relationships which he alone did not create—that social systems, just like himself, must relate themselves to an environment if they are to survive. And for this survival he learns that certain activities have to be performed and certain relationships have to be maintained for which he may have no liking. Although he learns to accept this, he becomes no slave to efficiency. Through dimension five (science) he learns the most difficult lesson of all. He finds that even "knowledge" and "books" themselves can block learning and that in spite of the popular myth of his day "science" is not the only road to understanding. In a world of uncertainty, imperfection, and inconsistency he finally has to learn what his whole educational system has carefully tried to prevent him from finding out. He has to learn to live in this world and make his peace with its uncertainties, imperfections, and inconsistencies.

PROBLEMS OF INVOLVEMENT

What our analysis has shown is that what is preventing the practitioner from learning about himself and others in his work-a-day world is in good part the culture itself in which he lives. For look at the five injunctions these five dimensions are making to him.

1. Conform or else—
2. Hold steadfast to the eternal verities or else—
3. Be true to yourself or else—
4. Be efficient or else—
5. Be scientific; make a controlled experiment or else—

Is it not obvious that our simple injunction "Take a good look—see for yourself or else" is falling on pretty barren soil? For in the first three of the above injunctions are the conditionings of the ages; in the last two are the major precepts of the modern world; in all of them reside the most powerful sentiments of society. By violating them, not only the Junior Senator from Wisconsin but society itself will get you. Society does not approve of looking too closely at yourself and your relations to others. It has ordered these matters long ago and it wants no experimentation. There is not "gold" but "dynamite" and "sickness" in "them there hills."

In terms of our frame of reference, the cultist, in spite of all the abstract knowledge he may possess, has little skill of dealing with his involvements with the multidimensional. And so it was with the trainees; they had little skill of dealing with these involvements. And this was what our program was about: how do you provide them with it? This was what we were trying to help them learn; this is what they were trying to learn. As we tried to do this, we found that we and they were engaged in no simple task. Had we been concerned with their involvements at the global level—their ideological beliefs and convictions—we truly would have been "sunk." But we were only concerned with their small day-to-day encounters and involvements with the concrete as observers, counselors, members, and leaders of small groups.

As they became more consciously involved in these simple daily encounters, all the dimensions we discussed previously came into play in a very simple but very central way. Their norms and ideals of behavior became involved; their conception of themselves became involved; their needs to survive in an environment became involved;

their "pet theories" and assumptions became involved. And because all these matters are fraught with tremendous personal significance (this was not a matter of just putting together a jigsaw puzzle), their feelings became involved quickly and strongly but in a very simple, direct, and immediate way observable to us and to them. These feelings needed to be expressed, recognized, sorted out, and worked through. They needed to be understood and "controlled" at this simple level. Remember we were not dealing with their feelings about republicans, democrats, communists, the underdog, democracy, and so forth. We were at a much lower and much more personal level. Remember we were carrying through two of our assumptions. (1) An internal development of maintaining a complexity of relationships within ourselves which must go hand in hand with the growing awareness of the complexity of relationships in concrete phenomena, and (2) it is from this process that "an organized system of capacity for response" develops and "skill" finally emerges.

As we have said before, for our trainees these encounters and involvements with the multidimensional territory presented a peculiarly significant conflict for them, because they were frequently accompanied by the need to be consistent with some cherished belief or principle of what one should be or how one should behave. But let us remember that just such involvements and conflicts—often expressed, of course, in forms quite different from the way our trainees expressed them—are the natural accompaniment of living. Each person resolves them—for better or for worse—regardless of whether or not he ever heard of human relations. We had no experiences which led us to believe that only our trainees exhibited these difficulties. Our training in itself did not create them. It did make the trainees more conscious of them, and it did not allow them to escape from them too easily or quickly.

HOW WE TRIED TO MEET THE THREE PROBLEMS

Let us summarize the ways in which we tried to meet these major problems of human relations training—the three problems of cultism, learning, and involvement:

1. By providing the trainees with experiences in different relationships which would make it difficult for them to cultivate one dimension exclusively, but which would allow them to develop their understanding of themselves and others along different dimensions at their own pace.

2. By giving them ample opportunity to discuss both in their own meetings and with us singly the conflicting feelings aroused by their involvements.

3. By helping them to think of these dimensions in terms of mutual interdependence, "organic wholes," and part-whole relationships—a way of thinking which allowed them "to make sense" of both their data and of their own feelings of inconsistency.

4. By trying to maintain an atmosphere of relaxedness, of not straining too hard, of not making a fetish of perfection, consistency, and certainty. In short, it was our belief that although normal learning was accompanied by frustration, once one could accept it, learning could also be fun, a lot of fun.

In the beginning we were interested in having all the trainees participate in all the five activities we provided, i.e., being (1) observers, (2) counselors, (3) members, and (4) leaders of groups as well as being (5) counseled when the situation required. The plan would not only give them a wide range of contexts in which to practice their skill but also was consistent with our conception of human relations skill. To us skill is a unitary phenomenon; it cannot be broken down into separate skills for special situations. In learning to understand others, for example, one is also learning to understand himself and vice versa. In learning to be a good group member, one is also learning the conditions for becoming a good group leader and vice versa.

Yet it is also true that one practices this unitary skill in quite different social contexts. At times—at least formally speaking—one is a member rather than a leader of a group. At other times he is in a formal position of leadership of a work or discussion group and is expected to exercise certain formal responsibilities. At times he is more a researcher than consultant or counselor to individuals and groups. At times he is involved in relationships where he is more concerned in understanding himself than others or in understanding others than himself.

In each of these different contexts human relations skill is practiced —in one sense, to be sure—differently, but not as a separate skill. What he sees and hears as a member or leader of or counselor or consultant to a group may not be much different, but the way he responds to what he sees and hears in these different contexts may be quite different. Nevertheless, in each case the skill of communicating ideas and feelings as well as responding to the ideas and feelings of others is present. That one's responses in these different contexts may vary does not make them different skills. It is this very character of the response which makes behavior skillful. Not to vary responses in these different contexts would be the character which would make them inadequate to a given point in a given situation. It would be failing to develop a growing awareness of the complexity of relationships in concrete phenomena and to respond accordingly.

Five Basic Contexts for the Practice of Human Relations Skill

Let us look again at the five contexts we had developed for the practice and learning of human relations skill. Each provided its own peculiar lessons.

Diagnostic Context. For this context the role of the trainee is primarily that of interviewer and observer. He is looking at and listening to the phenomena in the endeavor to understand them intelligently; he is not trying to help the people or groups understand themselves, although this aspect in our imperfect world cannot be completely ignored. In this context he is trying to diagnose as a totality what he sees and hears; he is trying to influence as little as possible by his own behavior the behavior of the people and groups he is observing. Therefore, his responses to what is being said and done in these groups are quite different on occasions from the way he would have responded had he been a working member or leader of such groups. He is not trying to be popular and liked; he is not trying to be unpopular or disliked. He is trying to gain acceptance for his role of impartial observer who is not evaluating favorably or unfavorably what he sees or hears or communicating such evaluations to others in the organization.

In this context the trainee is learning how to talk and think about people and groups intelligently and systematically. Granted that this way of *talking about* the phenomena is not the way of *talking with* the phenomena and to identify them would impede rather than facilitate communication, nevertheless this aspect of the trainees' skill cannot be ignored. To make of people merely objects of diagnosis—objects of one's own intellectual understanding—would be dangerous; on the other hand, to reduce human relations to being merely empathetic, intuitive, social, or to a matter of "feelings" would also be dangerous. It was our assumption that the head could work with (and not always against) the heart in matters of human relations. Rather than throwing the head out completely, we kept it in our "package" and through the process of sweating it out in other relationships, we hope these other experiences we are about to describe might pound some "sense" (skill) into it.

Counseling Context. In this context the trainee has the opportunity to learn how to listen to, observe, and *talk with* a troubled member of a group. He is not only trying to understand; he is trying to be of help and to secure understandings. Therefore his responses to what is said and done are different from what they would be were he merely trying to diagnose the "total situation" before him.

In this context the trainee also has the opportunity to observe the effect of what he says and does upon what the counselee says and does and also vice versa. He has the opportunity to recognize the counselee's feelings as well as his own and the effects of one upon the other. Here he begins to learn something about the previously described dimension three, "personality," why it cannot be ignored and also how it may be dealt with more skillfully. Of course all the other dimensions are present: how disturbed people are expected to talk and to whom they should talk according to the norms; what the ideal attitude toward people who are in trouble should be; how disturbed people should organize their lives more efficiently and scientifically. But, for the most part, these dimensions are in the background and need not trouble our trainee too much.

The major lessons we hope the trainee will learn—while doing the least harm and possibly being of some help—are that it is easier to *talk about* disturbed people than to *talk with* them; that also it is easier to want to help them than to be perceived as a source of help by them; and why in this imperfect world these things are so.

Membership Context. In this context the trainee is learning how to listen, observe, and *talk with* others as a member of a working or discussion group. Here he finds out further the limits of his diagnostic skill and intellectual understanding as such. To make of *his* group solely an object for his own personal understanding would be fatal. *This* group cannot be "used" for his needs alone. Neither can it be "used" as a place where, regardless of what he says and does, he can demand "complete" understanding of himself. He is now a part of the group whose purposes cannot be reduced to his feelings, hopes, expectations, and aspirations alone. He is a contributor to these purposes;

his contributions can help or impede these purposes. He is both in part determined by and in part a determiner of these purposes and of the way they are to be achieved.

In this context there are many difficult lessons for him to learn: how not to talk too much and yet how not to talk too little; how to express and not just repress his individual differences and feelings and yet how to repress and not only express his every little "precious feeling"; how to help in the chores which the members of the group have to perform; how to help other members of the group to express their feelings and differences and make their contributions, too.

In this context he has the opportunity to see the internal group structure emerge: the pairings and subgroups that form; the likings and dislikings that emerge among the members; the norms of behavior; the system of rewards and punishments that slowly but surely develop. Some of these patterns of behavior that emerge he may or may not like. But of these emergent phenomena he is in part a determiner as well as determined by them.

Usually our trainees do not see, understand, or appreciate these phenomena in their own group as well as they do in the groups they just observe. Their passion for intellectual understanding of these phenomena grows dim as they become themselves emotionally involved in them. This involvement is accompanied much more by wailing and gnashing of teeth than curiosity and intellectual passion for understanding. But these accompaniments are not from our point of view altogether bad. We knew of no better way for our trainees to gain some perspective and some "sense of humor." That in playing our part as members of a group we often are not "perfect members" but rather something approaching what for want of a better word we shall call "human"—frail, weak, and imperfect but still capable of some small learning—is no mean lesson to learn.

Of all the lessons our trainee can learn from being a member of a group, the most questionable, in our experience, is what he learns from the formal leader of the group of which he is a member. No other relationship is so fraught with the possibilities of misunderstanding and miscommunication. In this relation more than any other there is more opportunity of learning the "wrong lessons." Too often the trainee's ambivalences toward authority come sharply into focus. The leader becomes too often somebody to be copied and imitated, looked up to, and dependent upon or else somebody with feet of clay to be criticized, cajoled, gotten around, or rid and independent of. What the member of a group can usefully learn from the leader, of course, depends in good part but not entirely upon the leader's behavior. It is not until the member becomes the formal leader himself that he has the opportunity to learn some lessons that cannot be learned in any other context.

Leadership Context. In this context the trainee has the opportunity to listen, observe, and *talk with* others as the formal leader of a work or discussion group. Here he can practice in a position of responsibility all his understandings and insights about himself and others and groups. And here he can learn what up to now has been difficult to explain or "tell him"; he (the imperfect, uncertain, and inconsistent "he") is now asked to play the role of "perfection," "certainty," and "consistency"—the role he has asked others to play with such conspicuous failure. His members keep asking him, "Are you not the leader? Don't you know the answers? Should you not set the perfect example? Don't you know what is right on all occasions? Say, what the hell is going on here? Get wise to yourself, buddy!!"

Cast in the role of "perfection," "certainty," and "consistency," our trainee squirms. He does not like it. "You can't do this to me. I'm just one of the boys; I just work around here," he says. But remorselessly the wheels of the gods grind on. Up to now our trainee has expected to be understood. His parents with difficulty have tried to understand him, albeit from his point of view with great lack of skill. He has been misunderstood before, to be sure, but never has he been misunderstood when he is in that enviable position of gaining understanding—the leader. Now that he has the authority to get other people to listen to him and to do things (all his education has assured him) things will be easy. All he would have to do would be to be logical, lucid, clear, permissive, group-centered, democratic, efficient, and himself to boot and he would be understood. His parents and teachers had not understood these matters too well, but he has learned about them from courses in human relations, administration, and the social sciences. His success has been assured. The new behavioral sciences have guaranteed it!

But alas, things do not go along too well. Members do not understand him or his behavior too well; they don't hear what he says; they are not sure he himself understands what permissiveness means. "You never told me this," he bitterly cries. "You mean that I cannot expect to be understood; that my function as leader is not to get others to understand me. Say, what is going on here? Nobody ever told me that I had to learn to live in a world where if I did all the 'right things' I would still be misunderstood. Say, what kind of a world is this? How am I to practice understanding when nobody understands me? This ain't fair."

Our trainee is being sorely tried. His passion for intellectual understanding of himself and others grows dimmer and dimmer. This is not the game his education has prepared him to play. It is a bitter pill to swallow and some trainees swallow it more gracefully than others; some won't swallow it at all; some don't see the pill to be swallowed.

We don't press this experience.

Personal Context. In spite of what our critics may say, we are not sadistically preparing our trainee for the "analyst's couch." The processes we are talking about are very common ones which occur in each of us every day and night and which are not or need not be explored only in the office of a psychiatrist. As we become more and more consciously involved in the increasing complexity of relationships about us, feelings are aroused. These feelings are intimately related to the dimensions we discussed previously. As we have said before, our norms and ideals of behavior become involved, our conceptions of ourselves become involved, our need to survive in an environment becomes involved, our assumptions and feelings become involved. These feelings need to be expressed, recognized, sorted out, and worked through. They need to be understood and "controlled."

How do we learn to deal with these uncomfortable and contradictory feelings that our involvement in these "organic wholes" produces and from which there is no escape? These feelings we all have to deal with in some fashion or other, for better or for worse. Can we learn to deal with them—not perfectly but better? Our educational system has little to say on this subject. In real life it is left pretty much up to the individual himself—until his reflections become pretty "screwed up." The assumption upon which our educational system operates is that these feelings, will disappear as the student gains more "knowledge." But this was not our experience with our trainees, ourselves, or others. It seemed often to work in reverse. The more "knowledge" we acquired, the more acute these feelings became. To deal with these feelings, our trainees needed another experience in another context.

This is the context of learning to recognize, listen to, and respond to his own feelings. Could our trainees be helped in this process and how? Our trainees needed to learn to *talk about people* intelligently; they needed to learn to *talk with people* with understanding and skill. Did they not also need to learn *to talk with and respond to themselves* more understandingly and skillfully? This is the context where the trainee would have the opportunity of looking at and trying to make sense of his own preoccupations and feelings. If our analysis of "skill" is correct, must not these three kinds of learning be developed together?

To us, as we have said before, this last development is one of the most serious problems the human relations approach faces. In our present culture there is something morbid about this process. It smacks of pathology, introspection, introversion, and things of this sort often judged "unpleasant." As educators we wish to keep our hands clean, to leave this matter up to the psychiatrist. But can we escape the responsibility of looking at the consequences—both good and bad—of learning?

In this process of learning to control better this "internal chatter" we all have with ourselves about our involvements with people and groups, can we be helped by education? Or is this to be left alone to the individual himself and the aid of the psychiatrist? We could not quite accept this latter alternative. It seemed to us that in our complex industrial civilization these feelings were becoming more and more acute and were being dealt with not only by the psychiatrist but often in the first instance more or less adequately by many others. As a matter of fact, there were not enough psychiatrists to go around. We did not wish to intrude in this private domain; nevertheless, we could not ignore it. We did not encourage the expression of these feelings; we did not discourage them, but we tried to put no obstacles in the way of the trainees should they wish to explore and understand them. We gave them opportunity to do this on many occasions. They could do it by themselves, with other trainees, singly, with ourselves singly, and on occasions even in the group. And should they feel they still required more, they could go out of the group for help. Our only warning was that when we engaged in such activities, we wanted to do them honestly; "let's not pretend we are doing something else." By keeping this process out in the open, as something matter-of-fact, as something that did not need to be done surreptitiously, as a problem we all shared in common, we tried to keep it "healthy." On this difficult but sometimes amusing problem, it was our feeling that the last and most important lesson our trainee had to learn was that before he could learn to help others, he had to learn to accept help also without feeling humiliated —that last bitter pill which his educational system had not prepared him to swallow or even to see. And he had to learn that this help could come not only from "authority" (papa, teacher, or psychiatrist) but also from his contemporaries.

16 A Revolution in Thought

I made these remarks on October 25, 1956, in New York City when I accepted the Taylor Key Award from the Society for the Advancement of Management. The Society's journal, *Advanced Management,* published them in March 1957 and has granted permission for republication here.

The latent content of these remarks was to clarify the grounds on which I was honored to receive the Taylor Key Award. Although I had a great respect for Frederick Taylor, I was not sure that his road and my road to professional competence were quite one and the same, and I felt this needed to be clarified because I didn't want to sail under any false colors.

It seems to me that the philosophy of management is undergoing a revolution in thought comparable to the Copernican revolution of the sixteenth century. At that time the earth was regarded as fixed with the sun revolving about it. Copernicus suggested that a more fruitful conception might be to regard the sun as fixed with the earth revolving around it. This new conceptual outlook, although it explained more facts more systematically, was viewed with alarm and consternation. It seemed to run counter to the facts of common-sense observation. But, more than this, it seemed to dethrone man from his central position in the universe. If I may be permitted to draw an analogy it seems to me that our business world is going through a very similar upheaval.

The traditional and common-sense outlook says that management occupies the central and fixed position around which the organization revolves and that from this fixed position all things are to be evaluated and measured. This way of thinking fits well with the facts of our daily observations about the movements of the executive, just as the Ptolemaic or pre-Copernican way of thinking fitted well with the facts of daily observation about the movement of the sun. Just as we see the sun rise and set, so do we see the executive issue orders, make decisions, settle questions of policy, fix goals and objectives, and set the standards by which the activities of others are measured and evaluated.

But the pre-Copernican outlook failed to take into account a wider range of observations about the movements of the planets. In the same manner the traditional outlook of management as occupying the central position around which the organization revolves fails to take into account a wider range of observations about organizations and the behavior of people in them. What it has difficulty in accounting for are many observations that would seem to suggest that the more the executive practices literally the common-sense point of view, and the more he measures all things in terms of *his* standards, the more he loses the cooperation and personal development of the people he administers. This is a serious state of affairs for the executive. He cannot do his job alone; he needs the help and cooperation of others. What water is to a fish, so an organization of people is to an executive.

This state of affairs also poses a serious dilemma for the student of administration. For in trying to make sense of the common-sense outlook he finds himself in the awkward position of trying to conceptualize what the behavior of an executive would be if he were not involved in and a member of an organization, i.e., what a fish out of water should be like, besides being dead.

As a consequence some students of administration feel the need to change their outlook. The traditional conception of management as measuring all things from one absolute fixed point, they find no longer useful. A more fruitful way of thinking about organizations and the relations of executives to them is needed. What is required are measurements of an organization from different points of view as well as from a point of view which takes these different points of view into account. Therefore they conceptualize a business organization as a social system analogous to the solar system, i.e., as a system of mutually interdependent parts in which management plays an important but not the stellar role.

This new conception, quite naturally, is viewed with alarm in certain quarters. It sounds strange to our common-sense ears. It seems to deny the centrality of management's position around which all things revolve. For those who have these feelings, may I offer one observation. The history of civilization has shown that when man has divested himself of egocentricity and anthropomorphism he has become not only more effective but also more moral, mature, and civilized as well. In the same manner I believe that the more the executive can accept gracefully the fact that the organization does not revolve solely around him, the better executive he will become. When he begins to measure things from many different points of view and not only his own, what at first may feel like the beginning of his end will become the beginning of a new adventure and his growth into professional competence.

17   Management's Mission in a New Society

This was my contribution on September 5, 1958, to the Harvard Business School's 50th Anniversary Conference on Management's Mission in a New Society. It was published with other contributions from this conference in *Management's Mission in a New Society*, edited by Dan H. Fenn, Jr., copyright © 1959 by the McGraw-Hill Book Company, Inc., which granted me permission to reproduce my contribution here.

This paper was preceded by papers from Professor George F. F. Lombard and Professor Abraham Zaleznik on which I drew heavily in my remarks; and in the absence of those contributions it lacks some contextual reference. Nevertheless I am including it because it came at an interesting time. In 1958 at its 50th anniversary, the B-School was beginning to feel the effects of the so-called "second industrial revolution" and the "knowledge explosion." The new specializations had begun to arrive and things were no longer quiet on the B-School front. So I mounted my white charger again but this time I had some powerful allies. Research and development, or R & D, had come to town, even though the "D" in "R & D" stood mostly for "product development" and not "people development."

In this paper I make great use of John Kenneth Galbraith's concept of "conventional wisdom," to which he devotes a chapter in his book, *The Affluent Society*. By "conventional wisdom" Galbraith is referring to the acceptable ideas of our times—beliefs which we tend to accept without question. Those beliefs do not necessarily separate liberals from conservatives, or Adam Smith from Karl Marx. In terms of them, both sides are sometimes making the same assumptions.

Human relations research and training have a contribution to make to the theme "management's mission in a new society." Research can help to bring it down to earth by providing some facts on which to focus our thinking. Training can focus it on one aspect about which each of us can do something now if he so chooses.

What is the essential feature of our new society? For me it is the inability of its built-in ideas to cope with the march of events and problems. The obsolescence of today's conventional social wisdom—whether it be the conventional wisdom of conservatives or liberals, businessmen or academicians—is the most characteristic feature of our times.[1]

Such a daily exposure of inadequacy is anxiety-producing. It tends to excite an excessively vigorous defense of, or attack on, conventional

1. See John Kenneth Galbraith, *The Affluent Society* (Boston: Houghton Mifflin, 1958).

wisdom or a complete withdrawal from the scene of battle. Experience has shown that neither of these resolutions is entirely satisfactory. For the individual they spell frustration; for the society they mean that little gets accomplished. We wait for the march of events—a major war or a depression—to compensate for the limitations in our conventional wisdom, and, as we all know, this is likely to be wasteful and inefficient.

Research is a more efficient and rational way of changing our ideas before a catastrophe makes it imperative that we do so. Mr. Zaleznik gives us an example of this method. He takes an area, such as the motivation, productivity, and satisfaction of workers, about which the conventional wisdom makes many assertions. He observes a small work group, and in terms of his study finds the conventional wisdom wanting. He calls his findings paradoxes. Being more intellectually stimulating and less anxiety-producing, a paradox can be rationally resolved. Findings in themselves are not paradoxical. Paradoxes exist and persist only in relation to certain fixed beliefs which vanish completely under a different set of assumptions. It is thus that new and better theories are born.

Let us note some of the other attributes of this method. Although it bears other conventional names, it can be called the method of limited withdrawal, of piecemeal attack, and of minimizing the risk of being caught napping on the intellectual front. This is not the method of an angry, apprehensive, or dogmatic man; it is the method of a bemused man seeking order in his universe.

Thus, in the midst of battle when verbal arguments are flying thick and fast, we do not find Mr. Zaleznik mounting his white charger and doing battle for or against the conventional wisdom: i.e., talking louder and faster about things he has never observed or never could observe and verify. Rather, like a good strategist of verbal combat, he starts retreating to a level where he can observe something against which his ideas and the conventional wisdom can be checked.

With the competence of a man who knows his business, he knocks six small but sturdy nails into the coffin of conventional wisdom about matters of worker motivation, productivity, and satisfaction. This is no wholesale massive onslaught; rather, it is a limited, piecemeal approach which in the long run has some chance of success. One good nail well placed has put some pieces of conventional wisdom permanently to rest.

Let us not be too optimistic. We must remember that the march of events and circumstances can deal heavier blows to the conventional wisdom of our times than a few facts of research. Nevertheless, research does minimize the risk of being caught short when the time comes. In suggesting research as a way for management to minimize risks rather than to maximize profits in the new society, I realize that I am choosing an idea that runs counter to the conventional wisdom of our times and is therefore likely to be unpopular. This wisdom asserts that the businessman is by nature a risk taker, so that the reduction of risk is abhorrent to his soul. Instead, the search for and glorification of risk and insecurity are attributes more natural to him. Nevertheless, I shall risk this unpopularity and address my remarks to the way I find businessmen behaving, rather than to their portrait according to the conventional wisdom of the past.

Human relations has more to offer the thoughtful executive than some research findings against which he can test his preconceived ideas. It can also help him to improve his practice in relating himself to others in a work group. This approach is not in itself research, but it does include one of its essential features—observation.

Human relations has always retained the small group as a major focus of its studies. Let me cite some reasons for this:

(1) This focus has allowed theory and practice to be developed together.

(2) The small group is something which can be observed easily.

(3) Besides offering excellent opportunities for concrete observation, the small group is the concrete unit in which much of the world's work is done. Moreover, it is the unit in which men obtain those rewards and satisfactions that make them willing to work.

(4) It contains and keeps together all the major dimensions with which the administrator's job is concerned. It holds not only the specialized tasks that need to be done if the group's purpose is to be attained but also the individuals that are supposed to be doing them. In it we can find not only the unique individuals who do the work but also the relationships that are required and that develop among them. It contains values and sentiments which each member realizes in varying degrees. It includes followers and leaders, members of high and low standing, and members who like and dislike each other. It contains norms of acceptable behavior by which the regular members abide.

(5) All these dimensions exist together in one interrelated, organic,

living whole. Thus, the small work group is a little society; it is not society in general, or in the abstract; it is a small, living, particular social organism in which we are all intimately involved as members or leaders.

(6) Thus, as a formal leader of a work group, the supervisor or executive is not just a disinterested observer. He is also an involved member. This involvement brings in the most critical variables of all—the administrator's assumptions, which often determine his perception and feelings.

So the small group offers the executive or supervisor an opportunity for obtaining a better intellectual understanding of the medium in which he works. It also offers him a daily opportunity to practice and improve his skills in that medium. In the small group he can learn to make better clinical observation of his own behavior and the behavior of others under the burden of responsibility. He can see the fixed roles he plays and how he often fulfills his own needs through them more than the needs of the group. If he is interested, he can begin to become more perceptive of the roles that the group requires on different occasions to maintain its integrity so that it can secure its objectives. He sees how these contributions can be made without trying to fulfil! all these roles himself. To do this he has to learn to "control" (retrain and re-educate) his feelings, which too often get in the way.

The answers to the major question about management's mission, then, can be sought most fruitfully through this kind of hand-to-hand development of research and practice. Management's mission in a new society is not merely a matter for public proclamation or grandiose generalization; it is a subject for meticulous research that can result in better intellectual understanding and improved practices.

For the executive needs to understand not only his "relations to society" with a capital S but also his relation to society with a small s —the society with which he is intimately involved and which he can affect directly here and now. In this context, he can begin to correct and modify his behavior in the light of facts rather than in the glow of the conventional beliefs of his times. Here he can begin, for example, to understand the conditions of the "frozen groups" he often administers, the part he plays in these conditions, the more useful roles he might perform to assist in their unfreezing, and how he might go about performing these roles. At this level, his mission in the new society can become internalized in a code of professional competence. Short of this achievement, all we will get is grandiose talk and generalization.

The development of such a code must become the objective of our business schools. Business education will have to do more than train managers in the conventional wisdom of business for the fixed, inherent, and traditional managerial roles of yesterday. The managers of the new society will need a new kind of education to provide the intellectual understanding and skills that the new society requires.

This new training will need strong support, because the going will be rough. If we go in this direction, we will have to give up many notions of executive behavior—of what the conventional wisdom asserts that it is or ought to be. It will require, moreover, the cooperation of the "long hairs" and several other species whom businessmen have traditionally tended to view with suspicion and even alarm. But although the going will be rough, what is the alternative? To go it alone is a bit of intellectual arrogance that the manager of the new society will no longer be able to retain if he is to remain its leader very long.

18 Human Relations: Trends and Termites

I wrote this for the *Harbus News,* the Harvard Business School's weekly student newspaper, which published it on January 16, 1959. At the beginning of each new calendar year, it was customary for the *Harbus News* to publish economic forecasts for that year by the leading economists at the B-School. Being thought of as a *"here and now* butterfly chaser," I was somewhat nonplussed at being asked to become a *"there and then* crystal ball gazer." Nevertheless, I decided to forecast what the "knowledge explosion" might mean for the faculty and doctoral students at business schools, whom I classified into (1) termites, i.e. those who by their researches were undermining the conventional wisdom of business whether they knew it or not, and (2) nontermites, i.e., those that were still teaching it. I then classified the different kinds of termites among us. Let not the reader be misled by my facetious remarks. Behind the scenes there was much wailing and gnashing of teeth. The good old days at the B-School had gone forever.

When the editors of the *Harbus News* included me among 1959's forecasters, I was not sure whether this meant that human relations had arrived or that it had fallen into more disrepute. It is difficult to establish trends in something which has hardly gotten off the ground and where people differ about what it is—a good or bad word, an abstraction, a currently useful generalization, or something which exists outside of somebody's skin. The way it has of getting under some people's skins, although far from conclusive, suggests some external reality. So let me begin here.

Some thirty years ago human relations started as an inquiry into how people in organizations do behave—not should behave. This was a revolutionary idea at that time. In most quarters it still is; so there has not been much progress along this front. There is no evidence to suggest that this trend will change drastically in 1959. It is expected that during this year most business educators will continue to speak about how businessmen should behave. It is expected that this will continue to have about the same effect upon the behavior of business-men as it has had in the past.

Nevertheless in 1959 an increased number of non-organization men will continue to study behavior in organizations. They will continue to unearth more facts in this fertile field for research. All these new facts, there is reason to believe, will continue to reveal the same drift that the old facts have. Nobody in business from worker to president seems to be behaving, from any frame of reference except his own, the way he should. So long as no one insists upon knowing what this means, 1959. should be a peaceful year. But this is too much to ask.

In the early days of their exploration these "human termites," as we shall call these researchers of behavior in organizations, were naive. They thought that the facts would speak for themselves. Before their blast, the mythology of business administration, like the walls of Jericho, would crumble. But bitter experiences gradually showed them their error. Facts—particularly human ones—do not speak for themselves; they require interpreters.

But who are these interpreters to be? In fields like human relations there still exists quite a number of competing interpreters. For this reason it will be necessary to establish a rough classification of the major kinds of termites, each of whom slants the facts somewhat differently. For lack of space, not all species will be included.

1. *Pure termites:* Well-intentioned creatures but highly misunderstood by nontermites. Research creatures who collect facts and by theory transmute them into substance which, to nontermites, often still looks like sawdust.

2. *Applied termites (A):* Those creatures who interpret the above facts and theories for administration and administrators.

3. *Applied termites (B):* Those creatures who collect facts for students and executives to interpret.

4. *Pseudo or mixed-up termites:* Those creatures who have given up their undermining activities and want to make the facts palatable, or who have a conflict about undermining and supporting the conventional wisdom at the same time.

5. *Doctoral termites (A):* Younger termites who have the freedom (opportunity, challenge) to choose a traditional special business field to undermine.

6. *Doctoral termites (B):* Younger termites who have chosen to develop a new field which includes several disciplines to undermine.

But which of these kinds of termites is good or bad? This varies but it is settled for short periods of time by the intellectual and social climate which prevails at that time. Three very powerful forces and symbols of forces have helped to settle the intellectual and social climate for 1959—Professor Malcolm P. McNair, Sputnik, and the Ford Foundation. The climate which these forces have wrought is so well established that it is not likely to change during the year. Being able to treat it as a constant makes certain kinds of predictions relatively easy. It allows us to reduce the above six categories to three:

Categories 1, 2, and 6 become "good termites"; category 4 is composed of "bad termites"; and categories 3 and 5 remain "unsettled." That is, the abovementioned three forces are not working together in perfect harmony to produce clear, and distinct, good or bad termites. I am now ready to make my predictions.

1. The extermination of bad termites will continue in 1959. Although it is expected that all pseudo termites will continue to say they are not bad—not really—this declaration will not suffice. Plans are in progress to stop them from pleading good intentions and ignorance.

2. It is doubtful if these stern measures for stopping the infiltration of pseudo, mixed-up, and frustrated termites in the field of human relations will, in themselves, do the whole job that needs to be done in 1959. But they will help. For what these measures will do in the direction of exterminating bad termites will be complemented by the Ford Foundation with other measures in another direction for producing good termites, and so together progress is expected.

3. To meet the shortage of good termites, the Ford Foundation will continue to sponsor programs to produce good termites as quickly as possible. These programs, it is expected, will be installed in business schools to produce doctoral termites. As the Ford Foundation made no clear policy statements about how it stands on doctoral termites (A), business schools and doctoral termites (A) are likely to remain somewhat confused until this situation is clarified.

4. The vying of applied institutions for pure termites and the vying of pure termites for applied institutions will reach greater proportions in 1959 than they did in 1958. No respectable applied institution will be without a pure termite on its faculty. He will act as a multiplier of good termites and a builder of symbolic bridges between pure termites and applied termites (B), who it will be remembered the total social climate has not clearly defined as good or bad.

5. The policy of allowing younger doctoral termites (A) to choose a traditional special business field to undermine will have no appreciable effect in 1959. Short of a world crisis, the disappearance of these traditional fields is not expected in doctoral programs until about 1970 and in MBA programs until 2000 A.D.

So to summarize briefly: 1959 will be a bad year for bad termites. There will be some undefined termites who will be frustrated. Some will learn; some will be permitted to withdraw. But never will good termites have it so good.

19 On Elton Mayo

This is the introduction, dated January 1, 1960, that I wrote for the Viking Press edition of Elton Mayo's *The Human Problems of an Industrial Civilization*, copyright © 1960 by The Viking Press, Inc. I am reprinting it by permission of The Viking Press, Inc. The book had originally been published in 1933.

Writing this piece on Mayo was for me a great pleasure. I had been greatly indebted to him in more ways than one. I thought his great contribution had been much maligned and misunderstood and I was eager to try and set the record straight. I shared the opinion of a waitress in Harvard Square who when she heard of Mayo's death said, "Mayo was a great man. I don't know if Harvard knew it but we did; he understood us."

In what respects, other than historical, are the findings and conclusions of Mayo's *The Human Problems of an Industrial Civilization* still of importance today?

For me this question is not impersonal. I worked with Mayo for twenty years, from 1927, when I joined forces with him at the Harvard Business School, to 1947, when he retired. (He died in 1949.) I listened to him when he was preparing the chapters of this small volume in the form in which they first appeared as Lowell Lectures. I was involved in some of the experiments he was writing about. Insofar as any person is privileged to know another, I knew Mayo, not only in his different social roles of husband, father, teacher, researcher, and friend, but also as a person, as a restless, curious, creative mind.

It would be difficult to estimate the hours I spent with him in personal discussions of problems ranging from my own to those of the multiverse. But mostly these discussions focused on the nature of the scientific enterprise: more in particular, on the problem of how we learn to know about ourselves and others in their relation to each other, and more in general, on how such an understanding and knowledge might affect the leadership of our age.

During the past thirty years I have also witnessed the reactions of others to Mayo and his writings. On the one hand, I saw a group of younger men stimulated to do field research. I saw them forego the pleasures of arguing about unanswerable questions, or empirical questions for which there were no data, and instead go into the field and, as they say in anthropology, "talk with the natives," listen and observe, and with these "crude" (from the point of view of 1960) tools and data see what they could find out.

On the other hand, I also saw in the 1950's (the era of the cold war and the agonizing re-reappraisals of intellectuals) a mounting concern with Mayo's ideological and personal beliefs. Was he for or against trade unions? Was he a fascist or a Communist? Was he preaching the gospel of Saint Luke or "Saint" Freud? Was he the arch priest of conservatism, the tool of business, and the exponent of the status quo? Did he believe in democracy, progress, competition, and the free-enterprise system? Had he sired "the organization man"? Was he pro- or anti-intellectual? Did he believe in conflict or cooperation, freedom or determinism, conformity or independence? Was he for the individual or for the group? Was he a prophet of doom or a prophet of hope?

To have to admit that this war was waged by intellectuals and academics and by men called political and social scientists makes me still blush with shame for my "reference group." That men who called themselves "scientists" should understand so little the nature of scientific questions and evidence appalled me.

AS I SAW MAYO

Let's face it. I cannot talk about *The Human Problems* as if all these things had not happened. As I thumb through the book now, each page provokes only memories of the living reality that underlies the words, and for which the words are now but a pale substitute. For me, Mayo—the living reality I knew—was a man of imagination, a stimulator of thought, a promoter of clinical research, and the discoverer of a useful way of thinking about organization behavior that could be developed fruitfully in the directions of both knowledge and practice. This last is for me by far his greatest contribution. It is the one least understood. It is the one most relevant to a 1960 audience.

But before proceeding to this point, let me clear up one matter. Mayo was not a systematic thinker. Although he stated his ideas vigorously, he never stated them rigorously. His accomplishments are best seen in the context of face-to-face relationships. His chief products were the people that he influenced and helped to develop. Even the ideas that he developed in books were more often in the nature of seeds to be cultivated in the field than of rigorous hypotheses to be tested in the laboratory.

But let us observe more carefully. In the minds of some hardy investigators his seeds did grow into more systematic statements and more testable propositions. To give the devil his due, his ideas were at least capable of that development.

They were also capable of another development. They also had significance for the practitioner who was interested in improving his skills. From them there developed in the late 1940's and 1950's "the human relations in industry movement." During that period this development was one of Mayo's adolescent children. It incorporated all his enthusiasms, his sense of adventure, and his zest for living; in most of its phases it did not so well incorporate his more sophisticated and erudite side.

It was both Mayo's strength and his weakness that he never discriminated, in terms of professional, educational, academic, disciplinary, or social background, among the different people with whom he communicated. Regardless of backgrounds, he was interested in people who were curious and could work with ideas. Thus at this level he talked with practitioners and scientists alike, with grammar-school graduates and Ph.D.'s alike, with instructors and professors alike, with "ologists$_1$" and "ologists$_2$," alike, and with workers and presidents alike. It is little wonder that in these different soils his seeds grew in different forms and at different rates; some never sprouted at all and some, after a short bloom, withered on the vine.

Just the other day I had lunch with a man who had come in touch with Mayo some twenty years ago. This man was at that time a member of the younger generation and he was then, as a union leader, in the thick of the labor struggle at one of its most dramatic periods. I forget the occasion that brought him to Harvard, or what Mayo said that prompted him to talk. But very soon he was telling Mayo and the rest of us about his experiences and he regaled us with story after story. And what was the gist of his stories? How again and again, after all management's experts had gone into a work department to improve its productivity and had succeeded in raising it only zero to 2 per cent, he had gone in and listened to and talked with the workers, and productivity had increased 20 to 40 per cent.

At that time, around 1940, observations of the kind that this man made were rare. The air was so filled with accusations and recriminations that no one had much chance to look and observe. This young man's capacity to observe amidst the tumult and shouting intrigued

Mayo. He never let such capacities go unrewarded. As a result of this first conversation there followed many other conversations with Mayo and our group that were mutually rewarding. But then, as so often happens with the passage of time, we lost touch.

So I was interested to meet this now middle-aged man again the other day. He told me how he had left the union some years ago, gone into business, been very successful, and had recently sold his business because there was something else he now wanted to do—and this is what he wanted to tell me. For twenty years he had been writing a book on "What is America?" which he now wished to publish.

When, with some trepidation, I explored with him the contents of his proposed book, I found that the gist of his message was something like this. (I hope I do it justice when I put it in my own words.) He told me that what America stood for was *self-development for everybody, everywhere.* It was on this premise that he had been successful as a union and a management leader. It was on this premise that his business with his foreign customers had grown. He was very careful to tell me that his doctrine was not pro- or anti-union, pro- or anti-management, pro- or anti- any one particular nation. It envisaged growth for unions as well as for management; growth for the U.S.S.R. as well as for the U.S.A. It stood for growth for everybody, everywhere. This, as he saw it, was (is, could be—I did not press) America.

This is how he now stated what he felt was important in his more than twenty years of experience in different kinds of leadership. And to whom did he feel indebted for this discovery? To Mayo.

In a refreshing way, this man had stated Mayo's credo far better than I had ever been able to state it for myself. In a flash I saw the source of Mayo's genius as well as of his being misunderstood. At that moment I knew what it was that I wanted to say in this foreword to *The Human Problems,* particularly to the new reader for whom the "ists" and the "ologists" had not as yet pumped the book dry.

MAYO'S CONCEPTUAL SCHEME

Among Mayo's great accomplishments was his stubborn refusal to be "split by a false dichotomy." But the price he paid for this achievement was misunderstanding. Thus when Mayo advocated the development of society's elite as well as of its masses, he aroused suspicion. To many, we have to be for one or the other; we cannot stand for both.

But for Mayo, we cannot have one development without the other, and this is where his credo goes beyond sentiment and begins to take on the properties of a guiding hypothesis or conceptual scheme. The behavior of workers, to take an example, cannot be studied fruitfully apart from the behavior of management; one affects and is affected by the other; they are mutually interdependent. To Mayo this was no ideological dogma; it was a more fruitful hypothesis for observation. Note how in chapter after chapter he suggests a "natural system model" for the study of organizational behavior.

What are the conclusions, for example, of his first two chapters on "fatigue" and "monotony"? That these are not fruitful focuses for the study of the complex problems of modern industrial organizations. Why? "Fatigue is not an entity but merely a convenient word to describe a variety of phenomena" (Chapter I). "Monotony, like fatigue, is a word which is used to denote any sort of induced unbalance in the worker" (Chapter II). And what for him would be more fruitful? To *observe* "the many possibilities of such unbalance in different individuals and different situations." And what would be a more fruitful scheme for such observations? Alas, here is where Mayo's lack of rigor shows up. The answer to this question lies more in brilliant flashes of insight and in the total context of the book than in an explicit statement in any part of it.

Let us take, for example, a statement from his chapter on "Theories of Government and the Social Order": "The problem is not that of the sickness of an acquisitive society; it is that of the acquisitiveness of a sick society." When the new reader reaches this sentence, let him not immediately raise the question: "Is it true or false?" Instead, let him ask: "Which of these two hypotheses is more fruitful for empirical investigation?" Granted that Mayo's "twisteroo" is an overstatement; is it an interesting overstatement partaking of some of the growth properties of Copernicus' overstatement about the movement of the earth in relation to the sun? Does it allow new and more interesting observations to be made?

To the scientist who is primarily interested in the hypothesis-testing end of the scientific enterprise continuum, Mayo has little to say. But to the scientist who is also interested in the hypothesis-generating end of this continuum, he has plenty to contribute. Mayo, it might be said, was the enemy of the sterile hypothesis and of the meaningless correlation of high statistical significance.

Although Mayo was for the opportunity for growth for everybody, everywhere, he recognized the possibility of lopsided growth. He saw that many things, both desirable ones and undesirable ones, can be both functional and dysfunctional. Restriction of output among workers, for instance, although functional for the solidarity of the group and the emotional security of its members, is dysfunctional for the group's identification with the economic objectives of the enterprise.

But frozen states of equilibrium are not inevitable; they are man-made, and new ways of thinking can liquidate them. In *The Human Problems,* Mayo is giving birth to such a new way of thinking. Let the new reader concentrate on this agony of birth and he will be reading this book from the "growth" end up. What Mayo is saying is: Let's study organizations as natural organic wholes or systems striving to survive and maintain their equilibrium in different environments. Let's see if this way of looking at them will allow us to specify better the many factors in a complex situation and "wherever the general effect is unsatisfactory to the worker and to industry, to discover the nature of the disequilibrium and the source of the interference."

Let's note that this conceptual scheme is essentially a model for clinical and diagnostic inquiry with significant overtones for the practitioner. Mayo spells this out in his last chapter "The Problem of the Administrator." But let's not underestimate this accomplishment. What Copernicus, Galileo, and Newton did to Aristotle, Mayo's way of thinking also did to the dogmas of his day about organizational behavior. It reduced them to the status of empirical questions, that is, questions to be settled by observation and judgment and not by argument and debate.

On the relations of theory to practice and of knowledge to skill, Mayo's thesis is clear. The fruitful development of one is dependent upon the fruitful development of the other. Failure to achieve this balance leads to lopsidedness. In this lopsided growth, Mayo sees the human problems of our industrial civilization. He therefore stresses that "the earliest study must therefore be clinical" and that the first theories must be fruitful for the observation–skill end of the scientific enterprise continuum. Thus on the development of clinical and analytical knowledge, Mayo's position is: Not only can we not have one without the other, but also, we cannot have the second before the first. Analytical knowledge will flourish best only when the ingredient of logic is added to the observations, uniformities, and syndromes of preceding clinical studies.

THE QUESTIONS MAYO RAISES

What does Mayo have to say to a 1960 reader? Let me summarize by stating questions that he addresses to readers in several walks of life.

To the ideologically inclined: Are you as concerned with the development of society's leaders as with the development of society's masses?

To the scientifically inclined: Are you as concerned with the growth ideas of the scientific enterprise as with its products, technology, and hardware?

To the political leader (in economically underdeveloped or over-developed countries): Are you as concerned with the social development of your people as with raising their standard of living?

To the union or management leader: Are you as preoccupied with the growth and social motivation of your members or subordinates as with their wages and working conditions? Are you as concerned with the effect of your behavior on others as with the effect of their behavior on you?

To the business educator or student: Are you as concerned with the executive's social functions as with his task functions?

To the action-oriented: Are you as concerned with developing your understanding as with taking action? Are you as concerned with controlling your own behavior as with controlling the behavior of others?

To the individual person (regardless of reference group): Are you as concerned with your own self-development as with belonging and status?

ARE THESE QUESTIONS RELEVANT TODAY?

If you read this book carefully you will discover a way of thinking and methods that will help you find out whether these questions are still relevant today. And if you reach that stage, you will know what Mayo means by "lopsidedness" and the human problems of an industrial civilization and why he thinks that these problems are essentially *human* and essentially the same in Moscow, Peiping, Tokyo, Jakarta, New Delhi, Cairo, Rome, Paris, London, and New York. You will know why he says that "as ever in human affairs, we are struggling against our own ignorance and not against the machinations of a political adversary."

Cambridge, Massachusetts
January 1, 1960

20 Elton Mayo's Thesis

These unpublished notes were prepared by me in February 1962 for discussion in a seminar of doctoral candidates in the area of Organizational Behavior at the Harvard Business School. I am including them here because I think that Mayo's thesis is based upon one of the most perceptive diagnoses of the ills of the modern world that I have ever seen, and that it is as relevant today as when he first wrote about it. New words are used nowadays but the conditions to which they refer have not changed. As I see it, the "social disorganization" to which Mayo referred then is being expressed today (1968), for example, in terms of "alienation," "identity crises," "semantic confusions," "role conflicts," "hippies," "psychedelic drugs," "black power," "tell 'em like it is, baby," "urban crises," and "credibility gaps."

The footnotes in this piece, unlike those in the other essays in this collection, are being supplied in 1968.

Elton Mayo's thesis is composed of a large number of large-scale tendency statements at a fairly high level of abstraction, all of which, however, can be conceived of as pointing to where social science might begin to observe. Let me illustrate what I mean by stating first, Mayo's diagnosis; second, his proposed solution; and third, my comments about them.*

MAYO'S DIAGNOSIS

1. In the absence of an explicit understanding of the determinants of cooperative effort, rapid technological and scientific advance tends to be associated with increased social disorganization.

2. By "social disorganization" Mayo means a disruption (loosening, weakening, impoverishment, etc.) in the social ties, codes, and established routines (a) which regulate the relations of individuals to one another in a group, (b) which foster a strong identification of the individual to the group, and (c) which, therefore, constitute the essential conditions for cooperative effort among individuals and groups.

---

* Note (1968): In this statement I am summarizing four books by Mayo (1) *The Human Problems of an Industrial Civilization* (New York: Macmillan, 1933; New York: Viking, 1960); (2) *The Social Problems of an Industrial Civilization* (Boston: Division of Research, Harvard Business School, 1945); (3) *The Political Problems of an Industrial Civilization* (Boston: Division of Research, Harvard Business School, 1947) and (4) *Some Notes on the Psychology of Pierre Janet* (Cambridge: Harvard University Press, 1948).

3. When those elements are positively present, the nonlogical bases for cooperation are present and more rational bases for cooperation can emerge; when those elements are not present, the nonlogical bases for cooperation are also not present and more rational bases for cooperation are not likely to emerge.

4. Given the above condition of social disorganization, "obsessive" thinking rather than "rational" thinking is more likely to emerge.

5. The "obsessive" can be identified and "explained" in different ways. But in Mayo's terminology these are people who have not been trained (conditioned, educated) for cooperative effort either in terms of (1) the "social skills" of the established society or (2) the explicit skills of communication required by the adaptive society.

6. For such people caught in this human predicament, there is no turning of the clock back. To break through this predicament, the obsessive has to develop a new control of his preoccupation and to learn new ways (skills) of relating himself to others.

7. Likewise for modern societies there is also no longer any turning of the clock back. "This passage [breakthrough] from an established to an adaptive society has to be made." It also can only be achieved by improved administrative (social) skills on the part of the responsible leaders of the new industrial society.

MAYO'S PROPOSED SOLUTION

What is the solution? There is no heroic one. There is only the unheroic, pedestrian method of science. All of Mayo's large-scale tendency statements point in the direction of where this development in understanding can occur, i.e., the steps that will need to be taken in order to reach a solution—steps such as this:

(a) The development begins with a careful *observation* of the *character* of the *relation* of the individual to the group, that is, with observations of the processes of communication by means of which individuals and groups establish relations with each other.

(b) Only from such careful observations and by looking for the uniformities that reside in them will social science begin to develop systematic knowledge and in time achieve the status of a science comparable to the physical sciences.

(c) Better understanding will not be achieved by trying to integrate psychology and sociology at higher levels of abstraction. It will only emerge by starting from the very beginning to observe carefully those events and processes where the two interact and by building upon the uniformities in these observations to a better statement of the *character* of the relation between the individual and the group. It will be only on such a firm foundation that the new adaptive society can be built and the more adaptive individual can emerge.

(d) This development is not likely to occur from the observations of uncommitted and detached observers who are not responsibly involved; it is more likely to occur when the observer takes some responsibility for what happens in the situation he studies, i.e., when his data are collected under the burden of responsibility.

(e) The social scientist cannot remain uninvolved. He is involved in his data. He does not free himself from this involvement by denial. He can do this only by the acceptance of his predicament and the understanding of his involvement and by taking responsibility for it. This becomes the basis for his further complication, i.e., the development of his new understanding of his relation to his fellow men.

MY COMMENTS ON MAYO'S SOLUTION

1. Mayo supports many of the above extreme statements with evidence from the works of Janet, Freud, Le Play, Durkheim, Piaget, Pareto, Malinowski, etc. Each of these statements is extreme and can be challenged. Moreover, the voluminous evidence he cites in their support is *not* the method of verification in science. Such statements cannot be verified; one is wasting his time by trying. If Mayo had stayed at this level he would have remained a social philosopher; he would not have been a social scientist.

2. But note that he does not always stay at this level. Although he may juggle with words in order to state the problem, he does not try to solve it by this method. Over and over again he says, "If this is the problem, then we should look more carefully here in order to obtain better facts for its solution." This is why his books are unsatisfying for many. They contain no solution. Why? Because without more data derived from careful observation of particular situations it can not be solved. No facts—no solution, *Period*. Mayo only keeps pointing to where and how a solution might be found. Yet it is also interesting to note how many of Mayo's readers attribute to him a kind of solution that he never gave.

3. One of Mayo's most extraordinary talents was the way he could travel back and forth between his "system of ideas" and the "personal interview," i.e. the simple interaction between two people trying to communicate with each other, i.e. something that could be empirically observed. At one moment he would have you up in the clouds; at the next moment he would have you looking at the most ordinary, simple, down to earth here-and-now occurrence which you had experienced many times before but without any explicit understanding of what was going on. The way he used his "ideas" to illuminate the "interview" and the "interview" to check his "ideas" illustrated well the complexity of the attentive act and how reflection and attention could be fruitfully related.

4. It was this talent, more than anything else, that he brought to the Western Electric Company (Hawthorne) researches. Although the Western Electric Company started the experiments, it was he who saw the significance of the data that their experiments had generated and why it was necessary to continue generating new data to explain the results. He kept this process alive five years in a so-called "bureaucratic organization." Mayo never got "over the hump," however, so that the company *without his aid* could continue itself keeping the process alive. And when we discuss "the counseling program" in the seminar, we shall look at what happened to the people in the company who tried.*

5. Note Mayo's deep concern with the understanding of four "passages":
   (a) the passage from obsession to maturity,
   (b) the passage from skill to knowledge,
   (c) the passage from clinical (situational) knowledge to analytical knowledge,
   (d) the passage from the established to the adaptive society.
He keeps raising the questions, "how do you go from one kind of organization to another kind of organization of thinking, of knowledge and of social relations?" Let's keep these questions in mind as we follow the writings of the "Mayo group."

6. Note also that although these questions arose for Mayo in part from concerns with problems of practical significance, they can become

---

* Note (1968): Although the results were not formally available at the time, let me cite now William J. Dickson and F. J. Roethlisberger, *Counseling in an Organization* (Boston: Division of Research, Harvard Business School, 1966).

questions to be curious about for their own sake, regardless of their immediate practical application. They are also questions that need *scientific explanation.* Later in the seminar we shall see how George Homans tries his hand at explaining them.*

7. Mayo's best attempt at *explanation* is in his *Some Notes on the Psychology of Pierre Janet.* His greatest flight of fancy and his greatest number of extreme and emotionally laden statements occur in his *Social Problems,* particularly in his first chapter on "The Seamy Side of Progress." Note that this book was written in 1945 at the end of World War II. In this book, and in this chapter in particular, he reduces to a statement *intended to motivate* what all his experiences and researches as well as his understanding of the researches of Freud, Janet, Durkheim, Piaget, Pareto, Malinowski, etc., *mean* to him—the direction in which they point. It is a "call to arms" for social science— "Break through your Cinderella complex," "don the crystal slippers and walk into adventure." These are "rabble-rousing" statements. It is interesting to note, however, the "rabble" that Mayo was addressing and the specification of the "chains" that he felt that they only need fear loosing. It is this book and chapter in particular which provide Mayo's critics with the greatest amount of ammunition. His *Human Problems,* written in 1933, is a much more moderate statement. Note how in this book he starts with simpler and less emotional phenomena first—"fatigue," "monotony," "morale," etc., and then slowly proceeds to their wider social implications.

8. Note the difficult problem of communication Mayo faced: how he had to create a new frame of reference in order to get one to see the significance of certain clinical findings of human behavior. No one engaged in this kind of activity is likely to be easily understood. From the point of view of the values of the established society, Mayo's writings are bound to be perceived in a certain way, to be viewed with alarm. From this point of view they are implying a meaning and solution which from the point of view that Mayo was trying to develop had quite another meaning and solution. Let's not underestimate this difficulty of communication. It is still with us today and should provide an interesting focus of attention when reading the other social investigators with whom this seminar will be concerned. It's the same problem Douglas McGregor faces with his X and Y theories.

---

* Note (1968): See George C. Homans, *Social Behavior, Its Elementary Forms* (New York: Harcourt Brace & World, 1961).

9. Note that Mayo is not just saying "let's be 'scientific' about matters of human behavior." He is saying more than this. He is specifying the kinds of *questions, phenomena, observations, data, methods, uniformities,* etc., with which the science of behavior should be concerned. It is these injunctions which characterize in good part the "Mayo group" in its earlier period. These injunctions should also provide interesting focal questions for the remainder of the books we read. What new questions and problems arise when you "don the crystal slippers and walk into adventure?" How deeply involved in this adventure (or quagmire) can you get? By this route do you reach a firm foundation or only keep slipping deeper and deeper into the mud? Some of these questions, by the way, are a bit more "obsessive" than others. Some of them are not answered by the method of science but by the personal commitment of the scientist.

21   The Impact of Psychiatry on Management

The following essay was originally a talk given March 23, 1962, in New York City at a conference on the above topic under the auspices of the New York State School of Industrial and Labor Relations, Cornell University. It was published in the *Journal of Industrial Medicine and Surgery,* November 1962, and is reprinted here with their permission.

After comparing the psychiatric and management points of view, I described the new disease which I thought the modern manager was suffering from. To make it sound medical so as to intrigue the psychiatrists, I called it "role shock." But I was also trying to intrigue them in another way. It seemed to me that the modern manager no longer knew who he was and what was expected of him. In fact this disease had become so contagious that it was spreading to all kinds of occupational groups and I did not want the practicing psychiatrist to get infected too and start writing books about it instead of trying to help cure it.

Granted that psychiatry has influenced management, just how has this come about? Have these psychiatric ideas just crept in on management people, subliminally, so to speak, or are management people active participants in these ideas? How useful are these ideas to them; how knowledgeable about and committed to them are they?

These questions lead to still more questions: How can someone's theories relate to someone else's practice? In what sense is the practice of management related to the practice of psychiatry? By what stretch of imagination or conceptualization can managers and psychiatrists be conceived of as practicing in the same ball park?

Finally, even assuming that some conceptual bridge between the world of psychiatry and the world of management can be established, to what extent can the psychiatric model represent a useful one for the manager? What other competing models are there for managers to choose from?

These questions will give you some clues as to what I find intriguing. Please do not expect me to answer them. I simply want to explore some of them with you, hoping that you will find time later to reflect upon them.

Let me start my explorations by comparing the practices of psychiatry and management from the point of view of the territories to which their respective practices relate. Let us assume that both psychiatrists and management people are practitioners of something. But what are these "somethings" to which their practices relate? What do they have in common? But first, how are they different?

Although both are concerned with persons, they are concerned about them in different ways. Psychiatrists are responsible for the treatment of mentally ill people; management is responsible for the performance of so-called normal people. While one is helping, the other is directing people. One seems to be more interested in what people say; the other, more interested in what people do.

Morover, a psychiatrist generally is involved only in a relationship between himself and the patient. The manager generally is involved in a system of relationships involving more than two persons. The psychiatrist is seeking the cooperation of one person; the manager, of many interrelated persons.

In the manager's world the task component is very high; i.e., there is a job to get done. Moreover, the job to be done has a high organizational component. Each job is part of a system of related jobs. Therefore, the persons performing these jobs are part of a system of cooperative effort. In the psychiatrist's world this task component is not so high. The job, so to speak, is to get the patient to understand himself better, but this is a job of a different order than the job the manager has to get done.

If we turn from the territories to which their practices relate, to the bodies of knowledge and theories from which their practices derive, we can see again a big difference. The psychiatrist has some body of organized knowledge about the phenomena to which his practice relates. The manager, on the other hand, has no such agreed-upon body of organized knowledge. He has tatters and tears of knowledge; he gets his ideas and theories from many sources. By looking at any business journal today, one can see the smorgasbord of ideas with which the modern manager is deluged—ideas about materials handling, cost control, quality control, inventory control, present values, the marketing mix, linear programming, the corporate image, the soft and hard sell, and human relations, to mention only a very few.

Another way of expressing this is to say that the psychiatrist is a specialist while the manager is a generalist. The popular conception is that the manager hires specialists for the particular jobs that they can do well. This way of thinking would make the psychiatrist just one more of the many specialists that the manager hires to perform specialized tasks, but this relationship between the manager and the psychiatrist is not my subject. Psychiatry is related to management in some more fundamental sense. This is the tantalizing relationship that we are exploring. To do this we shall have to climb up a few rungs on the abstraction ladder.

THE CLINICAL AND SITUATIONAL ORIENTATION

I have called both the psychiatrist and the manager practitioners; i.e. they are both related to concrete phenomena. They are both under the burden of responsibility. They are both concerned with relationships and the interaction between persons. They are both involved personally in these relationships. Although from slightly different points of view, they are both fundamentally concerned with the performance of persons and the helping relationship. They are both trying to secure the cooporation of persons or trying to secure changes in their behavior. They are both trying to use ideas rather than solely to talk about them. In short, they are both clinically and situationally oriented.

The psychiatric clinician is engaged in concrete phenomena—he is not dealing with abstractions and words *per se*. He is dealing with raw live data, making first-hand observations of on-going processes. His mood and posture is one of diagnosis and identification. He is trying to identify what is going on before him. In this process he is depending a great deal upon the intimate, first-hand experience he has had with these phenomena and he is exercising judgment about them. Also, the clinician has established a good working relationship between his theories and practice; that is, he is not just talking about his ideas, he is trying to use them. He is inclined to be wary about ideas that can only be talked about and not practiced.

The manager, also, has in part a clinical or situational outlook toward his world. He, also, is dealing at times with raw live data and on-going processes and making first-hand observations; that is, he is dealing with situations that need to be properly diagnosed and identified. At the many conferences he attends, he has to decide what is going on before him, what "hidden agenda" are implicitly being discussed. Often he has to see things not only from a marketing, financial, or production point of view but also from an organizational–administrative point of view—from the point of view of a person in an organization who is under the burden of responsibility for the survival, maintenance, and growth of that organization as a total entity.

Let me compare this organizational–administrative point of view of the manager with the clinical point of view of medicine, because in this way we may see not only some important similarities but also some important differences.

THE ORGANIZATIONAL–ADMINISTRATIVE POINT OF VIEW

A good clinician has a point of view which specifies the class or classes of phenomena with which he is essentially concerned and the way he is going to look at them. In medicine, for example, he thinks of the human organism as a "natural system," surviving and developing in an environment. Therefore, he is interested in the functions that the different organs of the body perform for the survival, maintenance, and growth of the total human organism. As he looks at the organism in this manner, he begins to differentiate those organs that relate the organism more directly to its external environment from those organs that are not so directly related but which have also important functions to perform if the organism is to continue to survive and to relate effectively to its surroundings. In this way he abstracts the "internal environment" of the natural system he is observing. This abstraction helps him to observe more carefully the regulative and maintenance functions of this internal system of the human body. From this way of looking, modern physiology was born and the practice of internal medicine was developed.

The social psychologist also views the individual as a "natural system" surviving and developing in an environment. In his case he abstracts the "personality system" of the individual. For him, this is the inner system that has to be maintained if the individual is to develop an effective relation to his surroundings. A popular way of saying this is that a person has to be true to himself as well as to others in order to get along with his fellow men. He has to develop and maintain his identity as he also tries to adjust to his external social environment. From this way of thinking modern social psychology was born and the practice of psychiatry was developed.

Let me point out that these ways of thinking do not specify the way things should be; they help the practitioner to make more empirical observations of the way things are. They help to specify the class of phenomena that he should observe more carefully in order to seek the uniformities residing in them that will help him to improve his practice. It is around this clear specification of the phenomena with which his practice is concerned that his professional competence, knowledge, and identity also are developed.

At this level of abstraction, let us turn to the management of a modern business organization. Any purposive organization also can be viewed as a "natural system" surviving and developing in an external environment, which for business can be conceived as "the market." In fact, some thirty-five years ago, a group of researchers began to look at business organizations from this point of view. They, too, were forced to abstract the internal system of the organization, i.e., the system of interpersonal and intergroup relations that also had to be maintained and developed if the business firm was to improve its relation to its market. In this internal environment they found as rich and lush data and as interesting uniformities as the psychiatrists found when they looked at the internal environments, i.e., the personality structures, of their patients.

When we were much younger and more enthusiastic thirty-five years ago, this discovery of the firm's internal environment had tremendous implications for administration. We felt that we had discovered the class of phenomena with which the executive was and should be essentially concerned, and around which his practice, competence, professional identity, and knowledge could develop. We gave speeches, wrote articles and books, developed courses, consulted with management, and did further research about the implications of this discovery.

There is no question that some managers found this way of thinking about organizations useful to them in their practice, but for others it became more a way of talking than a way of thinking to be practiced. Anyway, the fact remains that today there is no such consensus among managers in this way of thinking about an organization as there is among practitioners of internal medicine and psychiatry in the way that they think about the human organism and the individual. Why is this? There are many reasons, of course, but I want to mention two that for me still represent major obstacles not only in building a viable two-way bridge between management and the social sciences but also in building a systematic body of knowledge about organizations and administration.

One reason is that the "natural system" model has a strong competitor in what is sometimes referred to as the "rational" model of organization and, in so far as I know, there is at present no good theory that adequately synthesizes both of them. The second reason is that the manager is an involved member of the organization in which he tries to secure change and there is still no good theory to explain how he utilizes his knowledge about organization under this constraint. As a result, the manager is receiving many conflicting ideas about what his job is or should be, and is suffering slightly from "role shock," if I may coin a phrase that I think, sociopsychiatrically speaking, reflects the condition in which the experts have placed the modern manager. Let me describe this new "disease entity" or "syndrome," not because I want to end on a pessimistic note but because I think there is some hard work still ahead of us in which both sociology and psychiatry have important contributions to make.

THE "RATIONAL" VERSUS THE "NATURAL SYSTEM" MODELS

From the point of view of the "rational" model, organizations are "instruments." That is, they are conceived as rational means to the attainment of collective ends. According to this conception the organization has no natural internal organs or structures, no guts nor insides. Its internal environment, in so far as it has any, is populated with much purer entities, that is, with logically conceived standards and programs, in terms of which its goals are more rationally and efficiently attained. This is also a useful way of thinking about an organization and it has achieved results far more visible and attractive than the "natural system" model, even though, according to the proponents of the latter, at a high human relations cost. But this is not the point I want to make. What I want to focus upon is the confusion that this unresolved conflict between these two quite different ways of thinking is creating for the modern manager.

One school of thought, for example, says that the manager is the brain who makes the decisions, plans, and policies that relate the firm to its competitive environment. Therefore the "external system" should be his proper habitat and chief concern. The other school says that the manager is not the big decision maker; instead, he facilitates the decision-making process. He sees to it that the proper resources are being brought to bear on the decisions to be made and that the people most qualified to make them are doing so. He is not doing the work of the organization but seeing that the work is done. Therefore the "internal system" should be his proper habitat and chief concern.

Under conditions of modern industry neither position in itself is completely tenable and if the manager tries to do both, he suffers from "role shock." For example, if he tries to play exclusively the first role he finds himself in competition with specialists that are coming into modern industry by the thousands. With their programs and computers many of these specialists can make better business decisions than he can. It is they who specify to the "poor old manager" how he can make more rational decisions under the uncertain economic conditions in which he and his organization live. But now they are performing functions which according to the rational model he should be performing himself, and this is very disconcerting indeed.

On the other hand, if the manager tries to play the role of the facilitator, he feels guilty. He does not know what he has accomplished. His posture is unheroic. The conventional wisdom tells him he should be doing something else. For playing this role he gets little support or reinforcement from the society, from the organization, and, let us be more concrete, from his boss.

To avoid the risk of becoming either obsolete or unheroic, some managers try to fulfill both roles. They try to do at the same time what both the mathematicians and the psychiatrists advise. But this is the road to madness, so let us not dwell upon it.

Here, then, are the three interesting career choices with which the modern manager is faced. The first choice leads to obsolescence, the second choice leads to a sense of guilt and futility, and the third choice leads to a mild case of schizophrenia. Around these anxieties it is not easy to develop the professional administrator—even, I might add, at the Harvard Business School.

One solution to this difficulty would be to ask why there should be just one role model for the manager. Is it not becoming obvious that the second industrial revolution has created the need for a multiplicity of roles—even some slightly new ones—to be performed in organizations at both middle and top management levels? The single word "executive" and the imagery it arouses does not specify clearly these different role requirements. Rather than searching for one ideal role model for managers, should we not be searching, therefore, for an effective constellation of roles to manage our modern corporations? Research has started in this direction and I believe it will increase rapidly during the next decade and be very fruitful.

I do not think it will quite do the whole trick, because I fear that about this new constellation of more effective roles, old questions are going to be raised: Who is to play the stellar role and who are to play the satellite roles? Of whose constellation am I a satellite? And for the stellar role is the "natural system" model or the "rational" model more fitting?

CHANGE UNDER CONDITIONS OF INVOLVEMENT

To grapple with the problems that these questions raise, the professional manager will need help from the psychiatrist on problems about which the latter does not often speak. Let me explain what I mean by climbing still higher on the abstraction ladder. (Those suffering from acrophobia should hold on tight a little longer.)

Along one very important dimension, the psychiatrist who is practicing psychotherapy and the modern manager who is trying to secure changes in the behavior of persons in his organization share a great deal in common. They are both instruments of change and they both have to secure their results not outside but inside a relationship. In order to communicate with the mind of his patient the psychotherapist has to develop a relationship with him. Similarly, the modern manager has to secure changes through a social structure of which he is an important, involved part. Now this is quite a feat when you stop to think of it, for it raises the question of how a part can effect a change in another part of a whole of which he is an involved member. In explaining this mystery I think the psychiatrist could help not only some managers but also some of his social science brethren.

I do not wish him to reveal all of his trade secrets, but, for example, instead of telling managers about the personalities of his patients, let him describe better how he establishes communication with them. Let him explain how and why, in order to do this, he has to develop a unique relationship with them—one that is quite different from an ordinary social relationship. In fact, it is so extraordinary, as the cartoons in the *New Yorker* and the jokes of Mort Sahl well testify, that it is excruciatingly funny. Let him explain how and why in order to help his patients he has to behave in ways that run the risk of having the society call him and not his patients "nuts." And above all have him describe how he "sweats out" this predicament.

Then there is another mystery which he should reveal. Let him explain how he manages to practice a theory in relation to his patients without talking to them about it. As I understand it, a psychiatrist is not trying to get his patient to understand personality theory or theories. He is trying to get the patient to understand his own personality and he uses personality theory or theories toward this end. But this use of a theory should not be confused with talking about the theory itself. As any seasoned psychiatrist knows, the less confusion there is on this distinction, the more likely the outcome of this practice is to be successful.

As I see it, these are the great mysteries that the modern professional manager needs to understand better. Not that I think it will cure him completely of the disease I have called "role shock," but it will help him along the way. And when he beccmes more knowledgeable about these matters, he may become not an obsolete but an indispensable member of the industrial society which modern science and technology have created; he may even become its "top banana."

22 The Generalist and the Revolution

This was a talk to the 32nd National Business Conference of the Harvard Business School Association on June 8, 1962. It was published with illustrative cartoons in the *Harvard Business School Bulletin,* October–November 1962, with the title, "What Is Guff and Not Guff?" Although permission to reprint it has been granted by the editors of the *Bulletin,* I am reproducing my original manuscript here with the original title and without the cartoons.

For many years the B-School had operated under the policy that it was training "generalists" and not "specialists," and up to about 1958 this distinction made a great deal of intuitive sense. But with the "knowledge explosion" and the many specialists it produced, this distinction became more difficult to state. The query arose about who this generalist was—besides being just a superficial jackass who knew something about everything but nothing in particular. Believing that the conceptual scheme of "human relations," in which an organization was viewed as a "natural social system" instead of as a purely "rational system," could rescue the "generalist" from this embarrassing dilemma, I entered the fray. Ouch!

What new fields of knowledge will the top executive of the future need to acquire? I fear that the chances of my talking sense on this topic are not very high. In fact, the difficulty of talking sense in our modern world is in my opinion one of its most serious problems. In the good old days the distinction between sense and nonsense was somewhat clear, but today the line between the two has become increasingly shadowy. No one is any longer sure of what is guff and what is not guff. This has a very real significance for the modern manager. Let me try to explain what I mean.

WHAT IS GUFF AND NOT GUFF?

It is very unfortunate that we sometimes have one word to refer to quite different things. Such a word is "development." We have, for example, product development, individual development, group development, economic development, executive development, and scientific development. From reading the business literature today I gather that development is something that always seems to be moving in a positive direction and hence is something which we cannot have enough of, and so is something which we are all 100 per cent for.

I don't know how it is in yours, but in my experience I find that words referring to values of which we cannot have enough have properties that make them fertile breeding grounds for guff and not guff. When a writer spends much time telling you that he is for "creativity" or "progress" or "development," for example, it is difficult to ask a discerning question that does not make you look and feel as though you are against it.

But these values, besides being difficult to say "guff" to, have another interesting property. They tend to express more clearly what man ought to want than what he really does want. If recognized, this would not be serious, but it does become serious when man confuses what he really wants with what he ought to want. This would mean, for example, that what advertisers tell them they ought to want, all consumers would believe they did want. Although this might make for good consumer development, it would not make for good individual development. This would be the rankest form of conformity development and would be one of those developments most of us would want as little as possible of.

In order to avoid this kind of negative development, all positive thinkers use the word "development" only in conjunction with those things that are moving in the right direction. Now again, if recognized, this would not be serious so long as we do not assume that all things moving in the right direction also move along merrily together in the same way without conflict, that is, that we do not assume that the way a "good" product or a "good" theory is developed coincides on all fronts with the way a "good" individual, a "good" group, a "good" organization, or a "good" executive develops.

So here is where I see how the problem of what is guff and not guff comes up for the modern manager, because amidst this plethora of developments, each zooming along at full tilt and each good in itself, the modern manager sits uneasily. In the olden days the manager knew what guff was. He was its chief arbiter and dispenser. But the technological revolution has slowly stripped him of this privileged role. Today he is not sure whether he is or should be developing a research laboratory, an educational institution, a mental hospital, or an open community; and although he would like to say guff to many of these developments that seem to be taking him away from his traditional task, he can no longer say it with his former gusto.

THE SEARCH FOR THE IDENTITY AND COMPETENCE
OF THE GENERALIST

This change has not come about overnight. The technological revolution has only sharpened the focus on a number of questions which have been with us for some time, such as, for example, what is the relation of the specialist to the manager? What particular skills and knowledge does the manager require? With what phenomena is he essentially concerned? What are his distinctive roles and contributions? Can administration be a science, be made a profession, and so forth?

Whenever I start reflecting upon these questions I keep coming back uneasily to the old distinction between the generalist and the specialist. I say "uneasily" because I realize that the generalist has fallen into disrepute. I have qualms about reviving a tired and outworn category. Yet it keeps haunting me that we may have buried the old man too quickly. But still more disturbing is the possibility that my analogy, or "model," as we would say today, is incorrect. The generalist may not be like a "tired old man" but more like an "adolescent boy" who has not realized or actualized himself and is suffering from underdevelopment.

You will remember that the generalist established a beachhead on the School's shores very early in our history with Dean Wallace B. Donham. He, more than anyone else, emphasized that we were not just a School of Business but a School of Business Administration and that business administration was something more than applied economics or engineering. I don't think it would be incorrect to say that under his leadership the School established the method by which the generalist should be trained and taught.

These ideas of Mr. Donham captured the imagination of his faculty and established the School's early unique posture and identity. But not only did Mr. Donham give the School its early identity, he also gave the faculty an "itch" to search for the underlying processes upon which the professional identity and competence of the administrator could be based. The generalist was Mr. Donham's name for a problem where he thought we might begin fruitfully scratching. It was clear to him that the generalist is not a common-variety specialist. But who he is in his own right was not so clear. It is this that Mr. Donham left for his faculty to find out and that I am calling the "itch" which

Mr. Donham bequeathed us and which we have not been able easily to get rid of. What more can any great educational leader do?

I think the intellectual history of this School could be written in terms of the many different ways the faculty—and students, too—chose to eliminate, outwit, or develop this itch. Some of us chose to keep scratching it and making it worse and some of us chose to learn to live with it and try to make it pay off, with many other resolutions in between. But this is beyond the scope of my paper. I just want to mention some of the problems we had in searching for the identity and competence of the generalist.

One of the chief characteristics of the generalist is his disinclination to conceptualize or be conceptualized. As in many diseases, his symptoms can be named but not explained. But since in business there was then no clear name-sanctioning body, such as existed in medicine, anyone was free to name the generalist in any way he chose. As a result, he was labeled in many ways that were not entirely consistent with one another.

At times the generalist could only look at facts or cases; he was not allowed to make generalizations except very occasionally to make currently useful ones. The generalist had no explicit conceptual schemes or methods in terms of which to analyze or diagnose his cases. He had no theories to explain his findings. All he was allowed was a "point of view" and this point of view also flourished implicitly under different labels. It was sometimes called the clinical point of view, the situational point of view, or the administrative point of view. But more often it was called "common sense" and "good judgment." But regardless of how it was named, once you had it, you became a member of the club and were allowed to practice it in any business specialization you pleased.

In fact it had an extraordinary way of being in many different places at the same time. Wherever and whenever the going got analytically tough, up would pop the generalist with his common sense, good judgment, sound opinions, and administrative point of view, and all conceptual difficulties were resolved. Confined to the concrete and the particular, the generalist's point of view was extraordinarily useful, but outside these limits it floundered badly.

THE UNDRESSING AND REDRESSING OF THE GENERALIST
BY THE SPECIALIST

As you can imagine, this state of affairs provided a field day for a particular breed of specialists, called "scientific." This breed suffers from another kind of itch. Its members like to specify clearly the questions that they are trying to answer and the kinds of data that they will need in order to answer them. They like to specify the methods that they will use to collect these data and to verify the uniformities that they find in them. These men abhor chaos; they have a passion for order. They do not like just to name things; they want to explain them. In order to do this, they like to write short sentences such as "x varies with y under condition a, b, and c" and they like to arrange these sentences in a deductive order. For example, they specify the decision rule from which the decision should rationally follow. As you can see, these scientific specialists are long on all the dimensions that the generalist is short on.

So when they caught up with the generalist and heard about the intuitive skills that he exercised in relation to judgment, decision, and getting things done through people, they said, "Tut, tut, this cannot be. Underlying these matters there must be certain, logical, psychological, and sociological processes that you—the generalist—are unaware of." So, like the eager beavers that they are, they began to dig in and establish the foundations upon which the generalist's intuitive skills were based. But instead of being grateful for this help, the generalists exhibited those same symptoms that the worker during the first industrial revolution exhibited when his traditional skills and art were reduced to science. They said, "You can't do this to me. It isn't fair." But the scientists were relentless in stripping the generalist—one by one—of his arts and crafts.

I'm not sure quite when, but I believe it was some time in the middle 1950's, a rumor got started that the generalist had no clothes left. At first this rumor was treated condescendingly and no one quite dared look to see. But the damage was done; the rumor could not be stopped, and so, in order to settle the question, emissaries came from all the great intellectual and cultural centers of the land. The hubbub was terrific. Some said he wasn't "decent" although some said he was. But the majority view was that although he was not naked, some of his clothes were a bit shabby, and he could use a few new ones.

So all the universities of the land cooperated in providing the generalist with clothes more befitting his stature. The results were startling. In no time generalists began talking like computers, human relationists, or Hamlet, depending upon which university they attended. A generalist in specialist clothing was a sight to behold. He no longer knew who he was; he was trying to do everybody else's job except his own.

This has serious consequences; it leaves no one concerned with how all these desirable specialist developments can be kept related to one another. There is no one left to do this job.

THE GENERALIST OF THE FUTURE

If the problem I see is as formidable as I think, it may provide the clue to what new fields of knowledge the generalist of the future will have to acquire. As I see it he will need a better understanding of (1) *the nature of science,* (2) *the nature of society,* and (3) *the nature of himself* as they relate to (4) *the nature of organization.* This is a tall order, I realize, but all the riddles and ambiguities of the generalist point of view lead me in this direction. I do not know today where this knowledge exists or where it is taught. I do have a few ideas of how the shape of this new knowledge might look and how in time it might be acquired.

The new knowledge I am envisaging will assign high priority to understanding the limits of useful and desirable things. Thus the future generalist will need to know what science can and cannot do, what society can and cannot do, and what man can and cannot do. Science can say what are the most efficient ways under certain specified conditions to reach certain specified goals; it cannot specify what these goals ought to be. Society can tell man what is expected of him and what he ought to want; it cannot tell him what he does want. Man can choose what he does want but he cannot get it for nothing. And here I am referring not only to his economic wants but his needs for belonging, status, competence, and self-development as well.

This new generalist will have to know what *words* and *books* can and cannot do, what *theories, definitions,* and *mathematics* can and cannot do, what *clinical* and *analytical knowledge* can and cannot do, and what can and cannot be done in *groups* and by *formal organization, informal organization, centralization, decentralization, delegation,* and *policy*. (Don't think that these exhaust the list of things I could have named. I could add some more, such as, for example, what can and cannot be done by *rules, regulations, standards, budgets, incentives, participation, human relations,* and *rewards* and *punishments* of all sorts.) This new generalist will have to know what *specialists, workers,* and *unions* can and cannot contribute and above all what *he as a manager* can and cannot do.

Without an understanding of these limits the line between guff and not guff rapidly approaches zero. In the physical world these matters are well understood. Nobody uses a monkey wrench for what a screwdriver can do better and nobody looks down upon the screwdriver for not being able to do what the monkey wrench can do. It is their limitations that make them useful. But in matters regarding organization, many persons today—in business and out of it—seem to behave as though no such limits seem to exist.

How often do we hear statements by executives saying that they are for or against group meetings, participation, decentralization, and so forth, and how seldom do we hear statements specifying the conditions under which these organizational forms are and are not effective. The manager often makes decisions that he could leave better to experts; he allows experts to make decisions that he could make better himself. He uses group meetings for matters that could be done better alone; he does alone what could be done better in a group. He uses participatory methods, for example, to reach decisions about matters that are well within his subordinates' zone of indifference and even sometimes that he has already decided himself, and he does not use them under those conditions where they might be more appropriate. He uses personal and group meetings not only to tell people what is expected of them but also to make them say they like doing it.

This new knowledge of limits is essential because the generalist is a utilizer and not a creator of knowledge. And the utilizer of knowledge needs to understand its limits, that is, to what classes of phenomena and under what conditions it can be applied. In order to understand its limits he will have to become less enamored with the scientists' new hardware and products and more concerned with the nature of the thinking that has produced them, and why it is so useful for its purposes and why it may be limited for other purposes.

This future generalist will be the upholder of the reality principle not only in matters of economics but in matters of psychology and sociology as well. He will understand that in these latter areas brute and stubborn realities also exist—for example, that you can't "kick people in the teeth" and be liked at the same time. You can have the pleasure of one so long as you are willing to forego the pleasure of the other, but you cannot have the pleasure of both. And with regard to matters of individual development the future generalist will understand that he cannot make people learn, grow, and be responsible. He can provide the conditions favorable for growth but the growing itself is done by the individual himself.

Toward this objective of understanding limits, science can be of tremendous help to this new generalist of the future. Science states well its limits to itself even though it may not communicate them as well to the layman. Science can help to make explicit what the manager does, what unique roles he does fill, and what his unique contributions to the organization are.

Let the social scientist assume for a change, however, that the manager is acting in relation to some reality and that he has learned from long experience some useful ways of coping with it, and let the social scientist start making his observations there. In this way he may help to provide sanctions for many things which the manager does and about which he feels guilty because the social stereotype says he should not be doing them. In what the manager knows and does well implicitly but does not know and do so well explicitly, he may find the substance of Mr. Donham's vision of the generalist. But in turn let the scientist remember that he cannot tell the manager who he is, where he is going, what he wants, and how good he is, but he can help him to find out.

It may happen that what both may find out is that the manager and the organization that he administers are open-ended natural systems that cannot be completely closed. This would be a really important and useful discovery because it would help the manager from undoing with his left hand what his right hand is doing. It would offer a beginning understanding if not a complete explanation of the predicament that the manager is in and why he responds to it in the peculiar way that he does. His predicament is that he is an *involved* member of an open-ended system through which he is trying to secure results. So far as I know, no scientist has come up with a satisfactory theory of and for this predicament. Most theories I know tell him how to escape from rather than how to cope with it.

In conclusion, then, let me say something which I don't think is as simple-minded as it sounds. In my opinion when the generalist of the future knows who he is by understanding the unique relation that he bears to his organization and the limits that this sets for what he can and cannot do, then he can be himself and cease to be defensive; and when by being himself and not a "copy cat" he will be doing what he ought to be doing in the first place, then "happy days will be here again."

23 The Contributions of the Behavioral Sciences to a General Theory of Management

I wrote this paper for a seminar on management theory and research at the Graduate School of Business Administration of the University of California at Los Angeles, November 8–9, 1962. It was published along with the other contributions in *Toward a Unified Theory of Management*, edited by Harold Koontz (McGraw-Hill, 1964), and is being reproduced here with the permission of the editor and publisher.

In this piece I have omitted only some introductory remarks that I felt I needed to make in the seminar because, with such a formidable assignment, I felt I was sitting on a hot seat and I did not wish to have my learned colleagues make it any hotter than it already was. In those remarks I told my colleagues that I did not feel competent to represent all the behavioral sciences or make them add up to some unity, that general theory building was not my particular forte, and that perhaps we were not ready to do this anyway. But I implied that in the true Harvard spirit I would give it a good try. But all this folderol I am sure will not be necessary for the kindly readers of this volume.

As I read the current literature it seems to me that amongst those of us who have chosen *organizations* as a fruitful place in which to study man's behavior, the more we have agreed about the place where we should study the less we have agreed about what it is we should be studying there—that is, what our unit of analysis is: (a) man, (b) organization, or (c) man-in-organization.

I want to present one particular approach toward the study of organizational behavior and administration. I want to look at this approach with a twenty-year perspective and to review its early formulation with its associated hopes and aspirations, its contributions, and its problems and limitations. It will be primarily the story of those persons in the behavioral sciences who, in spite of serious terminological difficulties, were essentially concerned with trying to carve out a new disciplinary entity in which the focus would be an empirical study of man's behavior in organizations and what this meant for administration. They had come to organizations in order to study the problems that organizations presented for administration in particular and not for society in general.

As I am not multilingual, I will tell this story in my own language system. This will very probably create the impression that I am making a case for just one school of thought. I wish I could get around this problem but I just do not know how. I would like to believe that if I had the skill I could tell essentially the same story in another language system.

Although I shall be borrowing ideas from others freely, and in this sense there will be nothing original in my account, I shall quote no names. This is not because I should not like to acknowledge my personal indebtedness but because I would like us to look at the ideas for themselves and not in terms of the people with whom they tend to become associated. Moreover, many of the ideas that I will be discussing have been expressed by so many different persons, even though in different ways perhaps, that it would be difficult for me to ascribe them to one particular person.

THE EARLY FORMULATION

Following World War II there was a strong movement in the direction of breaking down some of the artificial barriers that it was felt existed among some of the disciplines in the social sciences, particularly those of social anthropology, social psychology, clinical psychology, and sociology. Among some of the members of these disciplines it was felt that in certain respects their respective subject matters overlapped and hence that in certain areas they could make more hay by getting together than by going it alone. Although there was never anything like complete consensus on this point, nevertheless a sufficient number of members from those different disciplines felt this way to warrant the formation of new interdisciplinary combinations for purposes of teaching and research. In time the name "behavioral sciences" came to be applied to these disciplines, and labels such as "social relations" and "human relations" came to be attached to their combinations.

Among the many different places in which these different disciplines could fruitfully meet, there was one which seemed to hold promise, namely purposive organizations. These purposive entities had not been overly cultivated by any one of these disciplines separately; no strong claims had been staked out there by any one of them alone. It was obviously the most neutral territory in which to meet, but more than this it provided an excellent place in which they could study some of their common concerns.

Two important concerns loomed fairly high. For many behavioral scientists the balance between the rational and nonrational elements of human behavior was one of the critical issues of modern life. Since organizations provided some of the best examples of man's successes and failures to achieve rational behavior, where could this concern be better studied? And also, for many behavioral scientists, organizations provided a fruitful place to study some of the most important problems of a democratic society—the problems of order and freedom, control and initiative, and centralization and decentralization of authority.

But there were also other ideas associated with this new focus for the study of man's behavior, in which there was considerable intellectual excitement at the time and in which I became involved and in time committed. This excitement arose from the fact that organizations could provide a concrete setting where all the elements of behavior that the individual disciplines traditionally sought to explain singly were present together. For example, both institutional behavior and individual behavior were going on. Both what was expected of man and what he wanted were present and could be empirically studied together in their relation to each other.

How We Drew Our Lines

But how was this to be done? To put it oversimply, we would try to do this by drawing an arbitrary and imaginary line around an organization and treating the actual behavior that went on inside as the phenomena to be first observed and in time explained. All the important elements of behavior that the individual disciplines traditionally sought to explain would be there, so to speak, but as givens or boundary conditions of the actual behavior to be first observed and in time explained.

For example, the different values that the various persons in the organization brought to the organization would be treated as givens, i.e., as something lying outside of the line which we would undertake to explain. This did not mean that we would ignore them as important determinants of behavior. Obviously they were one of the important determinants of the behavior we would be observing and of course we would have to identify what these values were. But why people had the values that they did we would not be concerned, as such, with explaining. This did not mean that we could not explain them or would not accept or make use of the explanations that common knowledge or the individual disciplines concerned with their explanation provided. And moreover, if in particular situations we needed to know, we felt that we knew where to look, i.e., in the personal histories and social backgrounds of the particular individuals involved. But this was not to be our chief concern.

Likewise the rules of and the activities required by the organization, although not ignored as important determinants of behavior, would also be treated as given and as constant during the period under investigation and not as matters to be explained. They too, like the values that different individuals brought to the organization, we would treat as one of the boundary conditions under which the actual behavior evolved. Again let me state that it was not because we felt that we could not explain the proliferation of rules and requirements that seemed to develop in organizations as they grew larger and entered into the world of science and technology. If necessary we felt that we knew in what direction to look, but this was not our first order of business.

Formal and Informal Organization

Underlying this way of thinking was the notion of a natural social system. Organizations were to be conceived fundamentally as natural social units, but they differed in one important respect from other kinds of social groupings and social organizations that emerge whenever men are living together and that sociologists generally try to explain. They were different in the sense that they were social units that had been established for the explicit purpose of achieving certain goals. Built into them by the goals to be achieved and the means by which they were to be achieved were certain prescribed and planned relations that had not spontaneously emerged in the course of social interaction. We used the term "formal organization" to refer to these prescribed rules as well as to the required activities and interactions and their coordination that have been established for the explicit purpose of achieving certain prescribed goals.

But this official plan and prescribed ways about who should be doing what, where, when, and how it should be done, we did not think were to be treated as descriptive propositions of the actual behavior that was going on in organizations. Nor did we think that they should be treated as higher-order general propositions—principles so to speak—from which the actual behavior could be deduced and thereby explained. If so, we were out of business. Our job was done, and no empirical investigation needed to be made in order to find out what was going on; this could be learned by reading the official manuals and job descriptions. But as no empirical investigations that had been made thus far had come up with this finding, we felt that instead of treating them as simple descriptive propositions of actual behavior or as general propositions from which actual behavior could be deduced, it would be more apropos to treat them as normative propositions about what behavior should be. As such they were influencing what the behavior was, but they were not the behavior itself nor did they explain it.

To the emergent patterns of behavior that evolved within this formal framework we gave the name sometimes of "informal organization" and sometimes of "social structure." It referred to the practices, values, norms, beliefs, unofficial rules, as well as the complex network of social relations, membership patterns and centers of influence and communication that developed within and between the constituent groups of the organization under the formal arrangements but that were not specified by them. These patterns of behavior could not be obtained only from observing and interviewing the members of the organization. Although they developed within the framework of the formal organization, they were not all completely determined by it. But neither were they completely independent of the formal organization. Many of them seemed to be nurtured by it.

However, this question about just how the formal and informal organization were actually related in particular cases, it seemed to us, was an empirical question, to be decided by the results of the investigation and not before it. For purposes of investigation, therefore, we would treat the formal organization as constituting one of the important dimensions of the immediate environment in which the actual social structure of the organization developed, and we would collect our data accordingly. Just as there was only one organization so was there only one social structure; formal and informal were analytical concepts to refer to two different dimensions of the territory and not to two different separable things in it. It was this concrete social structure which emerged from what was *put there* by the formal organization and what was *brought there* by the individuals who came there that we would be trying to observe, identify, and diagnose and from which we would obtain the elementary descriptive propositions that we would have finally to explain.

Structure, Function, and Equilibrium

In its earlier formulation this new conceptual focus for the empirical investigation of man's behavior in organizations had also associated with it, beside the notion of social structure, the notions of function and equilibrium, as they were then being used by social anthropologists, before the concept of "functional analysis" had been refined by sociologists to refer to something more disciplined in nature. As these ideas have been the source of so many disputes and misunderstandings, I hesitate to add anything now that will help to increase their number; certainly nothing that I can say now briefly is going to clear anything up. But at least I will put them on the record and make a few general comments.

It has been said that scientific investigation begins and ends with theory; it has also been said that it begins and ends with observation. Be this as it may, it has also been said that the scientific investigator in any particular field starts with a theory that is quite different from the theory which he later develops. For some scientists this difference is sufficiently great to warrant the use of two different words to refer to them. Sometimes the words "conceptual scheme" (for investigation) are used to refer to the former and the word "theory" (of explanation) is used to refer to the latter. Although there is no general agreement on the use of these words, this will be the way I shall use them.

It has also been said that in order to be fruitful for investigation conceptual schemes do not have to be too precise and clear. Why? Because their function is not to explain but to fix attention upon what is to be first observed and in time explained. Their attributes are utility and convenience for purposes of investigation, not truth or falsity or clarity for purposes of explanation.

So from this point of view I am putting to bed now (but not for later discussion) these notions about structure, function, and equilibrium, by placing them in the category of conceptual entities which in themselves may not explain and perhaps in time may need explaining themselves, but which nevertheless, in the first instance, because we cannot do everything at the same time, may help to produce findings that are well worth explaining. By such a cavalier disposal of these very important ideas I do not think that I am downgrading them or misrepresenting the use that was made of them by the early investigators. These investigators, because of their empirical leanings, were more interested in the heuristic value of these ideas than in their logical consistency and metaphysical implications.

Moreover, it seemed to them that in purposive organizations—because of their goal orientations—the notion of function could be used without implying any great mystique. What was going on in a firm, for example, could be viewed from the point of view of the function that it had for (1) achieving the goals of the organization, (2) maintaining the ways of life of the constituent groups of the organization, and (3) satisfying the needs of the individuals comprising these groups. In this sense the functional point of view did provide a framework or rationale for understanding what was going on. It could easily be seen that what was functional for one might not be functional for another, so there was no built-in pre-established harmony in this way of looking at things. There was plenty of conflict around, as all the early investigations showed.

But no final pronouncements were made about the inevitability of these conflicts. Rather they were viewed as characterizing the setting in which the administrator worked, made his decision, and exercised his authority. What could provide a better opportunity to look and see how he went about it?

The Development of Knowledge and Practice Together

Therefore, associated with this new conceptual scheme for the empirical investigation of man's behavior in organizations was the notion that this behavior could be more concretely observed from the point of view of the problems that it presented for the people who were responsible for administering organizations. By doing this it was not our intention to slant things in the direction of management values or of being exclusively practical. Although these dangers were present, they were overshadowed by an idea that captured our imagination. In this way we felt that we could develop theory and practice together. We would be looking at organizations, not from the point of view of the problems that they presented for society in general, but from the point of view of the problems that they presented for persons who were doing something about them or could do, if they so chose, something different about them. Knowledge about the behavior of people in organizations would be developed hand in hand with knowledge for someone who could utilize it in a professional way.

Any idea has associated with it certain imagery and, as I remember it, the medical analogy was often used to make this idea vivid. The clinical practice of medicine was often compared with the clinical practice of administration. Just as the descriptive laws of physiology could help in the improved practice of medicine, so these descriptive laws about the behavior of persons in organizations, when found, could help to improve the practice of administration, and from them more competent professional management would more likely emerge.

A Situational Orientation

One other element—and it will be the final one upon which I will comment—was associated with this early conceptual scheme for the empirical investigation of man's behavior in organizations. Many of us had gone through a period of "wild psychoanalysis"; we did not wish to go through another period of "wild functional analysis," i.e., of speculating about the possible functional benefits to some system or other of every piece of behavior that we looked at.

We felt that this danger could be best contained by being situationally and clinically oriented, i.e., by being oriented to the functions of certain pervasive patterns of behavior that appeared in concrete situations that we were studying and for which we could obtain some first-hand clinical evidence. This dictated for many of us in the beginning a field research and a single case approach to the study of organizations. This raises some methodological issues that I will return to later.

Summary

In summary, then, let me comment briefly in general about some of these early ideas that I think set the stage for many of us who were starting an empirical investigation of man's behavior in organizations.

1. There was nothing new about any one of the ideas singly. They had all been borrowed from the behavioral sciences—for example, the notions of social structure, function, and equilibrium.

2. Although isomorphic to the territory, these ideas were not defining what in particular the territory was; they were more ideas of how it might be investigated in order to obtain the data and, in time, the propositions upon which a more scientific explanation could be built.

3. We drew our boundary lines between what we would treat as "givens" and what we would try to explain, so that neither traditional psychology nor traditional sociology could pre-empt the field and so that a premature reduction of one to the other could be avoided.

4. These ideas constituted a long-term step-by-step research strategy for empirical investigation; the payoff was not going to be immediate because there was nothing to be explained until the findings were in.

I think that I could have made many of these same statements had I been using the conceptual and terminological system of "force field theory" and stating it as a tool for investigation and not as a system of explanation. Anyway, it was this new long-term research strategy embodied in a conceptual scheme for investigation that captured the imagination and created the excitement for many of us at the time. It was far from being sheer empiricism. As I have tried to show, a set of explicit ideas were being brought to the investigation. It was hoped, however, that they would carry with them the least amount of preconceptions, i.e., the least amount of metaphysical notions about what organizations or man's relation to them should be. It was hoped that they would help to get results that in time would throw a new light and perspective on some of the traditional problems of management and labor, to break through some of the old distinctions and traditional concerns and ways of talking and thinking about these matters, and even to cut across the traditional distinction between pure and applied research.

It was hoped that this empirical investigation could be developed together in the direction of obtaining both improved knowledge about organizations and improved administrative practices on the part of responsible people in them. Improved knowledge would come by establishing first the simple descriptive propositions about man's behavior in organizations. These propositions would come slowly by patient, pedestrian effort in the field and well-documented case studies. When more carefully tested and verified, they would provide the basis for improved knowledge and practice.

SOME FINDINGS AND APPLICATIONS

I have spent some time on these ideas—what I have called the conceptual scheme for the empirical investigation of man's behavior in organizations—because they set the stage for two decades of research around two aspects of organizational behavior: (1) morale and employee productivity, satisfaction, and motivation, and (2) leadership and supervision. In these two areas not only were the findings the greatest but also the direction in which they pointed for the improvement of administrative practices was the clearest. As this development has been well documented in the literature, let me review it only briefly.

Some General Findings

It seems to me astonishing how at one level of analysis the findings of different investigators checked. Again and again these findings pointed to:

1. the inadequacy of the motivational assumptions underlying the traditional principles of management;

2. what little influence the employee was supposed to exercise, what few interpersonal transactions he was supposed to have, what little two-way communication there was supposed to be, and how doing what he was told and being obedient to authority seemed to be the sole integrative force under the traditional principles of management;

3. the conflict between the principles of scientific management on the one hand and the determinants of cooperation on the other, i.e., how the application of these principles seemed to be at odds with the way members of an organization became identified and committed to its goals;

4. how the more a supervisor managed in terms of what he was supposed to do in accordance with the principles of management, the less of an all-round, long-term job he seemed to be doing;

5. how supervisors and managers who seemed to get the best over-all, long-term effect seemed to be displaying a leadership style quite different from those who did not;

6. how supervisors and managers who were displaying a leadership style different from what they were supposed to be doing received little support from (a) their superiors, (b) the traditional theory, (c) any accepted new theory, or (d) any feedback of results, other than those of the traditional kind, that would reflect the good over-all long-term job that they were doing;

7. how, under the traditional principles of management, informal leaders tended to appear in many work groups in order to take care of the maintenance functions that the task leaders failed to perform;

8. "the restriction of output syndrome," i.e., how, under the principles of scientific management, employees tended to develop a concept of a day's work that was not too high or too low to get them into trouble;

9. "the man-in-the-middle syndrome," i.e., the different ways supervisors resolved the conflict of trying to get the cooperation of their employees while at the same time trying to get them to do what they should be doing at the proper time and place and with the proper methods, and as a result, the different leadership styles which tended to emerge and to which many different names have been given, such as, for example, institutional, autocratic, laissez-faire, accommodative, personal, production-oriented, person-oriented, group-oriented, democratic, permissive, supportive, and transactional;

10. "the staff–line syndrome," i.e., how staff people, who were supposed to be helping line people by setting standards for evaluating the results of employees, tended to be regarded by the line people more as a source of interference than as a source of help;

11. "the distributive justice syndrome," i.e., the many complaints that took the form that it isn't fair or just that what I'm getting is not proportional to what I should be getting in terms of my age, seniority, education, sex, etc.;

12. "the vicious cycle syndrome," i.e., how the unintended dysfunctional consequences of the traditional methods of control tended to encourage a continued use of them, e.g., the breakdown of rules begot more rules to take care of their breakdown or the breakdown of close supervision encouraged the use of still closer methods of supervision, and thus led to a continuous search for new control systems to correct for the limitations of previous ones;

13. "the specialist–generalist syndrome," i.e., the sharp difference of outlook, skill, knowledge, and influence required and acquired by those who do the work of the organization (whether they be workers, salesmen, clerks, technicians, or scientists) and by those who are responsible for facilitating that the work gets done, well illustrated by the differences, for example, between the optimizing of this *or* that and the "satisficing" of this *and* that;

14. "the frozen group syndrome," i.e., the kind of static accommodation which many work groups seemed to make to the organizational environments in which they had to survive; and

15. "the underdeveloped individual development syndrome," i.e., the amount of apathy, uninvolvement, and uncommitment which existed among some members of an organization, particularly at the work level, and the needs for belonging, competence, self-development and identity which were not being tapped by management and which could not be tapped by the traditional principles of management.

The Development of Human Relations Training

For many investigators as well as practitioners who wanted to do something, the action prescription to which these findings pointed was relatively clear: supervisors and managers needed to have a better understanding of cooperative–conflict phenomena in order to do a better job of supervision and management. This educational develop- ment of supervisors and executives has proceeded in ever-increasing stages of sophistication which I will review very briefly as follows:

1. At an obvious manifest level, these findings pointed to the need for more participative management, two-way communication, and permissive leadership. These ideas were not entirely new to some managements, and to those who were interested in going in this di- rection, the findings helped to give support. But to those who were not, these findings had little impact and so exhortations to be more participative, permissive, and two way-ish fell on deaf ears. Anyway, for many of these managements, how you become this way presented for them a difficult question.

2. Even to the investigators it became obvious that although more participatory methods needed to be utilized, these methods were not capable of being abstracted and learned apart from the concrete be- havior of the persons who were to practice them. The development of new styles of leadership involved a re-educational job. In order for the supervisor to be able to understand and to deal with the phenomena of cooperation and conflict that the institutional type of leadership ignored, he needed more fundamental training.

3. From these ideas, the beginning of human relations training at the supervisory and foreman levels developed. In many early programs this training took place at a persuasive and anecdotal level, going little beyond that of urging supervisors to treat their employees more like human beings. But among the better programs—at least in intention and ignoring for the moment the question of how well they were doing

it—there was an attempt to reach a more cognitive level, and through case materials, discussion, and lectures, to give the supervisor an understanding of the nature of cooperative–conflict phenomena and the skills that were associated with them.

4. In some programs a further refinement took place that I think is worth underscoring. It became clear that the fruitful ways of thinking for empirical investigation, outlined earlier, could also be utilized for the improvement of practice. If supervisors could be taught these ways of thinking and could learn to explore their problem situations in terms of them, better diagnoses of particular situations could be made. And from better diagnosed situations, better actions, it was hoped, would follow. Not only would the utilization of this way of thinking direct their attention to matters of feeling, sentiment, social structure, informal organization—matters which the traditional principles of management ignored—but also it would counteract the supervisor's search for the one right way and the one right answer. It was more important for supervisors to have the spirit and tools of situational investigation than to have assigned role prescriptions. (This development probably took place more in courses that were being developed at business schools for potential executives than in training programs for supervisors in industry.)

5. As these programs developed, the clinical psychologist came more and more to the fore. He had been present from the beginning as one of the important contributors to the interdisciplinary combination involved in the empirical investigation of man's behavior in organizations, and if I have neglected to mention his contributions earlier, it is only because I have been cutting corners in order to cover a large amount of material rather quickly. Anyway, his methods of interviewing in helping persons to talk about matters that were important to them had been borrowed and utilized freely during the period of investigation. But they were equally useful for the development of practice in trying to help supervisors to listen more intelligently and understandingly to the members of the work groups that they were supervising.

6. As time went on, however, some unanticipated problems began to appear. One of them appeared around the question, "Were these programs not being developed under some rather unrealistic assumptions?" For example, they were being addressed mainly to the super-

visory–foreman level. How could new styles of leadership be developed among them while their bosses continued to manage in the traditional way? How unrealistic could you get? Supervisors were neither free agents nor independent variables, and yet human relations training seemed to be making the assumption that they were.

7. Another set of problems appeared around the relation of knowledge to practice. It was felt that supervisors did not readily change their behavior from reading books and being told about the determinants of behavior or even from discussing case materials about the experiences and problems of others. Changes in behavior were more likely to occur when they could re-examine their perceptions of themselves and others in supportive settings, that is, under conditions where they would not have to fear being unjustly criticized and misevaluated. Although these ideas were coming from the clinical insights of psychotherapy, they were also receiving a great deal of support from the results of many training programs where it had been found that it was easier to get the supervisor to talk about the new styles of leadership than to practice them and where it was difficult to get them to feel the difference between the intent and the consequences of their behavior.

8. To take care of these problems many different modifications were introduced. Programs began to appear at higher echelons of management; executive development became the new thrust. Trainees were taken away from the organizational environments in which they worked and placed in new and more unstructured situations where they could "unfreeze" their old ways of doing things, experiment with new roles, get some confidence in becoming more role-flexible and reflect upon how they could apply this new learning when they got "back home." This kind of learning emphasized the need to examine more "here and now" data and less "there and then" data, i.e., to look more at the data (group processes) that were being generated and were taking place *here and now* in the group while it engaged in discussions about its task and to be concerned less with prefabricated materials in the form of "written cases" about somebody else's experiences.

9. This development, which is known as Laboratory Training or T-Group or Group Dynamics or Sensitivity Training, aims to reach a much deeper level of understanding of cooperative–conflict phenomena than any other previous version of human relations training. It is heavily influenced by social psychology, group dynamics, and psycho-

therapy; it is deeply concerned with humanizing bureaucracy; it has become the newest and for some behavioral scientists the most exciting instrument for organizational change; and around it has developed a new professional group of "change-agents" and a new field of "change-agentry."

10. As can be seen, human relations training has traveled a long road from its early days of trying to urge superiors to treat people as human beings to the present-day sophistication of the T-Group. But, it would be incorrect to believe that this is its final or only version; revisions are continually being made; different combinations of theory and practice are being sought and tried in different programs of human relations training.

11. Nor would it be correct to believe that the present T-Group version is not being criticized by some behavioral scientists. One question that keeps cropping up is "Has it not gone too far down the road of psychotherapy?" On this question, although the intent of its practitioners is clear (i.e., "T" in "T-Group" stands for training and not for therapy), the evidence is not clear because the line between certain aspects of social learning and psychotherapy is not clear. But more serious still for some is the question, "Can bureaucracies be humanized and democratized?" How successful has the T-Group been in achieving its own aims? What do the results show? Here again the evidence is difficult to obtain. Testimonials do not provide very good evidence, but also, because these questions cannot be easily made operational, they cannot be easily tested.

12. As a result two doctrinal positions have arisen in the area of organizational change, and the underlying tone of the current literature on the subject reflects them well. There is one school of thought whose members, though willing to admit that a bureaucracy is strongly resistant to change and that there are "bugs" in their position, nevertheless believe that it is worth while trying to do something and that in time the "bugs" can be removed. They support their position with evidence and insights from psychotherapy and clinical psychology, and this evidence, although not quite germane to the point, is nevertheless difficult to discount completely. Then there is another school of thought which says in effect that "it can't be done," that bureaucracies are bureaucratic for very good functional reasons and hence that human relations trainers who are trying to humanize bureaucracies are "incurable romanticists" and deluding themselves.

13. So this is the stage which one development of the findings has reached. Although each side of the above dispute can cite some evidence in favor of its position, it is doubtful that these doctrinal positions can ever be resolved by this method. So I should now like to turn to other developments which to some behavioral scientists not only are equally promising and exciting but also need to take place before some of the problems raised by human relations training can be resolved.

SOME UNFINISHED BUSINESS

Let me return to the findings. Some behavioral scientists have raised questions about these findings that were quite different from those questions with which the human relations training group was concerned. They have asked questions such as: (1) Had the findings been contaminated by the conceptual scheme? (2) Had they been sufficiently tested and were they in the form to be tested? and (3) Did they not themselves need to be explained? The first question has raised considerable discussion, some of which I feel has not been fruitful; the second and third questions have stimulated a great deal of fruitful research and speculation.

Problems of Slanting

Many criticisms have been made of the early formulation. Although I shall list some of them below for purposes of our discussion later, I will not attempt to consider each of them. Rather I will raise a more general question which to me underlies many of these criticisms.

It has been said that the original formulation, which I have called the conceptual scheme for empirical investigation, slanted things in the direction of (1) irrationality or nonrationality, (2) harmony and conservatism, (3) the organization's internal environment, and (4) management values. It tended to overlook (1) the more rational problem-solving behavior of organizations, (2) conflict, (3) the organization's external environment, and (4) union values. It had basically an anti-economic, anti-scientific management, anti-engineering, anti-legislative, and anti-formalistic bias. These biases have so contaminated the findings that they cannot provide a solid foundation upon which to build.

If we remove from these criticisms any implications of a lack of intellectual integrity on the part of the investigators—and this is the assumption upon which I will proceed, namely, that there was no deliberate slanting in terms of the investigators' ideological beliefs and that this issue is not being raised by the criticisms—then we are left with a problem that has never ceased to intrigue me.

Any conceptual scheme slants; this is what makes it useful. Because one cannot look at and talk about everything at the same time (a most unfortunate human predicament), a conceptual scheme says "look *here*" instead of (or as well as) "there." And in a certain sense persons who use it will find what they are looking for. But this is not as serious as it sounds, so long as one understands why this is so and how it can be corrected.

The conceptual scheme that I stated earlier, for example, was saying in effect: (1) Don't just look at actions; look also at interactions and their associated sentiments; look at the interactions between persons and groups and in the organization. (2) Look for both the intended and unintended consequences for some involved system (e.g., personality, small group, formal organization) of certain pervasive patterns in the organization. (3) Look for the patterns of behavior that keep recurring, that have seemed to settle down in some kind of practical equilibrium, i.e., that are expressing some long-term accommodation to the environmental forces about them. And, *above all,* (4) seek for descriptive propositions—not *normative propositions*—about these pervasive phenomena that are being observed.

The confusion between descriptive and normative propositions. I wonder how many persons realize what a serious confusion this is. Organizations, and business organizations in particular, are highly normative worlds. They are bristling with normative propositions about how things *should be* and *should be done* and what rational behavior *should* be. The world of organizations, as any field worker knows, is teeming with these notions of what is "right" and "wrong" and what is "good" and "bad," what is "rational" and "irrational," and what is "good sense" and "bad judgment." Many of the propositions of traditional management theory and scientific management are of this sort. They are the kinds of propositions that the practitioner wants.

As a result many difficult problems are encountered when one tries to slant things in the direction of stating descriptive propositions about man's behavior in organizations. The introduction of descriptive propositions into this highly normative world is as welcome as a "hole in the head." For this reason it may have unanticipated dysfunctional consequences that far outweigh the functional consequences that are intended. Among those who have tried it, this problem is understood, but among those who have not, the underestimation of the importance of this problem never ceases to astonish me.

One of the problems is that these propositions which are intended to be descriptive from the point of view of the speaker do not remain descriptive very long from the point of view of the listener. How often have we underscored, when using words such as "bureaucracy" (in relation to a certain kind of formal organization), "democratic" (in relation to a certain style of leadership), and "nonlogical" (in relation to a certain kind of behavior), for example, that we are using these words in a descriptive and not an evaluative sense. Does anyone hear this? Even words like "group," "conformity," or "deviance" do not remain descriptive very long. For many persons, statements to the effect that "democratic" (good) styles of leadership may have sometimes some dysfunctional (bad) consequences, that "nonlogical" behavior (bad) may perform sometimes some highly useful (good) social functions, and that "rational" behavior (good) may sometimes have some dysfunctional (bad) consequences imply for them some very serious contradictions.

Even the form of the findings previously stated, although intended to be descriptive of certain clinical uniformities in organizational behavior, can easily generate sentiments which will involve evaluative judgments and metaphysical suffering, such as for example that management people are not very bright; or that there is an irreconcilable conflict between the demands of organizations and the creative, self-developmental needs of man; or that bureaucracies are unfortunately a necessary evil in this world, etc.

In view of these problems, which exist among ourselves as well as among businessmen and laymen, I am not assigning a very high prior probability that anything I can say now will clear them up. But because, in these matters of conceptual clarity, hope springs eternal, let me repeat what has been said over and over again in one way or another by many, namely that the concept of "function" does not make behavior thereby "irrational," "nonrational," or for that matter even "rational." It is not stating how people should behave according to some normative model of behavior. Rather it is providing a rationale for behavior, a model for the analysis of behavior that can be applied to managers as well as to workers.

Applied to any individual, it is stating the benefits a person is getting from behaving the way that he does. Hence from *his point of view,* even though his behavior may not be "rational" from the point of view of an outside observer, even though his behavior may land him in a "looney bin," even though his behavior does not coincide with a normative model of how under conditions of uncertainty he should behave in order to maximize his expected monetary value, his behavior is not thereby "nonrational." What this means is that from the functional point of view one can make some sense of it. So it is possible that from some normative point of view the behavior is "nonrational" and still from the functional point of view one can make some sense of it, if one so chooses.

The confusion between external and internal. Equally slanting was the way in which we sliced our cake for the purpose of investigation, and which in turn determined what became for us "external" and "internal." As I have stated before, we chose to treat as boundary conditions for what we would be observing in the organization (a) the values that people brought there and (b) the prescribed ways in which things should be done in order to achieve the organizational goals. Thus, for us "a" and "b" became the environment for the actual behavior that we were observing. As a result the actual behavior (social structure) that emerged from these environmental conditions became the internal environment of the organization. This was *not* the organization's external environment in which the organization had to survive, such as the marketing environment in the case of a business organization.

Obviously this formulation slanted us in the direction of looking at and trying to understand the organization's internal environment, i.e., how the actual on-going social structure operated and was administered in order to survive in its external environment. This did not mean that we ignored the organization's external environment; we were very interested in any changes going on there that would have consequences for the social structure and the way it would cope with them. But why these changes were going on "out there," we were willing to leave to the economists and the sociologist to explain. We were interested in trying to explain how the internal system, i.e., the organization from within, was going to assimilate and cope with this external environment.

Although in theory it is recognized that these ways of slicing cakes for certain investigatory and explanatory purposes have nothing God-given about them, in practice this is sometimes forgotten. When someone treats as given what someone else wants to explain or vice versa, bitter disputes sometimes occur, even among those of us who are theoretically sophisticated about these matters. But among those of us who are not and who believe that some higher authority settles these questions, the confusion, in my experience, is very difficult to straighten out with words—no matter how clearly we try to define them.

Anyhow, it was this way of slicing the cake that allowed us to obtain an understanding of the executive's behavior that ran counter on almost all points to what the traditional principles of management said that his behavior should be. Let me illustrate this sharp contrast.

a. According to the traditional principles of management, the internal environment contains only the explicit control mechanisms that the manager and his experts put there. Once these controls have been set up so that everyone knows what is expected of him, the executive spends the remainder of his time making decisions that affect the organization's relation to its external environment. This way of thinking emphasizes the external environment as the executive's chief concern. It is the external environment to which he should be paying the most attention, toward which his fundamental posture should be directed, with which he should be acquainted, and about which he should have knowledge. In the case of a business organization, for example, his habitat becomes the market place. According to this point of view, a general theory of management would be derived from a knowledge about this external environment.

b. According to the way we sliced the cake, the internal environment is populated with the values and norms that have been *brought there* as social precipitates from the backgrounds and experiences of the individuals comprising the organization, as well as with the standards, controls, rules, and programs that have been *put there* for the purposes of achieving the organizational goals as well as the practice, norms, and values that have *developed there* under these conditions. This environment is not solely the executive's creation; it is not something independent of him; he both affects and is affected by it and in it he is highly involved. According to this view, the executive's job is not in the market place, buying and selling. This is the work of the organization, and the executive's job is not to do the work of the organization but to facilitate the getting of it done. His job is not to make all the decisions himself but to see that the proper resources are being brought to bear on the making of them. These decisions have to be made within the internal environment of which he is an involved member. It is this insight upon which the human relations training programs have been built. How does the executive secure changes in the internal environment under these conditions of involvement?

Moreover, the internal environment—not the external environment —is an important referent for many of the executive's most important decisions, e.g., where do I want to go? What do I want to be? What business do I want to be in? What share of the market do I want to have and what price (not only economic) am I willing to pay for it? Toward all these questions the external environment is neutral, except to state the conditions under which these goals can be realized, i.e., the price which would have to be paid for their realization. But the involved executive—not the external environment—has to decide what price (not only economic) he is willing to pay. According to this point of view the executive's natural habitat is the internal environment and from an acquaintance with and a knowledge about this internal environment, the professional competent manager as well as a general theory of management would be developed.

Problems of Verification

Let me return to the findings again, because besides arguing about them some behavioral scientists have tried to verify them. But this has presented some difficult problems and I will cite only some.

1. A re-examination of the previously mentioned findings will show that they consist mostly of clinical uniformities which were obtained from field research of single case studies. A single case may help to reveal this uniformity; it does not verify it. For this, not evidence from one case but evidence from many independent cases is needed.

2. But, in order to do this, social categories have to be created, in which it is often difficult to include the network of social relations between individuals and groups, that is, the social context under which these uniformities revealed themselves in the first place.

3. Moreover, many of these uniformities are not stated in the form which allows them to be verified easily. The anthropological–sociological concept of "function" (i.e, x fulfills function c for system y), for example, is not the same as the mathematical concept of "function" (i.e., y is a function of x) and it is often not easy to translate functional statements of the former kind into functional statements of the latter kind, although some of them can be.

So the verifiers have had plenty of trouble, but because these troubles involve difficult technical problems upon which they are diligently working and in time will make some headway, let me pass on to another problem.

Problems of Explanation

As may have been noticed, throughout this paper I have been concerned with questions of explanation, e.g., what are we trying to explain? What constitutes explanation? Is there not an important difference between investigation and explanation? May not the confusion between the two underlie some of the arguments about our classification schemes and terminologies? By confusing investigation with explanation may we not be trying to do two different things at the same time and thus misusing the instruments of one for the purposes of the other?

Recently in the literature I have detected a school of thought about scientific explanation which interests me because I think that it could be used to help us not only to reduce the amount of our disputes about words, concepts, and classification schemes but also, more important, to get on with the job of explaining our findings. If I understand this school of thought correctly it is saying something like this:

1. Let us stop being so concerned with differences in conceptual schemes, with looking for logical inconsistencies in them, with torturing ourselves with their metaphysical (ultimate, final, irreconcilable) implications, and with trying to make them logically consistent and metaphysically impregnable.

2. When things get tough and our findings seem paradoxical or contradictory, let us stop trying to seek for explanations by means of new words, labels, and concepts that are more logically consistent, psychologically appealing, or culturally attractive.

3. Instead let us concentrate upon the findings that our conceptual schemes have helped us to obtain. Let us keep looking at these findings

for the simple uniformities which they may reveal in the form of *"x varies with y."* These simple empirical propositions are our most enduring possessions. With them explanation begins; without them there is nothing to be explained.

4. Let us look for the boundary conditions under which these simple uniformities reveal themselves, and if under condition A our colleague has found that they reveal themslves in state P, while under condition B we have found that they result in state Q, let's not rush to give the lie to our colleague. No contradiction is necessarily involved. This result, if A and B are understood correctly, may help to confirm and not refute them.

5. Once these simple empirical propositions have been established, let us search for a set of more general propositions of the same order, from which under specified conditions the simple descriptive propositions that we have observed—as well as others that we may not have as yet observed—may be derived.

6. Let us state clearly what we are treating as given and what we are trying to explain. This is not the problem of just one school of thought or one investigator; it is a problem for all investigators of any school of thought.

7. Let us not try to reach *deductively* the general propositions by which our simple propositions are to be explained; these general propositions are arrived at *inductively*.

8. The deductive way that a theory of explanation looks *when completed* (i.e., as a set of higher-order general propositions from which under specified conditions the lower-order descriptive propositions can be deductively derived) is not the way this theory is *arrived at*.

9. The simple descriptive propositions are reached in many ways; field research is a good way, although not the only one; the simple propositions are confirmed by survey and experimental methods but the general propositions from which they are derived are inductive creations and inventions.

10. This is why it is futile to try to repatch our conceptual schemes in order to seek for better explanations. It doesn't go that way. The processes of investigation are not to be equated with the processes of explanation. Let us not confuse them.

I find these statements both reassuring and exciting. They say to me, "Let's start making an inventory of our simple descriptive findings and let us search for more general propositions to explain them." To me this approach, if done explicitly, offers some hope of cutting down our interminable.conceptual arguments and of making some progress in explaining our findings.

SOME CONCLUSIONS

The underlying theme of much of what I have been saying has been something as follows:

1. Some interesting clinical findings have been obtained about man's behavior in organizations; some of them have been verified by statistical procedures.

2. These findings were obtained by focusing (a) not upon man *per se,* (b) not upon organization *per se,* but (c) upon man-in-organization. They are therefore limited to this domain or subject matter.

3. In the obtaining of these findings no canons of scientific methodology were violated which make them unworthy of explanation. Many of the findings do not need to await further refinement before we try to explain them.

4. Although the findings have been argued about and different ultimate meanings have been attached to them, they still remain relatively unexplained, i.e., in the sense that there exists no set of more general propositions which explain them.

5. These findings are begging for explanation. Few investigators would argue that they are unrelated. But up to very recently their explanation has been sought for more in a set of logically interrelated concepts than in a set of general propositions.

6. There is no reason why any investigator should try to explain these findings if he is interested in explaining something else. But likewise there is nothing in science which says that if he is interested, he should not try to explain them or that he should be explaining something else.

7. For those who are interested, then, let's get on with the job of trying to explain our findings. Let us not keep rediscovering America over and over again; let's begin to try to explain what we have discovered. If and when we do, we may have the beginning of what we are looking for—a general theory of management.

24 How a Functionalist Thinks and Acts

I am including here a set of unpublished notes I prepared in December 1962 for discussion by doctoral students at the Harvard Business School in a seminar on "Clinical Observation and Interviewing." I realize that these notes, read by themselves, might be meaningless, but I think that if they are read in connection with the previous essays and particularly the last one (Chapter 23), they might help to clarify the way the area of organizational behavior might be developed for those who were to become engaged in it professionally as researchers, teachers, or consultants.

In these notes I was talking to doctoral students who not only would go into the field to collect cases but later would teach those cases. I was addressing both the *research field worker* and the *teacher practitioner*. I put my remarks in the form of questions that the doctoral student might be asking of himself and his clients *in the field* as well as himself and his students *in the classroom*. The proper names I used referred to cases about individuals-in-organization with which all the students were familiar.

Let me try to state how a functionalist thinks and acts in terms of the questions he would be asking when trying to diagnose a concrete situation in the field or in the classroom and to decide what, if anything, he should do about it.

1. FORMAL REQUIREMENTS, EXPECTATIONS AND STATUS

1.1 What is the stated problem? For whom? (The remainder of the questions can be viewed as trying to clarify the total situation of which the stated problem is a symptom.)

1.2 Who are the persons directly and indirectly involved in the problem?

1.3 What are their *formal* relations to each other? What is (are) the formal unit(s) or subunit(s) which for purposes of convenience I will treat as the *social system* to be examined?

1.4 What are the persons *supposed* or *ought* to be doing? What are their *required* activities and interaction? the *primary* tasks (activities) involved? the *standards of performance* to be met? the institutional *givens*? the *role requirements*? What activities are *required? permitted? prohibited?*

1.5 How are the tasks (jobs) spatially arranged? How are they differentiated in terms of *Territory, Time* (e.g. shifts), and *Technology?* What is the flow of work? What from the point of view of a T, T, and

T analysis is bringing people together? keeping them apart? requiring them to interact? providing them with opportunities to interact? What *legitimate activities* are going on in what *legitimate spaces* at what *legitimate times?* What legitimate *objects* appear in these spaces, places, and times? For example, would I expect to find a roll of toilet paper in the living room? Would I expect to find a pin-up girl in the office of the President of the X National Bank? Why not?

1.6   What is the *amount, frequency, duration,* and *origination* of the required interactions? *Who* is *originating* interaction upon *whom, how much, how often,* and *how long?* If A is supposed to initiate action for B, what is this telling me about the relation of A to B?

1.7   How do the different jobs rank in terms of status factors relating to the job (e.g. pay, autonomy, variety, etc.)?—*job status.*

1.8   What social backgrounds (status factors) are the individuals bringing to the situation (e.g. age, service, education, ethnicity, sex, etc.)? What status factors do they (individuals and groups) have in common?—*shared values.* How do they rank in terms of these status factors?—*social status.* (I should remember that these data are sometimes not provided in many written cases. In some cases reasonable inferences and assumptions can be made about these matters but I should realize that I am doing so.)

1.9   What are the possible trouble spots—ambiguities—out-of-line-nesses—conflicts such as, for example:

(a) Treating job status factors as "rewards" and social status factors as "investments," where are rewards out of line with investments (e.g. low pay, long service or high pay, short service) such that job status is out of line with social status such that R > I or R < I?

(b) Where is job or social status not well established as high or low? —*status incongruence.*

(c) Where does a low-status person by the requirements of the job have to originate action upon a high-status person?

(d) Where is a high-status group not high in all status factors so that it is not clearly differentiated from a lower-status group on all status factors?

2. COMPLAINTS AND THE CONDITION OF FELT INJUSTICE

2.1   What are people complaining about? When are they saying something isn't "fair" or just?

2.2　Do I see any connections between (1.9) data and (2.1) data?

2.3　Researches have shown some connection between them. Do I know what they are? How do persons talk and behave when $R < I$? $R > I$? Am I listening? observing? What is the functionality of this kind of talk and behavior for the person in the situation? By the way, do I think it is "fair" that some movie actresses earn more money than the President of the United States? Why not?

3. MEMBERSHIP AND INFORMAL LEADERSHIP

3.1　What is the emergent behavior?
(a) What are the expressed norms and values of groups?
(b) What are the friendships, subgroupings, pairings, etc.? Who is asking help (advice) of whom for what?
(c) What individuals are engaging in what non-work activities?
(d) In terms of (a), (b), and (c) what is the membership pattern (e.g. regulars, deviants, isolates)?
(e) Who is (are) the informal leader(s)—the norm-setter(s)? norm-policer(s)?
(f) Who is (are) the task leader(s)? the social leader(s)?
(g) How cohesive is the group? (I should remember that in many written cases the above data are not provided too well. Sometimes reasonable assumptions and inferences can be made. But I should not make them without any evidence.)

3.2　Can I now connect some of the data of 3.1(d), (e), and (f) with the data in 1.4, 1.5, 1.6, 1.7, and 1.8? For example:
(a) Can I now specify a person's position in a group by two conceptually different dimensions—status and membership—established by different and independent criteria so that now I can ask: Who are the (1) high-status regulars, (2) high-status deviants, (3) high-status isolates, (4) low-status regulars, (5) low-status deviants, (6) low-status isolates?
(b) Are some of these "positions" more congruent (in line) or incongruent (out-of-line) than others? Can I see and hear these differences behavioratively expressed? Am I listening? observing?
(c) Is a low-status isolate, for example, by the requirements of the job having to initiate interaction upon a high-status regular?

(d) In what *spaces,* at what *times,* and in what *activities* (technologies) do I find the persons in the above *six status–membership categories?* Are they randomly distributed? If not, why not?

(e) Are there high (low) status objects, places, distances, locations, and times?

(f) Do I find many (any) low-status persons who are informal leaders? If not, why not?

(g) By the way, where did I find those pin-up girls in my trip through the plant?

3.3 What are the *consequences* (functions) for *productivity* and *satisfaction* of the above emergent behavior?

(a) Who are the high, on-the-line, and low producers?

(b) Who are the high and low satisfied?

(c) Do I find any connections between my findings to questions 3.1(d), (e), and (f) and my findings to questions 3.3(a) and (b)? Researches have shown some. Do I know what they are?

(d) Do I see why some high producers are not very happy? And why some investigators have found an inverse correlation between productivity and satisfaction?

(e) What do I conclude from this, (1) managers should increase dissatisfaction to increase output, or (2) there is no positive relation between productivity and satisfaction, or (3) the relation between productivity and satisfaction is complex—not simple?

4. FORMAL LEADERSHIP

4.1 What are some of the formal leadership styles of the supervisors and managers?

4.2 How have these styles been characterized in the literature? (a) production-oriented, (b) person-oriented, (c) group-oriented, (d) autocratic, (e) institutional, (f) laissez-faire, (g) accommodative, (h) democratic, (i) permissive, (j) participative, (k) transactional, etc.

4.3 (Perhaps I should realize that these labels are not too clear or precise—that some of them are overlapping—that generally they are being used to refer to that dimension of the total situation to which the supervisor or manager is paying more attention or assigning more importance and value (e.g. *production, person,* and *group* oriented);

that some of them have more emotional connotations and are implying in addition something about the executive's notion about the source of authority (e.g. *autocratic, democratic*); that some of them are referring more to the responses (adjustments) made by the "man-in-the-middle" who is having difficulty (conflicts) in reconciling the institutional requirement with the group and personal requirements of his job (*laissez-faire, accommodative,* etc.).

4.4   Do I see that "leadership style" is a second-order abstraction, just as "role" is, and that both are derived from a combination of first-order abstractions such as *activities, interactions,* and *sentiments?* If I can describe a particular situation accurately by these first-order abstractions, do I need these words—role and leadership style—except for purposes of convenient shorthand?

4.5   In particular situations what are the functional and dysfunctional *consequences* of these different leadership styles for the *motivation, productivity* and *satisfaction, morale* and *development* of subordinate individuals and groups and for the leader himself? There has been considerable research on these questions. Do I know in general what the findings have been? What have the cases I've studied shown?

5. CONTROL AND MOTIVATION

5.1   What are the assumptions and logics of management about human motivation?

5.2   By whom are they most fervently and frequently expressed?

5.3   Who are the persons and groups formally responsible for setting management's standards of performance? output? quality? cost?

5.4   Who are the persons and groups formally responsible for setting management's goals—quotas, budgets?

5.5   Who are the persons and groups formally responsible for implementing these goals and standards?

5.6   What is the relation between the standard setters and the standard implementers; what is this relation supposed to be; what is this relation in fact? Why is it that those who are supposed to be a source of *help* (functional) are often perceived to be a source of interference? (dysfunctional)

5.7   In what way do standards of performance operate as incentives in helping persons to perform better or by helping them to identify better with the goals of the organization or by helping supervisors to supervise better? Do they also have sometimes some dysfunctional consequences? What did my findings to questions 3.3(c) and 4.5 show? Do they sometimes tend to facilitate more close than more general supervision? Why?

5.8   I understand that the degree to which a person realizes some standard of performance or expectation, i.e. the better he does what is expected of him as measured by some organizational standard of expectation, the more *effective* his behavior is, i.e. the more he is *adjusted* to his role requirements. This I understand is an external evaluation from the point of view of the organization and situation. Can a person be adjusted in this sense and not getting a kick from what he is doing?

5.9   Is this evaluation of a person's behavior in terms of an external standard different from evaluating his behavior in terms of the degree to which it realizes his system of needs? I understand that the more his system of needs are realized, the more *efficient* his behavior is and the more of an *integrated* person he becomes. But from whose point of view is this evaluation made? If this is an internal evaluation from the point of view of the individual, how do I evaluate a person from *his point of view*? Is this kind of evaluation common in business? Let me look at my cases again. How many supervisors and managers do I find who are evaluating a person from the latter's point of view? One, two, just how many? Is this evaluation worth making? If so, why? If not, why not? Have I answered these questions "functionally" and "under what conditions?"

6. NEEDS AND ROLES

6.1   I understand that persons are bringing *personal* as well as *social* backgrounds (see 1.8) to their work situations. They are also bringing certain needs, e.g. physiological, as well as needs for *membership* (to belong), *safety, status, competence, influence, self esteem, self development, identity,* etc. But how well are whose and what needs being satisfied? rewarded? reinforced? Are needs for membership for some workers stronger than their needs to exceed management's standards? What did my findings to question 3.3(c) show? What have research findings shown? Do I know what they are?

6.2 I understand that persons also have conceptions of themselves that they have developed from experience. These *self concepts* also in-

fluence the way they behave. Experiences which reinforce their conceptions of themselves are rewarding and hence sought; experiences which
threaten their conception of themselves are painful (unrewarding) and
hence avoided. Can I see what is rewarding and threatening to the self
concepts of the persons involved in the situation I am studying?

6.3   Perhaps I am now ready to make a role-need analysis of the persons of the case and tie together some of my data from 1.4 and 1.5 with
6.1 and 6.2.

(a) For what persons and relationships is the role requirement (i.e.
what is expected) not clear and ambiguous?—*role ambiguity*. Are
Cox, Hearn, Pulson, Durand suffering from this a bit?

(b) For what persons and relationships is what is expected by one
group in conflict with what is expected by another group?—*role
conflict*. Is the man-in-the-middle suffering from this a bit?

(c) For what persons is there a conflict between their needs and what
is expected of them?—*need-role conflict*. Are the deviants I found
in 3.1(d) suffering from this condition?

(d) What persons are making conflicting demands of their situation?
—*need-conflict*. What about Betty Randall, Al Ruskin, and Victor
Rallenitis? Are they suffering from a conflict between a need for
approval, friendship, being liked, being loved, being wanted, membership, etc. (choose your own way of saying it), and a need to
maintain their conception of themselves?

(e) (Perhaps I should not push these different kinds of ambiguities
and conflicts too hard. The point is not to fit people in these different labels. Many times I do not have enough data to make a clear
diagnosis or any diagnosis along any of these dimensions. The
point is: Does my attempt to answer the above questions help me
to see more in the situation than I did before? Do they help me to
tie some things together?) For example:

6.4   Do I see why, when no big gap between role requirements and
need dispositions exists, as in the Marshall Company case (i.e., where,
by tradition and long role training, people obtain satisfactions from
doing what they are supposed to be doing), the previously mentioned
leadership styles tend to blur, that is, it becomes more difficult to say if
the supervisors and executives are production or person oriented, institutional or personal style leaders, etc., i.e. a good case can be made
either way?

should be, how they should feel, what their values should be, what they should do, and how they should behave? Isn't this my responsibility?

(j) There may be one role conflict for which I do have some responsibility. Have I been clear in telling persons for whose performance I am responsible what I expect of them?

(k) But do I have to accept responsibility for (feel guilty about) people's feelings, conflicts, and ambiguities? Am I responsible for lonely Betty Randall and her conflict—when she wanted the approval, love, and friendship of her fellow workers and also wanted to express her superiority toward them at the same time? Am I responsible for the high-status isolate and his condition of felt injustice? Don't they have to take some responsibility for their feelings too?

(l) Who put the high-status isolate, for example, in his condition of felt injustice? Did I put him there? Did my concepts put him there? Did he put himself or find himself there? Am I responsible for his being there? Are these feelings of injustice *my* feelings or *his* feelings? Can I distinguish his feelings of injustice from my feelings of guilt? Can I do something about his feelings? What? Can he do something about them? What? Can I do something about my feelings? What? Does this mean that I don't have to sweep conflict and ambiguity under the rug?

(m) Just what kind of leadership style am I expressing when I am intervening primarily in order to clarify ambiguity? Am I institution-oriented, person-oriented, or group-oriented? Hell's bells what kind of a leader am I? Am I just maintaining a continuous *transaction* with the multidimensional situation in which I am involved? This is like walking a tight rope. This is not my picture of the administrator. This is not how the textbooks tell me I *ought* to behave. Who am I? What is my role model? Do I want to be an administrator? an expert? a teacher? a researcher? Am I too suffering from role conflict? role ambiguity? need-role conflict? need conflict? Does this mean that I am subject to the same ailments of the people I have been diagnosing? Does this mean that the Doctoral Program is no refuge from these problems? They are not going to tell me who I am, what I want, where I'm going. This ain't fair!

25 Twenty Years of Management Development

This piece was given as a talk on February 28, 1963, at a conference in New York City on the above topic under the auspices of the New York State School of Industrial and Labor Relations, Cornell University. It was published in the *Training Directors Journal,* September 1963, copyright © 1963 by the American Society of Training Directors, and it received the award from that society as the best article of the year in their journal. They have given me permission to reproduce it.

My assigned task is to place in perspective the phenomenon of management development as it has emerged on the American scene during the past twenty years. I will assume that the primary question is not whether we are for or against management development but instead what are its objectives and problems and how can they be better understood and evaluated. Probably the key questions are: Who and what are being developed? For what purposes? By whom? and, How? I intend to poke around these rather formidable questions.

It may seem naive to ask, "Who is being developed?" when the answer by verbal association is so obvious. But who are managers if we are not satisfied with the answer that they are persons who manage? What are they managing? If the answer is "organizations," then what are organizations? How do we conceive them? During the past twenty years a number of different answers have been given to these questions and in this welter of answers management development has flourished and floundered.

Let me review briefly, then, six versions of the manager that have flourished during this period:

1. The Manager as an Implementer of Standards.
2. The Manager as Having Social Responsibilities and as the Savior of the Free Enterprise System.
3. The Manager as a Motivator, Relator, Communicator, and Leader.
4. The Manager as a Goal Formulator.
5. The Manager as a Decision Maker.
6. The Manager as a Self-Actualizing Person.

Let me warn you that these six categories are not mutually exclusive and collectively exhaustive of the phenomena being considered. This is the trouble with them and I shall turn to this problem later. Secondly, these six versions cannot be placed on a normative continuum so that it can be said that we have progressed from the manager as an implementer of standards on one end of the scale to the manager as a self-actualizing person on the other other. Instead they all seem to flourish at the same time and this is also a problem to which I will return later. Thirdly, these six categories did not come from any great book or authoritative source. They are not the product of any great research. Instead, they are just categories that I have created for the purpose of providing some order to what I want to say. If you treat them other than this, this will be your problem, not mine, and this problem I, too, will come back to later in my concluding remarks.

THE MANAGER AS AN IMPLEMENTER OF STANDARDS

The manager as the implementer of standards has its roots in the classical theories of management and in what is often referred to as the rational model of organization. According to this view the chief function of the manager is to see that jobs are organized, methods are prescribed, standards are set, and performance goals and budgets are established, and to administer his organization in terms of these "controls." Once these controls have been set up so that everyone knows what is expected of him, the executive sits at his desk looking at reports and *manages by exception*. So long as people are doing what they are supposed to be doing, he can relax and sit back at his desk and take a snooze, if he so chooses, because the theory does not prescribe on this matter.

But once his reports shows a variance from the standard, the required posture is either to sit up or get up from his desk and say, "How come?" This is not exactly an exploratory question because according to the theory only two alternatives are possible: (a) either the standard is not a good standard, or (b) someone is not doing what he is supposed to be doing. These two possibilities, however, boil down to the same thing because the person who did not set a good standard was not doing what he was supposed to be doing. So in either case someone, either the standard setter or the person who failed to meet the standard, has "to get hell" of some sort. This is not because the manager is a "meany" but because the theory has no other way of dealing with the problem than to say "you are not doing what you are supposed to be doing, and you know, old boy, we can't have that kind of behavior around here."

Stated in more technical lingo, compliance with the standard can only be obtained through the use of hierarchical and economic pressures because the model provides no other instruments of control and motivation than these.

As it is popular among the newer theories of organization and management to make a whipping boy of this version of the manager, let me caution you not to go overboard. First, it is well to remember that no manager in fact has ever behaved this way. This is not a theory of how a manager does behave. It's a theory of how a manager should behave —it's what sociologists would call a role model of behavior. Such models of behavior are functional when they help a person to establish an identity with the group for whom a certain kind of behavior is a value and is relevant to the requirements of the situations with which he has to deal.

So the second point to remember is that this role model does emphasize one important dimension of the territory of the executive. In some sense the superior has the responsibility for evaluating the performance of his subordinates. No matter how you slice up an organization, there are certain primary activities that have to be performed if the purposes of the organization have to be achieved. No new version of management or organization can deny or overlook these realities.

However, it was not these realities that popularized the management development movement. The manager who managed by exception never became a popular public image. This model localized the manager's concern too narrowly to the hows of internal management, and although it was consistent with the corporate mission of running a good business that makes a profit, it did not reflect well the manager's place in the new economic society and the important part that he was playing in its development.

THE MANAGER AND HIS NEW SOCIAL RESPONSIBILITIES

So in the early fifties some business leaders and educators shifted from a sole concern with the "hows" of daily managerial life to a concern with its broader "whys." This shift arose in part from a curious anomaly. Here was business at the peak of its achievement in the production of goods and services, and from this point of view managers were doing a good job, indeed. But instead of being rewarded by society with affection for the taut shops that they were running, managers felt that they were being discriminated against in legislative halls, union offices, and classrooms.

This anomalous situation, of course, required explanation. In my experience man has never been found wanting in being able to provide ready explanations for social injustices and simple solutions for their correction. More often than not we try to correct them before we understand them. Anyway, two solutions appeared on the scene which became closely associated with the early development of the management development movement. One was to try to change the public's image with regard to the businessman. Obviously the public had the wrong image and they had to be educated. Another was to educate businessmen with regard to their broader social responsibilities. These two approaches were often combined by the miracle of words and by the many ways in which they can be associated so that it was possible to educate managers with regard to their broader social responsibilities on one hand while they were being justified as the sole saviors of the free enterprise system on the other.

Anyway, a new role model for the business manager appeared. No longer was he supposed to be looking just for exceptions to the way things should be. No longer was he supposed to be solely concerned with his immediate self-interest. No longer was he supposed to be solely responsible toward investors; he had responsibilities as well toward employees, customers, suppliers, distributors, the local community, and society as a whole. He had commitments which bound him to purposes far more extensive than his immediate self-interest. Obviously this new role model was much better than the previous one for educators to latch on to and they did so—one might say—with a vengeance. As some of you will remember, many eloquent speeches and articles were devoted to this subject.

But this new role model was not just the stuff for excellent speeches; it also was incorporating a hard reality. In the new world that science and technology had created, the business manager was locked into a role from which there was no escape. There was no way he could turn the clock back to the good old days; he had reached the point of no return; he had to face up to the consequences of his monkey business. He had a bigger role to play in the scheme of things than to say "how come" to "red flags." Although the businessman was no social reformer in his own or the public's image, he with the help of the scientist and technician had produced social changes far greater than any social reformer had ever dreamed of. In this new world this role model helped to provide him with his new professional identity.

One of the difficulties with this new role model, however, was to make it "operational," as we say in scientific circles. This means, to put it more simply, it did not specify very clearly what the business manager was supposed to be doing differently on Monday morning at nine o'clock, besides saying, for example, "how come" to "red flags."

MOTIVATOR, RELATOR, INTERACTER, COMMUNICATOR, AND LEADER

For this another role model was required and fortunately one was latently on hand. More than twenty years ago certain researches had come up with some findings that led to this new version of the manager. This new model conceived of the manager as a motivator, relator, interactor, communicator, and leader. Under it the management development movement came of age, at least to the stage of adolescence.

Let me list briefly just a few of the discoveries that led to this new version of the manager's role. First, it was found that investors, employees, customers, and distributors were not only economic categories but also people. They were important contributors to the organization, and inducements—both economic and non-economic—had to be offered them in order to secure their contributions. Second, it was found that people had feelings, attitudes, and sentiments, and that these attributes could not be completely ignored without some unfavorable consequences. Third, it was found that man does not like just to live alone; he also likes to associate with his fellow men, and from these associations and his desire for them, new phenomena emerge which control him, sometimes much more powerfully than the controls of management. So, fourth, as a result of all these little discoveries, the bigger discovery was made that the internal environments of organizations were populated not only with the standards that management *put there* but also with the social and personal values that people *brought there* and the social structures that *emerged there* from their interaction.

As you can see, these discoveries were not very original in and by themselves. Managers had known these things for some time but now someone decided to pay some attention to them, just as some centuries ago someone decided to pay attention to the fact that water tended to run downhill—a fact which people had known but about which, because of the very fact that they knew it so well, they could not get curious.

Anyway, from the slow but cumulative impact of these discoveries a new role model was born. No longer was the manager supposed to be concerned only with money markets, supplier markets, product markets, labor markets, consumer markets, and the like; he was now supposed to be concerned with the concrete people with whom he daily interacted and through whom he got his results. No longer was he supposed to be concerned only with that vague and fuzzy new and big "Society with a capital S," which existed somewhere *there outside,* which he had helped to create, and toward which he did not have a clear understanding of his new responsibilities. He was now supposed to be concerned with that new and smaller "society with a lower case s,"—which existed *here inside* his own organization, which in a much more concrete sense he had helped to create and which he could do something about on Monday morning at nine o'clock.

But this very closeness had its dysfunctional aspect because things that are too close are sometimes hard to see. This created all sorts of troubles for management developers who now had to get managers to see what by preconditioning ought not to be there. And as some management developers suffered from the same myopia, a kind of the-blind-leading-the-blind phase of management development developed. I shall not give this development a label, as you all know it.

Under this new model managers were now expected to ask a new kind of question. Instead of being expected to say "how come" to "red flags," they were now supposed to say, "what the hell is going on here." Under one interpretation, this question was not much different from the "how come" question because in either case the answer could be, "something that shouldn't be." But the question could be interpreted in a more exploratory way to mean, "I don't know, and I better try to find out."

This shift from a closed "how come" question to an open-ended "what is going on here" question, however, was a very difficult shift for some managers and management developers to make. For example, if the question of "what is going on" was really an exploratory one, this meant that management developers, instead of providing managers with specific answers about what they should be doing Monday morning at nine o'clock, were now supposed to provide them with ways of thinking and tools in order to find out. But this transition was hard on the nervous systems of both parties.

For the manager it meant that the "what is going on" question had to be preceded with an "I don't know" assumption because if the manager knew what was going on there was no good reason to ask the question except in the "how come" sense. But it was difficult for managers to say "I don't know" in a meaningful sense, because under the model of the managers I first described he should know what was going on and a manager who didn't know what was going on was, by definition, not a good manager.

This transition was hard on the nervous system of management developers, too, because the educational methods by which persons are taught to say "how come" to "red flags" are well known and have a long tradition, while the methods by which persons are taught to say "I don't know" are relatively new and untested, and very powerful social forces keep tending to drive them underground. For example, if management developers are expected to give answers to managers, management developers who are being employed by managers are reluctant not to give them because you will remember what happens under the red-flag version to people who do not do what is expected of them.

Stated now in more technical lingo, this shift *from* a rational model of organization, where members of organizations are viewed as passive instruments who are capable of performing work and accepting directions but who are not supposed to exert influence in any significant way, *to* a natural-system model of organization, where members are viewed as subjects who bring to their organizations certain attitudes, values, and goals that have to be taken into account in order to secure their participation, is a tremendous one. Questions that are relevant under the first model become irrelevant under the second model and vice versa.

However, people who do not understand this keep trying to get the second model to answer questions that are relevant only to the first model. After man discovered that the world was round, for example, the question as to whether one can get from New York to London by traveling east or west becomes a bit outmoded. But if a person who believes the world is flat asks this question and you parry it with the question, "How far or how long do you want to travel?" he is apt to answer, "None of this theoretical stuff please, Buddy; I asked you a straightforward question and I want a straightforward answer; I want to know how you can get to the same place by traveling in opposite directions." For him his question is still a question; his riddle remains still a riddle and your answer is no answer and sounds to him like theoretical quibbling.

THE MANAGER AS A GOAL FORMULATOR

Sometime in the 1950's it was discovered that organizations not only had *standards* and *people;* they also had *objectives*. With this discovery the posture of managers changed, at least a little. Now he was supposed to manage not *by exception* or *through people* but *by objectives*. It now became popular to ask, "What business am I in? What share of the market do I want? What kinds of people do I want to sell my products to? What image of my organization do I want the public to have?" and the like.

Under one mode of thinking, these were rather interesting questions because, strictly speaking, the manager could not go to the external environment for their answers as he was wont to go for them. The external environment was neutral toward them; it couldn't care less except to give some clues as to the price he would have to pay in order to get, for example, such and such a share of the market. But then it was up to the manager again to decide whether or not he wanted to pay this price.

Although this choice was not easy, the inner-directed manager was prepared to make it. But, for the outer-directed manager, this was so much stuff and nonsense. He was in business to maximize his profits, his share of the market, and his customers indiscriminately. So when he was asked about what business he was in, let us say, for example "was he in the cleaning or cosmetic business," instead of pondering this question deeply, he went to Madison Avenue for the answer and they told him he was in the business of making the world a more cheerful place to live in through linear programming or something like that. This "answer" allowed him to continue doing what he had been doing before; so there was no change.

This short-circuiting of the educational process was most vexing to management developers because they thought they had finally reached a set of questions that was going to make the manager think. But lo and behold he had outwitted them again.

This sorry state of affairs produced two different solutions that have appeared on the scene in recent years. One solution addressed itself to the question, "If we can't make men like machines, can we make machines that behave more rationally than men?" The other solution addressed itself to the question, "How can managers who have been trained to say 'how come' to 'red flags' be retrained to say 'what is going on here?' " Let me comment upon each briefly.

THE MANAGER AS A DECISION MAKER

The first solution was based on the discovery that not only was man a passive instrument capable of doing what he was told, and not only was he a passive subject who had attitudes, values, and goals which needed to be satisfied, but also he was an active decision maker and problem solver. This attribute of man, it was felt, had been left out or underevaluated in the previous role models of the manager I have described. They did not take sufficiently into account man's search behavior, particularly his search for rational behavior under conditions of uncertainty.

Mathematicians had been working on this question for some time but without much public attention. For a while it had been assumed that the theories that they had developed could be better applied in Las Vegas than in business. But nothing could have been further from the truth. Very wisely these theories were not applied first to the behavior of businessmen; they were applied first to the building of machines that would do more faithfully what the mathematicians told them to do. So, before anyone could become deeply concerned, machines were designed to solve first simple problems and then more and more complex ones, based on the decision rules which the mathematicians fed into them.

That machines can do things that man cannot do is not exactly news. This has been true since the days of the common screwdriver. Had no one attached the term "decision making" to what the machines were doing, everything might have been more serene. But someone did and "all hell broke lose." This consternation followed because decision making was one of the manager's major prerogatives and attributes; all of the previous models had presupposed this to some extent. So when a machine was able to do better than the manager what was supposed to be the manager's major job, this was a bit disconcerting to say the least, and some managers even began to worry about their jobs disappearing.

But this worry of managers could not be addressed under this new role model because the question of how persons *do behave* under conditions of uncertainty, whether they be managers or employees, had only one meaning under this new normative model of how persons *should behave* under such conditions. Under this new rational model any behavior that deviated from it was, as in the case of the earlier rational red-flag version, not the way a rational person should behave, and this time it applied to managers as well as to lowly workers. This was strong medicine for some managers to take, and so obviously management developers had to be brought in to make this medicine more palatable.

As I am not so conversant with this phase of management development, I shall have to depend upon my colleagues to correct the oversimplifications and exaggerations which by now you are well aware I am likely to make. But, as I get the story, someone got the idea that if business managers could be brought into contact with these machines and allowed to play games with them, managers might feel less threatened. Under these play conditions it was hoped that they would learn to see how these machines really worked and in time be slowly seduced to copy their behavior. At this present stage of the game it is difficult to appraise who is outwitting or seducing whom. But in terms of my personal assignment of probabilities, I know on which side I would place my bets.

THE MANAGER AS A SELF-ACTUALIZING PERSON

The second solution to this short-circuiting of the education of business managers was based upon another theory of learning. It had been discovered that managers were difficult to retrain on the job, because in their own organizations they found too many "red flags" to say "how come" to, and so were locked into this stereotypical response. To get them out of this bad habit, therefore, it was felt that managers should be taken out of their organizations and placed in "cultural islands" where there were no "red flags" to say "how come" to. In these so-called "unstructured situations," it was hoped that they would now have to ask "what the hell is going on here" in a meaningful sense and thus try to find out.

To make sure that this change in behavior would come about, however, these cultural islands sometimes developed their own norms of behavior which rewarded the new desired behavior and punished the old. These norms worked in the same direction as one retrains a pigeon to peck at a green target after he has been previously trained to peck at a red target. As you all know, this is done now by rewarding the pigeon with a piece of grain when he pecks at the green target and by dousing him with a bucket of cold water when he continues to peck at the red one. So likewise, in the case of these new cultural islands, those managers who played new roles were rewarded with "smiles" or some value equivalent for managers of what a piece of grain is for a pigeon, and those managers who continued to peck at the old red target were said "boo" to or given some value equivalent for managers of what being doused by a bucket of cold water is for a pigeon. Although punishment helped to extinguish the old behavior, just as in the case of pigeons, it also set up in turn some disturbing side effects. In short, some managers did not like what was going on and these feelings in turn prevented them from finding out.

Perhaps I should say now in all fairness that this reward–punishment theory of learning was not quite the theory of learning which this new school of thought espoused. Under their theory of learning these dysfunctional side effects were not supposed to appear and according to the theory they would not appear, if management developers could be trained not to say "boo" to managers when they kept still pecking away at the old red target.

At this point management development shifted from a major concern with the training of managers to a concern with the training of persons who trained managers. This long-awaited development of management development, however, presented the old problem at a new level. It now became the problem of how trainers could be trained so that they would not express approval or disapproval about the behavior of the persons whose behavior they were supposed to be changing.

I shall not consider all the different approaches that were recommended for the solution of this problem. But stated briefly and operationally, instead of saying "boo" to the executive who kept pecking away at red targets, the trainer was now expected to say (1) "why do you keep pecking at red targets which are no longer there?" if he belonged to one school of psychotherapy, or (2) "you feel uncomfortable when you have no longer any red targets to peck at" if he belonged to another school of psychotherapy, or (3) "what are you going to do about *your* feelings of uncomfortableness under these no-red-flag conditions, and are these not your feelings and don't you have some responsibility for them?" if he belonged to still another school of psychotherapy. By these kinds of questions it was hoped that managers would learn to find out what was really going on.

As you can see, this particular development of management development arose from the discovery that managers, just like employees, customers, investors, suppliers, and distributors, were persons who also had personal and role conflicts which they also had to learn to recognize, understand, accept, live with, and take some responsibility for. In fact, the very position of leadership posed some of the most difficult personal and role conflicts with which any human individual can be confronted. If the manager did not understand this, he was likely to project his own conflicts on others in the organization—his superiors, subordinates, and colleagues.

CONCLUSION

I hope that by now I have aroused your curiosity sufficiently so that you are all asking: "What is he up to?" "Why does he keep parodying these different versions of the manager?" "Is he for or against them?" In short, "What the hell is going on here?" Lord forbid that I should short-circuit the educational process by preventing you from finding out for yourselves that I, too, as an educator, have my own role and personal conflicts with which I have to learn to live and that joking may be one of the ways that I have learned to do this. But let me say at a more intellectual level what my method of presentation has been about.

1. I am both for and against each version of the manager I have presented. In the sense that each version represents one important dimension of the administrative reality, I am for it. In the sense that one version denies the reality of the other, I am against it.

2. For me the important problem for the manager is to think of these important dimensions of his territory in an integrated way. This lack of an integrated way of thinking about these different aspects of his reality is for me why managers can suffer from overdevelopment as well as underdevelopment, or lopsided development instead of balanced development.

3. In my opinion management development will come of age when we stop trying to reduce one of these versions to the other or to establish priorities among them in order to choose one or the other. Let's

face it: (1) organizations have *purposes;* (2) to carry out purposes, *structure* is needed and *roles* have to be assigned. Also, (3) organizations are *peopled* and (4) people have *needs.* These are for me no longer matters to be discovered, or to write eloquent speeches or articles about. For me these are the givens from which to go on to ask more interesting empirical questions for research, namely how these dimensions are related to each other and on the basis of this kind of understanding how might they be better related to each other.

4. In spite of the confusions that I find in the management development movement today, I nevertheless feel that something very exciting is going on. More than any other professional group I know, managers have submitted their modes of behavior to self-examination. For this I feel they should be rewarded. By joking about their trainers I have tried to express my sympathy for the punishment that the managers may have taken from those of us who with the best of intentions have tried to help them in their search for the source of their professional identity and competence. By all means let us not dampen this search. Even though not well understood, it is one of the most exciting and important things that is going on in the world today.

26 Hawthorne Revisited

This piece was delivered October 24, 1966, in Washington, D.C., before the Public Personnel Association. It was published in the association's *Personnel Report,* Number 671 (1967?) and is reprinted here by permission.

This is the last written speech I gave before the present volume went into publication. Although I wrote it in a facetious vein, I was actually quite disturbed about many things that were happening in the world at this period and about my inability to know what to say or do about them. In particular, I was concerned about the function of universities in the new world that science and technology had created. In trying to relate effectively to this world, the university was undergoing great stress and strain in its internal structure; and Harvard was no longer the monastic establishment I had joined in 1927. Change was in the air. In the midst of such change I felt that an unhappy change agent could only become a joker.

If the reader is puzzled by the fact that in a piece entitled "Hawthorne Revisited" I say nothing about the researches in the Hawthorne plant of the Western Electric Company, let me say that this omission is not as odd as it might appear. I was not revisiting a place; I was revisiting a point of time in my life which "Hawthorne" symbolically represented, that is, that glorious period of time in my early manhood when I thought I had a bear by the tail.

In this paper I want to talk about an itch I have been scratching for a long time, and I want to verbalize this itch at a fairly high level of abstraction and generality. Obviously I will try to objectify it so as to persuade you that I am scratching something that really exists and is worth scratching and that in some sense is relevant to jobs in personnel.

Let me begin with the year 1966 and look back thirty years to 1936 in order to see what, if anything, has happened. In what respects, if any, is the year 1966 different from 1936? What looks somewhat the same and what looks somewhat different? In this interim have we in the United States been moving upwards in a straight line or like a spiral or have we been just going around in circles?

If we look at man's human condition in this interim between 1936 and 1966, we do not find much difference. He is living, dying, and paying taxes today just as well or as badly as he did then. If we look at man's social life at an elementary social level, we also do not see much change. The social rules by which man lives in association with his fellow men may have changed and multiplied slightly but this does not seem to have made any substantial difference in his capacity or incapacity to live harmoniously with his fellow men. He seems to be doing as good or as bad a job now as he did then.

If we look at man's organizational life, we see a rise in the number and size of complex formal organizations. Every time life breaks down at an elementary social level, new formal organizations arise to repair the damage. So, whereas in 1936 I could be identified by only a few numbers, such as, for example, my local street number, telephone number, and automobile license number, I have now in 1966 a Social Security and Medicare number, an area code number, a zip code number, a bank number, and a payroll number, as well as an assortment of charge numbers in different stores, hotels, motels, restaurants, and bunny clubs of a wide range in status.

But formal organizations do not arise merely in order to keep track of me and give me a unique numerical identity. Other forces produce them. By far the greatest change from 1936 to 1966 has been in the area of science and technology. In this area in this interim there has been an explosion of great magnitude. It has not only created a big bang in its own right, it has penetrated and affected these other aspects of man's life that I have referred to—his personal life, his social life, and his organizational life.

In the short span of thirty years, this revolution has made the world of 1936 look like a horse-and-buggy period by comparison. During this period specialization has increased at an accelerated pace, and with it has come a host of newly generated languages to serve its purposes. The two major languages are those of applied mathematics and applied behavioral sciences. These are not natural languages like French, Spanish, German, English, or Russian; they are languages created for specialized purposes, but they are languages all the same; they have to be learned and used properly if communication is to result. So between 1936 and 1966 thousands of new words generated by these specialized pursuits have crept into the vocabulary of the day. It is in terms of this profusion of new specialized tongues that I now want to contrast 1966 with 1936 because they have penetrated every nook and cranny of man's life.

As a convenient shorthand, I will refer to these different aspects of man's life in terms of four spaces in which he dwells and has his being. I will call these different spaces (1) technological space, (2) social space, (3) organizational space, and (4) life space. I shall not define these words but hope that their meaning will become apparent.

TECHNOLOGICAL SPACE

It is here that the difference between 1936 and 1966 is most visible because the technological space of 1966 is populated not only with new words but also with new things. This is what gives this space its distinctiveness, since, as we shall see in a moment when we take a look at the other spaces, there is no guarantee that new words produce automatically new things; sometimes they generate only more words. But in technological space there is a much better correlation between new words and new things. This is a very important difference and one that I cannot emphasize too strongly.

For the first time in the history of mankind, university people began to build machines and they built them out of pure theory, that is, out of new ideas, words, concepts, models, and ways of conceiving things. Their products were visible—the atomic bomb, the missile, the rocket, and the computer. With this visible, tangible, concrete payoff, theory came into its own. No longer could it be summarily dismissed as something for the birds. Here was a new breed of birds who did not just talk about ideas. Instead they used ideas to produce things that had never existed before. Between just talking about ideas and utilizing ideas to generate new things, there exists a tremendous difference, as yet, too little understood.

SOCIAL SPACE

Obviously all of academia is not populated with this sort of bird. Most of academia is still populated with another species who for centuries has been more interested in man's social and human conditions, or, what I am calling here, his social and life spaces. From time immemorial these spaces have been talked and sung about by the laymen as well as poets, novelists, religious leaders, and philosophers in their own native languages. But when a small sector of academia, called social scientists, saw their natural science colleagues being courted by power centers and allotted huge research grants, they said, "Well, we can be scientific too. We can produce ideas that will make also a difference to those spaces in which we are interested. We too can build new models of man, organizations, institutions, and society."

And they did, and, alas, I got hooked into this game. We generated a lot of new words but these words did not seem to produce anything very concrete, certainly not any visible, tangible products like machines. For all our huffing and puffing there was nothing to show. We did not produce anything like the great society or more democratic societies or more humanized bureaucracies or more mature behavior. We did not even produce any sentences or propositions in a scientific sense to verify. We were still just reclassifying things, that is, giving new names to things that existed in 1936 but which had not been classified this way before.

One of the difficult problems we faced was that we could not make these new classification schemes stick. Whereas all the entities in the animal, vegetable, and mineral kingdoms, such as the animals, birds, bees, fish, trees, flowers, vegetables, and rocks had accepted the names the scientists had given them, the entities in the human–social kingdom resisted this name-calling. They refused to get stuck with the names we gave them. For example, the natural birds that got stuck with the name of "fuzzy-headed woodpecker" instead of "bluebird" might have preferred the latter name to the former; we don't know because the computer isn't as yet ready to tell us. But the human bird who is called a "fuzzy-headed woodpecker" instead of a "bluebird" just won't take it. He says, "You may be being just descriptive and not evaluative but it doesn't feel that way to me; I feel like a bluebird; I see myself as a bluebird; *ergo* I am a bluebird. And so nuts to you and your classification scheme."

In spite of these difficulties we remained undaunted. Not being able to write any sentences, we decided to produce more and more competing and rivaling dictionaries. Each new dictionary was heralded as a breakthrough. But as each dictionary maker likes his own dictionary better than that of his colleagues, there was no agreement about which dictionary was better. So a great fight ensued as to who had the best dictionary, but this fight was localized in academic institutions and learned journals. All the practitioner could do was to taste the dictionary of each school of thought or university and make up his own mind as to which one was the more useful for his own nefarious purposes.

ORGANIZATIONAL SPACE

By the mid-1950's things really began to get hot, particularly in organizational space. Everything that had existed there before got a new name. For example, in 1936, data were being processed but there was no "data processing"; information was being passed along but there were no "information systems"; employees and executives played games among themselves and with each other but there was no "game theory." In 1936 there was production control but no "linear programming." In 1936 "R and D" stood for Republicans and Democrats; in 1966 "R and D" stood for "research and development."

In 1936 managers grew up the hard way, because there was no "management development." People were exchanging values with each other but there was no "exchange theory." In 1936 there was competition but it was all "perfect"; by 1966 there was still competition but it was now all "imperfect." In 1936 there was conflict but there was no "conflict management."

In 1936 most executives counted things by tens instead of by twos; they thought that this was the one and only way of counting things or accounting for them. The language of go-no-go was still not current lingo. Decisions were being made but there were no clear "decision rules" for how to make them rationally, particularly under conditions of uncertainty, and there were no decision rules that could be put into a machine that could make certain kinds of decisions faster and better than the manager could. So, to make a long story short, although in 1936 there was a lot going on, there were no "role players," no "image makers," no "game players," no "leadership styles," no "hidden persuaders," no "organization men," and no "waste makers." All these jolly new names for jolly old things were still to come.

If one had asked of an executive of a corporation in 1936, "What business are you in?" his response would have been certain and immediate. "Holy smokes," he would have said, "what are you asking? I'm in the grass seed business." By 1966 this would have provoked a less emphatic reply. "Well," he might say, "we used to be in the grass seed business but now we are selling 'green lawns,' that is, we are selling fertilizers, lawn mowers, weed repellants, insecticides, and God only knows what else to make lawns green. To tell you the truth, grass seed is just an incidental part of our business now."

So during this short span of thirty years, not only did many new businesses spring up, but also many old businesses were no longer sure just what businesses they were in and just what they were selling or should be selling. Were they selling "green lawns" or grass seed? "Progress" or electrical toasters? "Better living for more people" or stockings? "Soft hands" or detergents? "No cavities" or toothpaste?

"Marlboro country" or fine tobacco? "Miss America" or cosmetics? Nobody knew. Almost overnight everybody was either in a new business or they didn't know just what business they were in anymore.

LIFE SPACE

But social and organizational spaces were not the only spaces affected by this technological revolution; life space got entangled too, From the simple models of man as a child of God or a creature of nature there developed competing models. For example, in 1936 man wasn't sure if he was one step lower than an angel or one step higher than an ape. But it became quite clear shortly thereafter that if man was one step higher than an ape he could get somewhere even though it might take a bit of time and doing, whereas if man was just a fallen angel, he could only become what he once had been, namely, an angel. So this latter conception, I'm sure you will agree, was not forward looking. It was what one might call downright enervating. It put all of man's values in a very distant past or in a highly improbable future and deprived his present existence of all significance. Man could only hang his head in shame and say, "I am a fallen angel."

Now somewhere between 1936 and 1966 I began to hear rumblings saying in effect, "Rise, fallen angels of the world. You have only your white robes to lose. Stop crying in your beer about your state of celestial disgrace. Find out who you are. This is your intolerable but glorious existential condition. Stop trying to get back to your original frozen state; try to become what you are."

So between 1936 and 1966 an avid search for new models of man began. At first some people did not quite get the message. They felt that so long as they couldn't be angels, they should try to become better apes, but this was evolution in reverse. So the economists offered their solution. They said that the greatest good for the greatest number would be obtained if man became a better machine. But the other social scientists, not to be outdone by them, offered their models in rapid succession—man as an id and superego, man as a security seeker and conformist, man as a power and status seeker, man as a role player and role performer, man as a myth and image maker, man as a rule and law maker, man as a problem solver and decision maker, and finally man as a self actualizer, innovator, and creator.

But it was while everyone was trying to determine among this assortment of models which model to choose for himself that the applied mathematician stole the show. He said in effect, "You verbal wood-peckers are on the wrong track; you are approaching the problem from the wrong end. It is much easier to build a rational machine than to make a rational man, and I'll show you how. When you've made up your mind about who you are and what you want to be and where you are going and what business you'd like to be in and subjective matters such as that, you come into my computation center and I'll show you how to get there."

No siren since Lorelei has sung a more seductive tune than this. It said in effect, "Let's seduce man into becoming rational by a machine which will be more rational than he is. Let's build a machine that will answer only rational and intelligent questions so that every time some bluebird asks of this machine a silly question, it will say, 'no go.' In time the bluebird will find this an unrewarding experience. So in time he will stop asking silly questions in his own imprecise indigenous languages; he will begin to learn the rational go-no-go language of the computer because this is the only language it can understand and give answers to. Confronted by his own rational image, the bluebird in time will be shamed into becoming a rational fuzzy-headed wood-pecker." And so, from this exciting idea somewhere in the mid-fifties, the second industrial revolution and a super-rationalism were born. In fact in this short space of ten years three generations of computers have been delivered.

SUMMARY AND CONCLUSIONS

So the best understatement I can make for the year 1966 is that there exists a lot of ferment and confusion but also a great challenge for the bluebirds. Let's see how this might be so. I have tried to show how each space speaks its own language, has its own logic and its own conception of what constitutes the rational and the real, that is, what really counts and is important and makes a difference. Each space specialist feels, like any true believer, that his space is the one and only true space and that all other spaces should be reduced to his own. Academia has helped in this process by organizing these spaces into disciplines so that to become an expert in any one space or subspace one has to have a Ph.D.

Now in these terms I am ready to state better the itch that for thirty years I have not been able to stop scratching. The question I keep asking myself is: What if nature may turn out *not* to be organized in disciplines in quite the same way as the universities are? What if the bluebirds are involved not only in all the spaces I've been talking about but also where they intersect? What if most of their problems reside in these intersections, so that they are involved not just in either one space or another but in both one space and another? What do you do? What kind of bilingual or multilingual languages do you speak in these intersections? Is it a pidgin English or the language of go-no-go, or do the bluebirds have a language of their very own?

Now, of course, you understand that by "bluebirds" I am referring to a certain class of birds. It is just my shorthand way—my completely descriptive and nonevaluative way of course—of referring to persons in positions of administrative responsibility in purposive organizations which still have some people left in them. As that's quite a mouthful to say each time, "bluebirds" is just a shorter and more convenient label by which to call them. It expresses my fondness for them and their predicament—the paradoxical and ambiguous lives that they live in territories that are being invaded more and more by fuzzy-headed woodpeckers, which is my shorthand term of endearment for applied mathematicians and social scientists, who are also my friends.

So my itch scratched down is this: "How are the bluebirds (i.e., personnel administrators) and fuzzy-headed woodpeckers (i.e., scientists) going to learn to live together in the same territory (i.e, in the same purposive organizations)? In order to survive are the bluebirds going to try to become woodpeckers, or are they going to try to change the woodpeckers into bluebirds, or are they going to try to become better bluebirds?" Or is there still another alternative?   .

Now in my thirty years of scratching this itch, the conclusions I've reached are these. If you take the first alternative and try to make like woodpeckers, you are abdicating your responsibilities. If you try to make woodpeckers into bluebirds, you just get fewer good woodpeckers and more conflicted bluebirds. So what about the third alternative which is to try to become better bluebirds? But here is the paradox. You are not going to become better bluebirds until you find a nesting place in the intersections of the various spaces I've been describing. But this is not a comfortable nest in which to lie, as I've been trying to tell you by my scratching. It may be difficult to nest there and remain a good old-fashioned bluebird. If you try to remain so, you may not become a better bluebird but a stuffed bluebird for a museum.

So my message to the bluebirds is a bit difficult to communicate. But it goes something like this. Stop trying to imitate your more operationally goal-oriented woodpecking fine feathered friends. Try to understand their languages but also capitalize on your own predicament. Learn to live happily in the intersections of the spaces that elude their grasp. You are the only nonspecialist bird left. If you don't want to become an extinct species, you will have to find out what kind of a bird you are and cultivate your own distinctive competence. I don't think the computer is going to help you find out. There is no grand architect for the kind of bird you are, certainly not the woodpecker. So don't let him tell you who you are. You can only become what you are the hard way. So bluebirds of the world, rise up and seek your own destiny. You have only your feathers to lose. But don't lose them by scrapping with the woodpeckers. Lose them in the process of becoming yourselves.

Index

Index

Index

318

Index